Science Fiction Television

Recent Title in
The Praeger Television Collection
David Bianculli, Series Editor

Spy Television
Wesley Britton

Science Fiction Television

M. Keith Booker

The Praeger Television Collection
David Bianculli, Series Editor

PRAEGER

Westport, Connecticut
London

Library of Congress Cataloging-in-Publication Data

Booker, M. Keith.
    Science fiction television / M. Keith Booker.
        p. cm.—(The Praeger television collection, ISSN 1549-2257)
    Includes bibliographical references and index.
    ISBN 0-275-98164-9 (alk. paper)
        1. Science fiction television programs.   I. Title.   II. Series.
    PN1995.8.S35B66   2004
    791.45′615—dc22   2004040056

British Library Cataloguing in Publication Data is available.

Library of Congress Catalog Card Number: 2004040056
ISBN: 0-275-98164-9
ISSN: 1549-2257

First published in 2004

Praeger Publishers, 88 Post Road West, Westport, CT 06881
An imprint of Greenwood Publishing Group, Inc.
www.praeger.com

Printed in the United States of America

The paper used in this book complies with the
Permanent Paper Standard issued by the National
Information Standards Organization (Z39.48-1984).

10 9 8 7 6 5 4 3 2 1

For Amy, Adam, Marcus, Dakota, and Skylor

Contents

Photo essay follows page 148.

CHAPTER 1

Early Predecessors to *The Twilight Zone*: The Birth of Science Fiction Television

This book is a history of science fiction television (SFTV) series that appeared in America from the 1950s to the early years of the twenty-first century. It describes the principal characteristics of the most important series, at the same time placing each program within the historical contexts of SFTV as a whole and of the American culture and society within which it was produced and consumed. Science fiction series have been among the most innovative and successful programs ever to appear on commercial television. Classic American series such as *The Twilight Zone* and *Star Trek* were among the pioneering programs that defined the phenomenon of cult television, continued by more recent, highly respected series such as *Star Trek: The Next Generation* and *Babylon 5*. Such series have had some of the most dedicated core audiences in the history of television, as evidenced by their ongoing popularity in syndication and, more recently, on DVD. In the 1990s, *The X-Files* boldly went where no SFTV program had gone before in terms of production values and mainstream audience appeal, while cable programs such as *Farscape* and *Stargate SG-1* carried the banner of science fiction television into the new millennium. It is also worth noting that science fiction programs such as *Space: 1999* have been, at least for short periods, among the most successful British imports in the American market, while near-legendary British programs such as *The Avengers* and *The Prisoner* have included strong elements of science fiction, along with elements of other genres, such as the spy drama and detective story—a characteristic that can also be found in *The X-Files*. And, in terms of British imports, there is always the incomparable *Doctor Who*, which ran for twenty-six years on the BBC (British Broadcasting Corporation) and still has a strong cult following in both Britain and the United States (and, for that matter, in dozens of other countries).

It should come as no surprise that some of the best television ever has been produced within the science fiction genre. Television, as an overtly technological medium, would seem to be a natural venue for science fiction. Moreover, the recent proliferation of cable channels (including especially the Sci Fi Channel) has opened vast new territories for programs, such as many science fiction series, that may not attract a huge mainstream viewership but do quite well with well-defined niche audiences, allowing them to explore more interesting and quirky possibilities without the necessity of widespread mass appeal. Though science fiction television has sometimes fallen prey to the same cliché-ridden sameness for which commercial television is often criticized, the genre seeks, by definition, to imagine worlds that are different from the one in which we now live. SFTV, by its very nature, explores thought-provoking concepts and alternative perspectives that can challenge its audience to rethink long-cherished ideas. In short, science fiction is, as a genre, particularly well suited to the kind of thoughtful and imaginative visions that demonstrate the positive potential of television as a medium.

In point of fact, however, the roots of science fiction television reach back in time well before the invention of television itself. As modern film technology began to take shape in the last decade of the nineteenth century, the pioneering Lumiére brothers of France saw tremendous potential in the realistic capabilities of the new medium. Accordingly, they produced a series of reality-based films in which they simply recorded real-life places and events for viewing by their audiences, thus making their films the predecessors of modern-day documentaries. At the same time, however, another early French filmmaker, Georges Méliès, saw the medium very differently. For Méliès, a magician by trade, the true potential of film lay not in the simple photographic representation of reality, but in illusion and visual trickery. By the end of the century, he had made dozens of films that relied centrally on what would now be referred to as special effects to create worlds of visual fantasy for his audiences. By 1902, he had made what is still his best-known film, the fourteen-minute *Voyage dans la Lune* (*A Trip to the Moon*). This work of whimsical imagination, based on a novel by the groundbreaking science fiction writer Jules Verne, was a major milestone in the history of film, and still has the ability to entertain and fascinate audiences even today.

It is, of course, no accident that this early landmark in the development of movie magic was a work of science fiction. For one thing, early film was as much science as art, and early filmmakers such as Méliès and the Lumiéres were inventors who had to develop, on the fly, the technology that was needed to carry out their cinematic visions. Indeed, much of the appeal of film to early audiences came not from the actual content of specific films, but simply from the technological marvels embodied in the medium itself. Attending an early film was itself almost like participating in science fiction. In addition, science fiction is perfectly suited to the kind of fantasy-based filmmaking pursued by Méliès: By definition, science fiction imagines worlds other than the one in which we live, and Méliès was simply the first to realize that the capabilities of the new medium were perfectly suited to the exploration of such alternative visions of reality.

Science fiction became a staple of filmmaking very early on, and it has continued as a crucial film genre from Méliès forward to *Star Wars* and beyond. A similar story, of course, pertains to television—and for many of the same reasons. Indeed, science fiction film was an important predecessor to science fiction television, and the two forms carry a close generic kinship. Perhaps the most direct predecessors to science fiction television were the film serials of the 1930s, in particular the three Flash Gordon serials and the Buck Rogers serial of that decade, all featuring Buster Crabbe in the central roles. These serials were in turn based on popular syndicated comic strips, extending the generic genealogy back even further.

The Flash Gordon and Buck Rogers serials were produced in episodes of fifteen to twenty minutes in length, with each serial running for twelve to fifteen episodes that were shown weekly in theaters in an attempt to attract young audiences to the movies. Each serial involved a continuous plot, and each episode typically ended with a cliff-hanger in which one or more of the major characters was threatened with some sort of dire danger (usually overcome rather easily at the beginning of the next episode). The plots of the various serials involved classic science fiction themes. For example, the first Flash Gordon serial, *Flash Gordon: Space Soldiers* (1936), is an alien-invasion story in which Flash and his attractive, rather skimpily clad sidekick, Dale Arden (Jean Rogers), foil the plans of Emperor Ming of the planet

Mongo to colonize Earth. In *Flash Gordon's Trip to Mars* (1938), Ming the Merciless resumes his assault on Earth, this time in an alliance with the queen of Mars. But Flash and a more demurely clad Dale (the Hays Code—a self-regulatory code of ethics created by the Motion Picture Producers and Distributors of America—having clamped down) take the battle to Mars, winning another victory over interplanetary evil. In *Flash Gordon Conquers the Universe* (1940), Ming is at it again, this time showering the earth with a purple powder that causes a deadly planetwide plague. However, Flash and Dale (this time played by Carol Hughes) manage to find an antidote and foil Ming once again. In the 1939 Buck Rogers serial, on the other hand, invaders from Saturn are actually the good guys, helping Buck and the rebel forces of the Hidden City defeat twenty-fifth-century dictator and criminal kingpin Killer Kane. This serial thus involves a dark, dystopian vision of the future, though all turns out well in the end. It also involves considerable interplanetary travel (as Flash shuttles back and forth from Earth to Saturn) and a sort of time-travel plot in which Flash, a test pilot from the 1930s, is placed in suspended animation, awaking five hundred years in the future.

By today's standards, the special effects of these serials, marked especially by their sparking and spitting rocket ships, were extremely crude. However, to a generation of young Americans, they offered thrilling images of other planets and other times that presented an exciting alternative to a dreary Depression-era world that was drifting toward global war. Despite the importance of the visual dimension, these serials depended primarily on their suspenseful plots and on identification with their swashbuckling heroes to keep their young audiences coming back for more. Indeed, both Flash Gordon and Buck Rogers also became the protagonists of radio serials in the 1930s, indicating that the stories worked even without visuals. Such early science fiction radio programs were important predecessors to science fiction on television, just as radio serials were important predecessors to television series in general.

Actually, however, it was not until the 1950s that science fiction radio really hit its stride, even as science fiction was beginning to appear on television as well. Radio programs such as Mutual's *2000 Plus* and NBC's *Dimension X* (both of which began broadcasting in 1950) were anthology series that offered a variety of exciting tales of future technology, with a special focus on space exploration (including alien invasion), though both series also often reflected contemporary anxieties about the dangers of technology. *Dimension X*, in particular, featured adaptations of stories by some of the leading science fiction writers of the era, including Kurt Vonnegut, Ray Bradbury, and Robert Heinlein, not to mention L. Ron Hubbard, later to become the founder of the Church of Scientology. That the first episode of *Dimension X* was a space exploration tale called "The Outer Limit" (actually, first broadcast as an episode of the *Escape* program before *Dimension X* even became a series in its own right) marks the series as a predecessor of the later television series *The Outer Limits*. Meanwhile, one of the most important science fiction radio anthologies of the 1950s was *Tales of Tomorrow*, broadcast on ABC Radio beginning in early 1953, then switching to CBS Radio shortly afterward. This radio program directly paralleled a science fiction television series of the same name, though in this case the television program, produced in association with the Science Fiction League of America, had begun broadcasting on ABC Television two years earlier, in 1951.[1]

Indeed, radio and television jockeyed for position in the science fiction race throughout the first half of the 1950s, as they did in other genres as well. Of course, by the end of the 1950s, television had established a clear dominance in this and other areas, and radio drama was forever banished to the margins of American popular culture. In the meantime, science fiction television of the 1950s was seriously limited by technological and budgetary restraints, employing special effects that were often, if anything, inferior to those of the movie serials of the 1930s. These serials clearly provided models for early SFTV series, and television versions of both *Buck Rogers* and *Flash Gordon* in fact appeared during the 1950s. While much of the SFTV programming of the 1950s was clearly aimed at children, these early programs also struck a chord in the popular imagination.

For one thing, television itself was such a new and amazing technology in the 1950s that it seemed almost like an example of science fiction in its own right. Meanwhile, it is clear that early programming of the 1950s reflects the deep ambivalence of that decade toward science and technology, which were opening bold new possibilities for mankind as a whole (and even within individual households), but which also had created the possibility of global nuclear destruction. As the decade proceeded, early children's series such as *Captain Video and His Video Rangers*; *Tom Corbett, Space Cadet*; and *Space Patrol* helped to establish science fiction as a central television genre, while the television version of *Tales of Tomorrow* established a tradition of thoughtful, adult-oriented programming that many see as a direct predecessor to *The Twilight Zone*, which can perhaps be considered the series that marked the maturation of science fiction television as a genre.[2]

One of the most sophisticated early productions of science fiction television was a series of three British miniseries, each consisting of a sequence of six thirty- to thirty-five-minute episodes. *The Quatermass Experiment* (1953), *Quatermass II* (1955), and *Quatermass and the Pit* (1958–59) all featured British rocket scientist Bernard Quatermass (played by Reginald Tate, John Robinson, and André Morell in the respective series) involved in various battles against alien invaders, government conspirators, and strange, demonic forces. In the first series, Quatermass must overcome a gigantic rampaging vegetable monster that comes to Earth by stowing away aboard a British spacecraft. The second series closely anticipates the classic science fiction film *Invasion of the Body Snatchers* (1956) by featuring an alien invasion in which Martians come to Earth inside meteorites, then secretly take over the bodies and minds of individual earthlings, including highly placed government officials. In the third and creepiest of the three series, excavations in London unearth evidence that the evolution of humans on Earth was furthered by Martian intervention, while also setting in motion a chain of events that threatens to re-activate the Martian influence.

The three series, though limited by the special effects technology available at the time, managed to produce a sinister sense of threat that was very much in tune with the anxieties of the 1950s. Quatermass himself, a flawed individual who often seems on the verge of madness, is a particularly interesting character whose battles against bureaucracy embodied the sense of many in the decade of being surrounded and engulfed by gray-suited conformism. Meanwhile, the motifs of conspiracy and looming hidden dangers anticipated such later science fiction series as *The X-Files*. Writer Nigel Neale, the creative genius behind *Quatermass*, also managed to make the three series consistently thought-provoking, despite the over-the-top plots and lame effects. Hammer Films eventually condensed each of the three original *Quatermass* miniseries into a feature film (in 1955, 1957, and 1967, respectively). The first two films were in black and white and starred Brian Donlevy in the title role; the third was in color and starred Andre Keir. The *Quatermass* franchise was renewed in 1979 (with Neale still as the writer) for a fourth series of four sixty-minute episodes shown on British ITV, condensed for distribution abroad as a 105-minute TV movie.

The spillover of *Quatermass* onto film calls attention to the impor-tance of science fiction film during the 1950s. It is surely no accident that the decade saw an explosion in the production of science fic-tion films as well as numerous now-classic science fiction novels, even as both science fiction radio and science fiction television were ex-periencing unprecedented growth.[3] During the 1950s, the American (and British) population was fascinated with science and its poten-tial consequences (both positive and negative) as never before, and the production of science fiction narratives in a variety of media re-sponded directly to this fascination. For one thing, the atomic bomb-ings of Japan at the end of World War II, quickly followed by the development of even more devastating hydrogen bombs by both the United States and the Soviet Union, led to the widespread realization that science had, for the first time, provided the means by which the human race could literally destroy itself. On the other hand, espe-cially in the United States, the proliferation of an array of new high-tech domestic appliances (including that amazing new appliance, the television set) transformed the texture of everyday life, while devel-opments in rocketry made the exploration of outer space, so long a staple of the science fiction imagination, an approaching reality.

It was little wonder, then, that science fiction became an increas-ingly important part of American television—and American culture as a whole—throughout the 1950s. Thus, science fiction motifs ap-peared not just in science fiction programs themselves, but also some-times in more mainstream programming. Even Lucy and Ethel got into the act, for example, dressing as Martians in one episode of the land-mark sitcom *I Love Lucy* in order to promote a science fiction film. The popular fascination with science also led to related nonfiction pro-gramming, such as the *Bell System Science Series*, sponsored by AT&T and featuring such creative talents as legendary film director Frank Capra.

The latter series strove for entertainment value and popular appeal in an attempt to reach the masses and fulfill their hunger for scien-tific knowledge, while reassuring them that science was not so far beyond the grasp of the ordinary mind as it sometimes seemed. At the same time, the *Bell System Science Series* was conceived as a prestige production that could proudly carry the banner of its sponsor. In con-trast, the science fiction programming of the decade increasingly gained a reputation as a subliterary form of culture designed to appeal either to children or to the kind of lowbrow plebeian tastes that became the object of much criticism in the 1950s. Indeed, numerous American cultural critics of the decade decried what they saw as the rise of a least-common-denominator "mass culture" that represented a serious dumbing-down of American cultural production. Television as a medium was absolutely central to this phenomenon, and the association between science fiction and television in the decade did little to improve the reputation of either.

Then came *The Twilight Zone*, surely the most important SFTV program of the 1950s, and the first to gain a widespread reputation for genuine artistic merit. This series again had extremely minimal special effects, yet its production values were extremely high. Well written, well acted, and well produced, *The Twilight Zone* quickly became (and still remains) one of the most respected television series of its time. Indeed, Rod Serling—the creator, producer, on-screen host, and frequent writer of *The Twilight Zone*—has long had something of a reputation as *the* genius of 1950s American television. Actually, however, the program did not begin airing until near the end of 1959 (the first episode to be broadcast by CBS Television was shown on October 2, 1959). Of the program's 156 episodes, only 12 were broadcast in the 1950s proper, though it is also the case that most of the period from January 1, 1960, to June 19, 1964, when the bulk of the episodes of the series aired, probably has more in common with the popular memory of the 1950s than with that of the 1960s.

The Twilight Zone, following the anthology series format that had already been established by predecessors such as *Tales of Tomorrow*, was almost infinitely flexible. Indeed, this format allowed the series to adapt to consideration changes in taste and context, which partly accounts for the fact that *The Twilight Zone* underwent two different reincarnations. It returned to its original home on CBS for the appearance of new episodes for an on-again, off-again two-year run from 1985 to 1987, then on to syndication in 1988. The series was then again resurrected for a run on the fledgling UPN, beginning in 2002. This latest version of the series is, at this writing, still in production. *The Twilight Zone* has also served as the prototype for a number of subsequent anthology series with similar themes, including *The Outer Limits* (1963–65), *Night Gallery* (1970–73, which again featured Serling as the on-screen host), and Steven Spielberg's *Amazing Stories* (1985–87, concurrent with the first attempted renewal of *The Twilight Zone*).

The original *Twilight Zone* included a wide variety of episodes that can roughly be categorized as science fiction, horror, fantasy, or some combination of the three. Meanwhile, the episodes that can clearly be considered science fiction are of a variety of types, including space exploration, alien invasion, time travel, and imaginative visions (mostly dystopian) of the future of human society. Though not all episodes could be considered science fiction by most definitions, *The Twilight Zone* as a whole still served as a virtual catalog of science fiction motifs, while at the same time demonstrating through its low emphasis on special effects that science fiction, as a genre of ideas, need not depend on the kinds of spectacular visual effects that would later come to characterize science fiction films. *The Twilight Zone* is rightly regarded as one of the most thoughtful television series of all time, partly because the ideas it explores so intelligently directly address numerous central concerns of American society in the late 1950s and early 1960s. This illustrates the fact that science fiction, no matter how distant its setting in space and time, generally comments first and foremost on the here and now, using imaginative settings and scenarios as a means of gaining new perspectives on contemporary problems.

Many episodes of *The Twilight Zone* can be linked quite directly to the show's historical context. For example, the cold war background of the original series is obvious in a number of episodes. "The Mirror" (October 20, 1961), for example, presents a superficial and stereotypical view of Fidel Castro as a typical strutting Latin American tyrant, while "The Whole Truth" (January 20, 1961) satirizes the fabled dishonesty of used-car salesmen, but ultimately suggests that being forced to tell the truth at all times might be even more embarrassing to Soviet leader Nikita Khrushchev.

Other cold war episodes were far more serious. "Four O'Clock" (April 6, 1962) comments on McCarthyism through its focus on a fanatic who is obsessed with keeping tabs on his fellow citizens, then informing on any who seem to harbor suspect ideas, especially communist ones. More effective as a satire of cold war anticommunist paranoia was the classic episode "The Monsters Are Due on Maple Street" (March 4, 1960). Here (under, as it turns out, the manipulation of aliens conducting an experiment), suspicion runs rampant along previously peaceful Maple Street, turning neighbor against neighbor, as mysterious events are attributed to the nefarious activities of human-looking aliens who may have infiltrated the neighborhood.

A similar theme is treated more comically (and less effectively) in "Will the Real Martian Please Stand Up" (May 16, 1961), in which Martian and Venusian invaders compete with one another, while the humans in the episode bicker among themselves, each suspecting the others of actually being aliens.

In "The Shelter" (September 29, 1961), a sort of companion piece to "The Monsters Are Due on Maple Street," the depiction of the attempts of a family to take refuge in their bomb shelter from a perceived UFO attack obviously derives from contemporary concerns about the possibility of nuclear war. When the family refuses to let any of their less-prepared neighbors join them, the neighbors batter down the shelter door; more violence is averted only when news arrives that the supposed UFOs were merely harmless satellites. This bomb shelter motif, meanwhile, indicates the way in which the concern of *The Twilight Zone* (and of much science fiction of the era) with the cold war frequently included the depiction of post-holocaust worlds and the exploration of the aftermath of nuclear war.

The classic post-holocaust episode of *The Twilight Zone* was "Time Enough at Last" (November 20, 1959). In this episode, mild-mannered, myopic bank teller Henry Bemis (Burgess Meredith) is the ultimate alienated individual, understood by no one and tormented by both his domineering boss and his hectoring wife. In particular, neither the boss nor the wife can understand Bemis's love of reading, which clearly serves for him as an avenue of escape from the dreary and regimented routine of his daily life, but which serves for them as something that marks Bemis as abnormal. As Serling's opening voice-over puts it, "a bank president and a wife and a world full of tongue-cluckers and the unrelenting hands of the clock" are constantly thwarting Bemis's passion for the printed page.

The Twilight Zone, however, supported such passions, and a love of books and literature is central to several episodes of the series. Bemis is thus presented sympathetically throughout the episode, despite the fact that his devotion to books has radically increased his alienation from the world around him. Desperate for a chance to get a little reading done, Bemis symbolically locks himself away from the world in the bank vault so he can read without interruption during his lunch breaks. One day, while he is in the vault, a nuclear attack destroys the entire city, and perhaps all of human civilization. But Bemis emerges unscathed, saved by the thick metal walls of the vault. At first, even though he is able to find plenty of food and other necessities, he feels despair at being the last man on Earth. He even considers suicide. Then, however, he discovers that most of the books in the public library have survived. He suddenly realizes that the nuclear attack was a godsend: now he can have all these books to himself, with all the time in the world to read them and no one to interfere or complain. He joyously begins to arrange the books in stacks, planning out his reading for years to come.

At this point comes the episode's famous, heartrending conclusion: Bemis drops and shatters his thick glasses, without which he is too blind to read. Now, with no one to help him, with no ophthalmologists, optometrists, or opticians left alive to provide him with a new pair of glasses, Bemis is helpless, and all those books are worthless. The point seems clear: it's not so easy to live without other people after all, an alienation-related theme that resounds through many episodes of the series. For example, a similar theme informs the less-successful episode, "The Mind and the Matter" (May 12, 1961), in which the bitterly alienated protagonist gains the power to make everyone else on Earth disappear, then relents and brings them back when he discovers life alone is even worse.

At the same time, the typical *Twilight Zone* protagonist is very much alone in the face of the strange circumstances that confront him or her. And these protagonists are typically treated sympathetically, in keeping with the individualist ideology that permeates the series— and American television programming as a whole. One of the best illustrations of this motif is "The Obsolete Man" (June 2, 1961), a companion episode to "Time Enough at Last," in which the protagonist's love of books again places him in opposition to the official values of his society. Here, a lone librarian, Romney Wordsworth (again played by Meredith, providing an intertextual link that emphasizes the parallel between Wordsworth and Bemis), confronts a totalitarian dystopia that declares both the librarian and the books he so loves to be obsolete and useless. Thus, books again are glorified, and the episode holds up print culture as a bastion of individual liberty and natural enemy of totalitarianism.

"The Obsolete Man" is one of *The Twilight Zone*'s most interesting-looking episodes, employing exaggerated expressionistic sets to enhance the dystopian atmosphere of the episode, in which a totalitarian State exerts total control over the minds of its citizens, having banned all books, all religion, and all independent thought. The episode begins as a chancellor of the State (played by Fritz Weaver) pronounces

Wordsworth "obsolete," a judgment that carries with it a penalty of death. In this thoroughly rational society, nothing that cannot be immediately put to use in the interest of the official goals of the State can be tolerated. Serling's opening monologue, meanwhile, emphasizes the symbolic nature of this State, declaring that it "has patterned itself after every dictator who has ever planted the ripping imprint of a boot on the pages of history since the beginning of time." This boot image probably derives most directly from George Orwell's *1984*, but it also reaches back to Jack London's *The Iron Heel* (1907), placing the episode in a long tradition of dystopian fiction. There are historical references as well, for instance, when the chancellor (employing a confused equation between fascism and communism that was a central motif in American cold war propaganda) later identifies both Hitler and Stalin as his predecessors, though declaring that neither went far enough in eliminating undesirables.

Though it is not entirely obvious in the actual episode, director Elliot Silverstein has stated that the texture of the hearing in which Wordsworth is declared obsolete was partly inspired by the infamous Army-McCarthy hearings, a fact that suggests that this dystopian State, while overtly linked with Nazi Germany and the Stalinist Soviet Union, may also have a great deal in common with the United States. Indeed, if the lonely Wordsworth is a paradigm of alienation, this society is the ultimate in regimented routine, a fact that Wordsworth well recognizes, complaining to the chancellor that "your State has everything categorized, indexed, tagged." However, other than such vague hints at criticism of American society in the 1950s, "The Obsolete Man" is pure orthodox Americanism. It presents Wordsworth (not surprisingly, given his surname) as a paragon of Romantic individualism, upholding the values of religion, traditional culture, and human rights in the face of a dystopian regime so extreme that few viewers would be likely to relate it to their own United States. Indeed, the political commentary of *The Twilight Zone* is quite consistently attenuated by the series' ultimate orthodoxy, something that might also be said for the cultural criticism of the 1950s. At the same time, the orthodoxy of *The Twilight Zone* is consistently undercut by unstated hints that all is not well with the American way of life.

Due to budgetary and technological restraints, *The Twilight Zone* actually shows us very little in the way of space travel and alien environments that are the stock-in-trade of "hard" science fiction. When spacecraft, robots, and other high-tech props are shown, they are typically recycled from earlier MGM productions such as *Forbidden Planet*, as when the model flying saucer from that film appears in episodes such as "The Invaders" (January 27, 1961) and "Death Ship" (February 7, 1963). Meanwhile, the alien landscapes explored on *The Twilight Zone* tend to be rather earthlike, allowing them to be filmed on location without expensive set designs. On the other hand, the series sometimes makes a virtue of this necessity, and one of its favorite motifs involves reversals in which the seemingly simple opposition between earthlings and aliens is undermined, often by leading audiences inadvertently to view this opposition from the point of view of the aliens.

Space travel is a central concern of the series, beginning with the initial pilot episode ("Where Is Everybody?"), in which the loneliness of the long-distance space traveler is clearly used as a metaphor for the sense of many in the late 1950s of being ultimately alone in the world, alienated from and unable truly to communicate with those around them. In this episode, the central character (played by Earl Holliman) apparently awakes to find himself the only man left on Earth, dramatizing the alienation felt by so many during the decade. Here, however, the scenario turns out merely to be part of a staged test to see if he, an astronaut-trainee, will be psychologically able to withstand the extreme loneliness and isolation of solo spaceflight.

The loneliness of outer space was also a central preoccupation of the next episode to deal with space travel, "The Lonely" (November 13, 1959). As this episode begins, James A. Corry (Jack Warden) has been convicted of murder (though he swears it was self-defense) and sentenced to serve fifty years of exile on a barren asteroid. Serling's opening voice-over explains to us that Corry is dying of loneliness in this barren, alien environment, though this loneliness is subsequently relieved when a compassionate spaceship captain drops off a female robot (named Alicia), which looks entirely human. In fact, the directions that come with Alicia suggestively tell us that "to all intent and purpose this creature *is* a woman. Physiologically and psychologically, she is a human being." Initially appalled by the idea of using a mechanical contrivance for company, Corry slowly warms to Alicia and falls deeply in love with her. Indeed, her lack of humanity seems to make her a perfect woman: with no real identity of her own, she simply becomes a reflection of Corry's own interests and desires. The episode thus comments, though in a subtle way that is not at all heavy-handed, on gender relations in the early 1960s, when the women's movement was beginning to gain momentum in its challenge to the objectification of women. Later, Corry is pardoned and the spaceship returns to take him back to Earth. Unfortunately, he can only take fifteen pounds of luggage on the small ship, so he is told that Alicia must be left behind. When he protests that Alicia is not luggage, but a woman, the captain provides a shocking reminder of her otherness by pulling out his gun and shooting the robot in the face, destroying it and revealing a mass of circuits and wiring. They won't be leaving behind a woman, the captain tells Corry, just his loneliness.

Perhaps the most memorable space-exploration episodes of *The Twilight Zone* are the several that present variations on a basic motif in which we see astronauts set forth to explore new planets and encounter alien species, only to learn at the end that the astronauts are actually aliens and that the strange new planet is Earth. For example, in "Third from the Sun" (January 8, 1960), a group of scientists takes off in an experimental spacecraft to avoid an imminent nuclear war. We learn only at the end that Earth is the destination, not the point of departure, effecting a sudden reversal of perspective that creates an ironic distance and allows audiences to recognize the episode as a commentary on contemporary cold war tensions, while at the same time enjoying the episode as entertainment.

"I Shot an Arrow into the Air," broadcast one week later, represented a variation on this same kind of reversal, in which three astronauts survive a crash landing on what they take to be a barren asteroid. One of the three kills the other two to extend their limited water supply, only to discover that they have in fact landed in the Nevada desert, with civilization (and plenty of water) only a short distance away. Meanwhile, in "The Invaders," a woman is terrorized by tiny invaders from another planet in an episode that reveals, only at the end, that the invaders are in fact astronauts from Earth who have landed on another planet.

Such reversals were highly effective at a moment in American history when many traditional "Us vs. Them" boundaries were being challenged. For one thing, in the wake of World War II, the United States had assumed an unprecedented prominence in international politics, largely assuming the role of global standard-bearer of Western civilization, a role that had been played for the previous two centuries by the British Empire. As a result, American culture was coming into contact with foreign cultures, including seemingly exotic, non-

Western ones, to an extent that Americans had never experienced before. Meanwhile, on the domestic front, a burgeoning civil rights movement was calling into question a number of traditional oppositions within American society itself. Indeed, much of the amazing hold of cold war rhetoric on the popular American imagination can probably be explained by the fact that Americans were eager for the kind of simple good versus evil oppositions that this rhetoric offered amid a climate in which so many traditional oppositions were losing their imaginative grip.

Gender was another such opposition, though *The Twilight Zone* was relatively timid about offering challenges to traditional gender roles. However, the series was bolder in exploring more conventional science fiction boundaries, such as that between human and machine. In what can be taken as a variation on the motif of human-alien reversals, several episodes of *The Twilight Zone* explore the notion that, as our machines become more and more sophisticated, the boundary between us and them becomes more and more difficult to discern. For example, in the memorable and frightening "In His Image" (January 3, 1963), the protagonist discovers, to his horror, that he himself is a humanoid robot. This latter episode thus addresses the fear of many by the early 1960s that they were in the grip of large, impersonal forces far more powerful than themselves, forcing them into mechanical, conformist, and dehumanizing modes of behavior. Robots were again used to address this particular fear in one of the very last episodes of the series, "The Brain Center at Whipple's" (May 15, 1964), which in fact served as a summary of numerous contemporary workplace concerns. In the episode, Whipple, a heartless company head, decides to replace all of his employees with machines in order to increase profits. Then, in a final plot twist of the kind that occurs in nearly all episodes of *The Twilight Zone*, Whipple discovers that he himself is being replaced by a robot, played by Robby the Robot, another prop borrowed from *Forbidden Planet*.

The Twilight Zone was more clever than genuinely scary, and its final plot twists often contained a delicious and wry sort of irony. This was especially the case in episodes such as "Static" (March 19, 1961), in which the series took satirical jabs at television itself. This episode presents television as a medium of a degraded and commercialized present, as opposed to a nostalgic vision of a more humane past, represented in this case by the medium of radio. Indeed, much of the pleasure of *The Twilight Zone* surely derived from the ability of the series to tap into so many anxieties that were haunting the American psyche at the beginning of the 1960s, while at the same time investing those anxieties with a distancing irony that made them seem less threatening. Nevertheless, especially in retrospect, the series is surprisingly pessimistic in many ways, especially when it ponders the possibilities of technology. Most of its science fiction episodes, in fact, are cautionary tales about the dehumanizing consequences of technology gone awry rather than uplifting tales about a future made glorious due to increased technological capabilities.

This tendency toward technological pessimism, certainly understandable in the cold war context of the time, would continue, though in different forms, to dominate science fiction television for the next forty years. Yet, despite this overall tendency (or perhaps because of it), some of the most beloved science fiction series of all time (especially the first two *Star Trek* series) are notably optimistic about the future. The remainder of this volume traces the history of science fiction television during the forty years following the original *Twilight Zone*. In so doing, it seeks not only to document the highlights of the history of science fiction television, but also to explain what is special and distinctive about the genre. By tracing the evolution of the genre over time, the following chapters explore the ways in which science fiction television constitutes a specific cultural tradition in which each series is importantly influenced by what has come before. In addition, it notes the many ways in which the evolution of science fiction television has responded to (and, in some cases, influenced) social and historical trends in the world at large.

Chapter 2 discusses the way in which SFTV series of the 1960s continue to show the effects of cold war tensions but are also (*Star Trek* being the paradigmatic case) influenced by a new sense of excitement and possibility linked to the oppositional political movements of that decade. By the 1970s, phenomena such as the energy crisis, Watergate, and the inauspicious American retreat from Vietnam had led to a new era of suspicion and cynicism, even as cold war fears of nuclear holocaust were in decline. As discussed in chapter 3, the decades of the 1970s and 1980s were largely meager ones for SFTV, though the success of the *Star Wars* film led to a brief flowering of special-effects-oriented series at the end of the 1970s, and the 1980s closed with the reemergence of the original *Star Trek* optimistic vision, as *Star Trek: The Next Generation* outstripped even its predecessor series in popularity.

Chapter 4 indicates some of the ways in which the complex climate of the 1990s—in which American society was informed on the one hand by unprecedented prosperity for the wealthy and on the other hand by unprecedented social problems for the poor, even at the end of the cold war—made the global political situation seem more, rather than less, threatening to American prosperity. As a result, SFTV programming of the 1990s took a decidedly dark turn. *Star Trek: Deep Space Nine* introduced sinister elements into the *Star Trek* universe, while *The X-Files* reached levels of violence, paranoia, and abjection (all tempered by self-conscious postmodern irony) never before attained by science fiction television. By the new millennium, as discussed in chapter 5, science fiction television had virtually abandoned the attempt to envision the future, concentrating instead on the strangeness of the present. Together, these chapters track the evolution of both science fiction television and American culture for the past half century.

CHAPTER 2

From *Doctor Who* to *Star Trek*: Science Fiction Television Comes of Age

On May 5, 1961, astronaut Alan B. Shepard, Jr., piloted his Mercury space capsule on a modest 302-mile suborbital flight that made him the first American in space, following hard on the heels of the first manned orbital flight, by the Russian Yuri Gagarin on April 12 of that year. By 1969, however, it was the Americans who held the lead in the space race, culminating in Neil Armstrong's small-but-giant step onto the lunar surface in July 1969. In between, American television carried numerous fictional accounts of space exploration. However, given the priority accorded the space race within the cold war context of the 1960s—and given the way the race to the moon ignited the imagination of the general American populace—narratives of space exploration played a surprisingly limited role on American television during the decade. Of course, one could argue that the real-world space race was so compelling that fictional narratives of space exploration simply paled in comparison. Indeed, the televised coverage of the early manned spaceflights represented some of the most compelling television programming to air during the 1960s. Meanwhile, the special-effects technologies (and budgets) of the time remained limited, making the representation of far-out space adventures very difficult. Still, even though television in the 1960s was dominated by Westerns and cold war spy dramas, it is still the case that the programming of the decade provided a pivotal foundation upon which all subsequent science fiction television would be based. In this sense, two series from the 1960s were particularly crucial: *The Twilight Zone*, which ushered in the decade, and *Star Trek*, which brought the decade to a close, its last episode broadcast on June 3, 1969, almost seven weeks before Armstrong's walk on the moon. A number of important series fell in between, including several important British series.

The first important American series to follow *The Twilight Zone*, showing a strong and direct influence by that series, was the original version of *The Outer Limits*, which was broadcast by ABC while *The Twilight Zone* was still in its original run on CBS. The original version of *The Outer Limits*, aired from 1963 to 1965, lasted only forty-nine hour-long episodes, though it nevertheless exerted a strong influence on the American popular imagination during that period. ABC seriously considered bringing the series back in the 1980s, but the failure of the 1980s revival of *The Twilight Zone* put an end to those plans. However, *The Outer Limits* was resurrected on the Showtime cable channel in 1995 for a successful run that spilled over into syndication, and the Sci Fi Channel, running into the twenty-first century.

Substantially darker (and generally more frightening) than *The Twilight Zone*, the original version of *The Outer Limits* nevertheless quite obviously owed a great deal to the influence of its illustrious predecessor, including not only the anthology format, but also the tactic of opening each episode with a distinctive and easily identifiable voice-over narration that held the episodes together as a recognizable unit. In this case, the series opened with a chilling "control voice," which announced to viewers that they should not attempt to adjust their sets because those sets were now under the control of the forces represented by the voice. "We are controlling transmission," the voice memorably proclaims. "For the next hour, sit quietly and we will control all that you see and hear. You are about to participate in a great adventure. You are about to experience the awe and mystery which reaches from the inner mind to the outer limits."

This opening thus addresses both the promise and the threat of the television medium itself, the motif of control particularly echoing the now-classic (but then recent) John Frankenheimer film *The Manchurian Candidate* (1962), a cold war spy thriller in which television broadcasts transmit signals that constitute a key element of a mind-control plot. Indeed, even more than *The Twilight Zone*, *The Outer Limits* often commented on television—and even on itself—making it one of the most self-referential series ever to appear on American TV. For example, even a relatively undistinguished episode such as the alien-abduction tale "Second Chance" (March 2, 1964) contains such commentary, as when the control voice describes the function of an amusement park in an opening narration that might well apply to the series itself: "When fear is too terrible, when reality is too agonizing, we seek escape in manufactured danger, in the thrills and pleasures of pretending."

Many episodes of *The Outer Limits* were quite reminiscent of *The Twilight Zone*, though their hour-long format generally allowed for more dramatic development. *The Twilight Zone* featured half-hour episodes, except for one brief (and unsuccessful) experiment with hour-long episodes in early 1963, when the series made a comeback after being taken off the air in the fall of 1962. The fact that *The Outer Limits* episodes were an hour long might also partly account for the fact that the series tended more consistently toward science fiction than did *The Twilight Zone*, the longer time allowing for the exploration of more complex ideas. On the other hand, the necessity to fill a longer time slot might also account for the fact that *The Outer Limits* was significantly more uneven than its predecessor. At its worst, *The Outer Limits* could be hokey and hackneyed, featuring ridiculous-looking monsters in rubber suits chasing uninteresting humans that few in the audience would be likely to really care about. Thus, in "The Mutant" (March 16, 1954), a would-be Earth colonist on an alien planet mutates into a bald, bug-eyed monster, whose very touch can be deadly to ordinary humans. He is, however, mortally sensitive to darkness—and is thus rather easily killed off by being lured into a dark cave by his fellow colonists.

At its best, though, *The Outer Limits* could be as literate, thought provoking, and multilayered as anything ever to appear on American commercial television. "A Feasibility Study" (April 13, 1964) is a classic example of such an episode, even though it involves a rather far-fetched premise that requires considerable suspension of disbelief on the part of the audience. In this episode, an entire middle-class neighborhood is scooped up and teleported to the alien planet of Luminos, where the inhabitants have contracted a contagion that renders them incapable of physical movement by the time they reach adulthood. The good news is that this immobility has helped the Luminoids to develop their mental abilities to astounding levels. Indeed, they spend their adult lives suspended in "Contemplative Energy Plants," where groups of them can pool their considerable mental resources to explore new intellectual frontiers. As one of them explains in the course of the episode, their immobility allows them to channel all of their energy to their minds, which are thereby "never drained, never dulled. Minds, like nuclear birds, soaring to the most splendored dreamings of the universe."

The bad news is that the Luminoids still need someone to do the physical labor necessary to sustain their society. Unable (and unwilling) to do that work themselves, they decide to scan the galaxy for potential slave labor. As the control voice tells us in its opening introduction, "They seek a planet on which life is healthy, vibrant, strong, and mobile. They need such people to do their work, to labor and slave for them, to manufacture their splendored dreams." They choose Earth as a likely candidate for this project, but they are uncertain whether earthlings will be able to endure the sultry conditions on their planet. Therefore, as the episode opens, they have abducted the inhabitants of a single neighborhood in order to conduct the feasibility study of the title. In the course of the episode, the abducted earthlings realize the situation and then decide intentionally to infect themselves with the Luminoid contagion, foiling the experiment and saving the population of Earth from a future life of slavery on Luminos.

On one level, "A Feasibility Study" is a rather straightforward science fiction tale that draws upon motifs so familiar as to border on clichés. Thus, we have the population of Earth, strong and vital, threatened with subjugation at the hands of an advanced but degenerate species whose mental development has occurred at the expense of physical weakness. Moreover, we see the earthlings resist this subjugation through personal sacrifice, preferring death to slavery in a final "give me liberty or give me death" demonstration of solidarity. In its rejection of the institution of slavery, the episode also offers the kind of obvious social commentary that can often be found in science fiction, television or otherwise. However, this episode has powerful allegorical resonances that go well beyond the simple opposition between defiant good-guy earthling slaves and manipulative brainiac alien masters.

For one thing, the episode is underwritten throughout by the reminder that the lofty lifestyle of the Luminoids is possible only through the exploitation of a lower class of workers. This brings the episode to the verge of an open critique of American capitalism, the increasing globalization that in the previous decade had helped to produce more and more material comfort for Americans at the expense of a

growing international division of labor in which American brain workers supplied management skills and expertise while much of the rest
of the world supplied manual labor and raw materials. However, as
it actually plays out, the allegorical critique of capitalism in this episode seems aimed less at this international situation than at the domestic economic situation within the United States. For one thing, the
very title of the episode identifies the Luminoids with the American
management class, aligning their "research" with precisely the kind
of drive for efficiency that had helped to make American capitalism
more and more productive since World War II. For another, the trade-
off offered the earthlings by the Luminoids is suspiciously similar to
the one that many saw as being offered to American workers at the
time. In return for their services, they are told, "Your lives here will
be comfortable and secure, and you will be free to worship and love
and think as haphazardly as usual." Thus, what they are essentially
being offered on Luminos is an extension of the conditions under
which they already live on Earth. This parallel clearly suggests that
they are already not as free as they would like to believe, having become the slaves of the things that are necessary to the maintenance
of their middle-class lifestyles on Earth.

The two families that we meet in the episode are headed (and that
is the right word—these are very conventional, patriarchal families)
by a workaholic businessman, Ralph Cashman (David Opatashu), and
a medical doctor, Dr. Simon Holm (Sam Wanamaker). As the episode
opens, we see Cashman heading to the office on a Sunday morning
without even having a decent breakfast. His wife, Rhea (Joyce Van
Patten), begs him not to go, warning of the "success compulsion" that
has come to dominate his life. Cashman ignores this spousal complaint and heads off nevertheless, only to discover rather quickly that
they are now on Luminos. Cashman comes off well by the end of the
episode, struggling heroically to warn the others in the neighborhood
of what is going on. However, his depiction clearly addresses the
concern of many in American society at the time that their newfound
prosperity was being bought at the expense of a virtual enslavement
to the gray-flanneled drive for success.

Gender also plays an important role in the social commentary
embedded in "A Feasibility Study." Early in the episode, Cashman
confides in Holm that he has been careful to avoid marrying an intelligent woman, and his dominance of Rhea seems almost total.
Holm, meanwhile, has married an intelligent woman indeed, which

leads to its own problems. We thus learn that the Holms (who live next door to the Cashmans, but—in another comment on American society in the 1960s—hardly know them) are in the midst of marital "disappointments" that have led them to agree to separate. We also learn the reason for their conjugal discord: Mrs. Andrea Holm (Phyllis Love) is a former crusading journalist who has given up her career in order to be a stay-at-home wife to the domineering Dr. Holm, who remains deaf to her complaints that this sort of life is stifling to her. It is so stifling, in fact, that she describes her domestic life as "a kind of slavery," while the doctor himself is caught so thoroughly in the grip of his preconceived notions about marriage and gender roles that he seems entirely unable to see her point of view.

On the surface, then, "A Feasibility Study" celebrates the official American belief in the sanctity of individual liberty, specifying that the earthlings of the episode sacrifice themselves because they prefer death to the loss of "choice." Yet we also see that, in the course of their everyday lives on Earth, they had tended to act out a scripted existence, in which all of their choices were predetermined. Within the marriages, both wives are thoroughly controlled by their husbands, even if one of them has opted to leave her marriage to escape this domination. Both husbands, meanwhile, are in turn consumed by the demands of their jobs and by their perceptions of what it means to be a successful male in modern America.

Such commentary often appears in episodes of *The Outer Limits*, a series that consistently pushed the envelope, leading to incessant battles with network censors and no doubt contributing to the series' rather quick demise. Indeed, "A Feasibility Study" is quite typical of the better *Outer Limits* episodes, both in its thought-provoking commentary and in its subject matter, which builds upon fairly standard science fiction motifs in unexpected and interesting ways. Variations on and complications of stock science fiction themes distinguished the series, which was often more interested in thematic commentary—or even on-screen artistry—than in believable science fiction premises. Indeed, one of the most admired and beloved episodes of the series, "The Man Who Was Never Born" (October 28, 1963), is truly awful as science fiction—filled with scientific inconsistencies and preposterous plot devices—yet nevertheless manages to be very good television. Artistically impressive, it quite effectively addresses its themes, which derive more from the tradition of the fairy tale than of science fiction, even though the basic premise of the episode has to do with time travel and runaway scientific exploration, two of the favorite themes of the science fiction genre.

In the episode, astronaut Joseph Reardon (Karl Held) blasts off in 1963 in a spaceship far beyond the technology of that year, signaling from the very beginning that this will not be an episode much concerned with scientific verisimilitude. On his flight, Held encounters a "time barrier" that hurls him forward to the year 2148, where he discovers that human civilization is in ruins, the race itself having been reduced to a few straggling and horribly malformed mutants, all due to the accidental release of alien bacteria on Earth as a result of the experiments of late-twentieth-century scientist Bertram Cabot, Jr. In the future, Reardon meets one of these mutants, Andro (Martin Landau), who explains the situation and shows him to the library where he has lovingly preserved all remaining records of the past. These records, however, consist largely of literature, and it is clear that Andro's vision of the past is filtered largely through such literary works as Tolstoy's *Anna Karenina*, Melville's *Moby Dick*, Fitzgerald's *The Great Gatsby*, and "Mark Twain's whole meandering Mississippi." Indeed, Andro's tendency to see the reality of the past through the filter of its fiction points toward his basically romantic nature and toward one of the crucial issues addressed by the episode—the sometimes complex relationship between reality and our images of it.

Andro agrees to travel back to the past with Reardon so that his gruesome disfiguration can serve as a warning of what is to come. Unfortunately, Reardon is killed (and then vanishes) on the way back through the time barrier, leaving Andro to confront the past alone. Then, through a series of extremely unlikely coincidences, Andro finds that he has arrived at a time before the birth of the scientist Cabot. Indeed, he takes refuge in a boardinghouse in which Noelle Anderson (Shirley Knight), the mother-to-be of Cabot, is living in the days just prior to her marriage to Bertram Cabot, Sr., a military officer. Realizing the situation and aided by a psychic ability that allows him to make others see him as a normal human, Andro decides to try to prevent the marriage so that Cabot, Jr., will never be born and can thus never conduct the experiments that would virtually destroy the human race.

After a series of misadventures, Andro succeeds in luring Noelle away from the handsome but soulless Lt. Cabot, convincing her to return to the future in Reardon's spaceship with him instead, even though she is treated to a sight of him as he really appears. However,

in a motif clearly borrowed from the fairy tale *Beauty and the Beast*,
Noelle is unconcerned with his appearance, realizing that she prefers his sensitive and romantic nature to the stern and unyielding
manner of her soldier-fiancé. In short, she prefers her imaginative
vision of him to the real vision offered by her eyesight. The fairy-tale
feel of the episode, meanwhile, is enhanced by its look, achieved by
some extremely creative camera work, including the use of unusual
camera angles and the filming of many shots, especially close-ups,
through a filter designed to produce a soft, dreamy look.

The episode ends with a rather clichéd time-travel twist: having
succeeded in preventing Cabot, Jr., from decimating the human race,
Andro himself (a product of that decimation) ceases to exist, becoming, like Cabot, Jr., a man who was never born. His disappearance
leaves Noelle alone on the ship, flying into an unknown future. However, the predictability of this ending does little damage to the episode. Instead, it makes Andro a more effectively romantic tragic hero,
at the same time leaving viewers to ponder the implications of the
plight in which Noelle's own romanticism has placed her. She has
definitely not gotten what she expected and hoped for, but she has,
after all, helped to save the human race through the power of her
dreams.

A similar defense of the imagination and of those who dare to
dream (many of them lone scientist figures) appears in many episodes
of *The Outer Limits*. In "The Children of Spider County" (February 17,
1964), a group of five young men (all born at about the same time
and under similar unusual circumstances) have developed unusual
intellectual gifts. Four of the five have moved away from their birth-
place in rural Spider County and have achieved considerable success
in the world. One of them, young Ethan Wechsler, has been unable
to escape because he was orphaned at the age of nine. He has thus
suffered his whole life at the hands of the locals, who, not understanding his unusual mental gifts, have labeled him a "witch-boy," treating him with suspicion and contempt. Indeed, as the episode opens,
he is being held in custody for a murder he did not commit. As the
episode unfolds, we learn that all of the men had been fathered to
human mothers by alien men from the planet Eros, where a long-term
quest for material wealth has created a society devoid of dreamers—
with the peculiar side effect that it can no longer produce male children and is thus dying out. Ethan's father returns to Earth to fetch
all of the young men back to Eros, but they ultimately decide to re-

main on Earth, which Ethan and the others conclude is more hospitable to dreamers like themselves than Eros could ever be.

Though not one of the more riveting episodes of *The Outer Limits*, "The Children of Spider County" is fairly typical in its concerns. It includes a vague critique of materialism in its treatment of Eros (which clearly serves as a cautionary model for Earth), while also endorsing individualism and difference (though in an oddly elitist way). The episode also endorses dreaming; it celebrates those who dare to be different. Indeed, it argues that such special individuals are the key to the success of any society. As the opening voice-over narration explains, the episode is based on the premise that "in light of today's growing anxieties, it has become more absolute that the wealth of a nation consists in the number of superior men that it harbors." Then, at the end of the episode, a second voice-over reiterates and embellishes this fundamental point by concluding that "the wealth of a nation, of a world, consists in the number of superior men that it harbors, and often it appears that these men are too different, too dreaming. And often, because they are driven by powers and dreams strange to us, they are driven away by us."

"The Children of Spider County" is an alien-invasion episode in which the alien invasion is largely beside the point, just as the space and time-travel motif in "The Man Who Was Never Born" is merely a pretext for the exploration of the episode's true romantic concerns. When *The Outer Limits* stuck more strictly to science fiction, it often did so in the form of cautionary tales that warned, in the tradition of *Frankenstein*, against the perils of unfettered scientific research. Bertram Cabot's deadly bacteriological research is an example of such investigations. Meanwhile, the series no doubt gained a certain energy from excitement over the space race at the time. In fact, the opening narration of "Specimen: Unknown" (February 24, 1964) contains a brief history of space exploration that (inaccurately) congratulates Project Mercury for being mankind's "first venture into space," forgetting that the Russians had been there before. Still, when *The Outer Limits* envisioned advances in space travel, it was usually far more interested in the potential deadly effects of space exploration than in the depiction of exciting new vistas for human adventure. For example, in "Specimen: Unknown," alien spores from space are brought back from a space station, inadvertently infesting the earth with killer flowers that spread rapidly, threatening to destroy all human life on the planet. When a rainstorm looms, the horrified authorities expect the alien contagion to spread even more quickly, but, luckily, water is deadly to the plants, which are killed off in the downpour, saving humanity similar to the way that relatively harmless (to humans) Earth microbes kill off the Martian invaders in H. G. Wells's classic, *War of the Worlds*.

"Specimen: Unknown" begins as a space exploration episode and ends as an alien-invasion story, but then the original *Outer Limits* was always more interested in the latter kind of tale. Alien invasions and alien abductions of humans were the bread and butter of the series, though the series tended to complicate this standard motif of cold war science fiction in interesting ways, often by blurring typical boundaries that would simplistically identify earthlings as good and aliens as evil. For example, in the series pilot, "The Galaxy Being" (September 16, 1963), well-meaning freelance scientist Allan Maxwell (played by film star Cliff Robertson) develops a device that whisks an unwitting alien to Earth from the far reaches of space. The peaceful and highly advanced alien means harm to no one, but he is greeted on Earth (described in the episode as an insignificant speck of dust in the cosmic scheme of things) with violence and hysteria, leading to his death. Maxwell and the ghostly galaxy being thus represent variations of the mad scientist and the invading alien, except that, in a typical *Outer Limits* modification, they are in this case both benevolent, while ordinary human beings are the villains of the piece.

If the complex treatment of the alien-invasion motif suggested an unusually sophisticated approach to typical cold war concerns, *The Outer Limits* was sometimes even more overt in its treatment of these political issues. For example, the classic episode "O.B.I.T." (November 4, 1963) is a sort of companion piece to *The Twilight Zone*'s "The Monsters Are Due on Maple Street" in its satirical treatment of cold war paranoia. In this case, however, paranoia is depicted as being justified by sinister activities within the U.S. government rather than by the threat of communism. The ultimate villain in the episode is identified as an alien invader, thus providing a measure of political protection for the program and its message.

"O.B.I.T." (Outer Band Individuated Teletracer) is the official designation for a piece of high-tech surveillance equipment being used by the government (with strong support from the military) to keep tabs on the researchers at the Defense Department's top-secret Cypress Hills Research Center, seeking thereby to ensure their loyalty and ideological orthodoxy. The device is able somehow to tap into the brain waves of individuals, providing both video and audio images of their activities, no matter where they are. The existence of this piece of equipment (previously known only to a few security personnel) is revealed when a murder at the research facility draws a congressional investigation. In particular, Senator Jeremiah Orville (Peter Breck) comes to the facility to conduct hearings into the killing, and discovers the existence of O.B.I.T. in the process. Horrified by the extent to which the machine is being used to monitor individual activity, Orville presses his investigation, insisting on testimony from Clifford Scott (Harry Townes), the head of the Cypress Hills facility, who has recently vanished following an apparent mental breakdown. When Scott does appear, he exposes the central role of facility administrator Byron Lomax (Jeff Corey) in promoting the use of the device. More important, he reveals that Lomax is actually an alien infiltrator involved in a plot to take over the earth.

Clearly foreshadowing such later "paranoid" series as *The X-Files*, "O.B.I.T." also builds upon contemporary cold war concerns about surveillance and the invasion of privacy in the interest of security. Indeed, the episode draws considerable energy from the fact that Corey, who plays the central villain, had been investigated by the notorious House Un-American Activities Committee in the early 1950s, then blacklisted for his perceived political beliefs, a development that forced him out of acting in films from 1951 to 1963.[1] The episode also includes a certain amount of commentary on the voyeuristic potential of television itself, as the similarity of the O.B.I.T. viewing screen to a television set is clear. Thus, when an army colonel who had formerly approved of the O.B.I.T. project suddenly realizes its sinister nature, he also grants the addictive nature of the viewing experience offered by the machine. "I can't *not* look," he admits. "It's like a drug. You can't resist it. It's an addiction!"

The colonel, of course, might also be speaking about television itself, the growing cultural power of which was becoming a cause of great concern to many in the early 1960s. Moreover, the episode's warnings about the potential spread of television voyeurism (seemingly verified in the proliferation of "reality" programming in the early twenty-first century) are made even more chilling by the way in which Lomax defiantly responds to the revelations about his activities. The machines are everywhere, he explains, participating in a surveillance project that goes far beyond what anyone at Cypress Hills might have imagined. Furthermore, they will have done their work even if the government finds and destroys them all, because the revelation of the very existence of the machines will create rifts in society and strike telling blows to the popular morale, making Earth a much easier target for an alien invasion.

If episodes such as "O.B.I.T." tried for serious social commentary, other series of the 1960s were designed more for fun. For example, the British series *Doctor Who* used its low budget, poor special effects, far-fetched premise, and ridiculous-looking monsters and aliens to such good effect that it ultimately became the most durable science fiction series in the history of television, running continually on the BBC from 1963 to 1989, amassing a whopping total of nearly seven hundred episodes. The series lasted so long, in fact, that it ran through seven different actors in the title role, plus an eighth for a 1996 television movie and a ninth (Peter Cushing) for two mid-1960s theatrical films based on the series. The other characters changed as well, as the doctor acquired an array of companions (often young, female, and highly attractive) on his travels. Indeed, this revolving-door casting of the central character and his companions, which might have seemed sure death for the series, was turned into a positive asset, adding to the amazing flexibility of the series, which, in the course of time, explored virtually every major science fiction motif, adopted a variety of tones and attitudes, and frequently changed its look and style, though always maintaining the basic low-budget feel that fans came to love.

Despite the frequent changes in casting (which was explained in the series by the fact that the doctor required occasional "regeneration" in order to keep going), Doctor Who himself became one of the most beloved characters in the history of science fiction television. Doctor Who is a renegade time lord who has fled his home planet of Gallifrey because he finds the discipline and conformism there intolerable. By turns eccentric, comic, forbidding, flamboyant, dashing, and mild-mannered, the various versions of the doctor played by the different actors offered something for everyone. Yet the doctor, as his name indicates, also retained a basic mystery. Audiences could ultimately piece together enough clues to conclude that he originated on Gallifrey, from which he fled with his granddaughter in an amazing craft, the TARDIS (Time and Relative Dimension in Space). In fact, the TARDIS (which from the outside looked exactly like an ordinary London police telephone box) was the secret to the flexibility of the series, because it allowed the doctor and his companions of the moment to travel instantaneously anywhere in space and time, thus opening unlimited possibilities for adventure. On the other hand, this particular TARDIS is a bit banged up, and its various malfunctions also provide considerable plot material.

The episodes of *Doctor Who*, generally running approximately twenty-five minutes in length, were usually broadcast in cycles of four to seven episodes devoted to a single plot arc. However, in one case (1978–79), a continuous plot arc ("The Key to Time") was maintained through an entire twenty-six-episode season, though this season still featured a sequence of several substories, each four to six episodes in length. One of the most memorable sequences of the series, "The Daleks" (aka "The Mutants"), was also one of the earliest. In this Season One episode cycle, the doctor (played by William Hartnell as aged and grumpy), his granddaughter, and companions Barbara Wright (Jacqueline Hill) and Ian Chesterton (William Russell) inadvertently land on the planet Skaro, a bleak world decimated by an earlier nuclear war. The sequence obviously addresses cold war fears of nuclear holocaust. However, the success of "The Daleks" depended not on topicality but on suspense, as the four travelers encounter a variety of harrowing experiences of a kind that would become a hallmark of the series.

The situation on Skaro draws upon a number of familiar science fiction post-holocaust images. It also echoes in a particularly direct way the future world of H. G. Wells's *The Time Machine* (1895), in which a degenerate humanity has split into two races, the passive and effete Eloi and the brutish Morlocks. In this case, Skaro is populated by the Thals and the Daleks, who had previously been antagonists in the nuclear war. Now, the blond Aryan Thals, once mighty warriors, have become pacifist farmers, dedicated to a principle of nonviolence in order to avoid a repetition of the previous holocaust. The Daleks, meanwhile, are horribly mutated creatures that now need radiation to survive and can function and move about only by encasing themselves in robotlike machines powered by static electricity drawn from the metal floors of their city.

In this sequence, the four travelers wander into the Dalek city, where they are captured. Meanwhile, they all begin to succumb to radiation poisoning. The Daleks send Susan, the granddaughter, back to the TARDIS to fetch some antiradiation drugs left there by the Thals, assuring her that the drugs will be used to save her and her companions. However, the Daleks actually hope to use the drugs themselves, establishing a tendency toward treachery that will mark this and their several subsequent appearances in the series. Later, for example, they employ similar trickery in an attempt to lure the Thals into the city so that they can kill them all and establish sole dominion over Skaro. Instead, with the help of the travelers, the Dalek power supply is destroyed and the Daleks themselves are seemingly wiped out. The travelers return to the TARDIS, leaving the Thals to rebuild a new civilization on Skaro.

This sequence was so popular that it was remade as the theatrical film *Doctor Who and the Daleks* in 1965. A subsequent Dalek sequence in Season Two, "The Dalek Invasion of Earth," was similarly remade for theatrical release as *Daleks' Invasion Earth: 2150 A.D.* in 1966, establishing the Daleks as the best known of the numerous villains and monsters encountered by the doctor in his long career. Indeed, in the fourth season (in which Hartnell, due to illness, was replaced by Patrick Troughton as a younger, more jovial—and disheveled—doctor), the Daleks were featured in two sequences. This season also introduced the young Scotsman Jamie (Frazer Hines), who would prove to be one of the doctor's more popular sidekicks. Also introduced in Season Four were the Cybermen, part-human, part-robot invaders from the tenth planet of Earth's solar system, intent on conquering Earth and making its human inhabitants into cybermen like themselves. The Cybermen were featured several times in the series, appearing in two episode cycles in this season alone. They were also particularly silly looking, being nothing more than men in shiny suits wearing robot helmets that looked like they were designed and made by children as part of a school project. But this look only added to their appeal and to the appeal of the series, which came to rely upon such motifs as part of its campy charm.

In one of Troughton's last sequences, "The Invasion" (November 2–December 21, 1968), the Cybermen once again plot to invade Earth. This time, however, they are opposed not only by the doctor, but also by a well-organized secret quasi-military force, UNIT (United Nations Intelligence Taskforce), the British branch of which is commanded by Brigadier Alastair Gordon Lethbridge-Stewart (Nicholas Courtney). UNIT and Lethbridge-Stewart would become semiregulars in the series from that point forward, anticipating the UN-sponsored SHADO group of the *UFO* series that began broadcasting in 1970, as well as more vaguely foreshadowing the later FBI X-Files unit.

The alien-invasion motif of "The Invasion" had clear overtones of cold war anxieties, just as *Outer Limits* episodes such as "O.B.I.T."

demonstrated the ongoing engagement of American science fiction with the cold war in the mid-1960s. *Doctor Who* would last nearly for the duration of the cold war, as will be discussed further in chapter 3. Meanwhile, it was also the case that television series keyed more directly to cold war themes often drew inspiration from science fiction during this period. Perhaps spurred by the tendency of the James Bond films to spill over into science fiction (with mad scientist villains inventing a variety of high-tech weapons of mass destruction), series such as *The Man from U.N.C.L.E.* (which aired on NBC from fall 1964 to January 1968) often involved plots and motifs that contained strong science fiction elements, in this case, ones that grew more and more far-fetched and fantastic as the series proceeded. However, the most striking engagement with science fiction on the part of television cold war dramas occurred in two British series, both of which also aired and eventually gained cult status on network television in America (except for a few episodes nixed by squeamish American censors). The first of these, *The Avengers*, had actually begun broadcasting on British ITV at the beginning of 1961, though it began as a noirish crime and espionage series, moving more into science fiction only later, especially during the crucial fourth and fifth seasons (which ran in Britain from 1965 to 1967 and in the United States from 1966 to 1968), when the series first came to American television and when Diana Rigg joined the cast as the memorable Mrs. Emma Peel, the new partner of longtime protagonist John Steed (Patrick Macnee). *The Avengers*, especially during the Mrs. Peel seasons, was the ultimate in 1960s cool, addressing a number of concerns of the period, but with a flippancy and style that made those problems seem like great fun. The other British series was almost the direct opposite. *The Prisoner* addressed many of the same issues as *The Avengers*, but in a decidedly serious style—which may account for its relatively brief run of seventeen episodes, broadcast on ITV in 1967 and 1968 and running approximately a year later on American television.

The Avengers, of course, is remembered mostly for its hip style and its "too cool to be concerned" treatment of cold war anxieties. Still, despite its devotion to style and its unconventional approach, *The Avengers* was, first and foremost, a work of cold war culture. In *The Avengers*, England is generally a country under siege, threatened by a variety of invaders, saboteurs, and would-be destroyers from within and without. These invaders are sometimes from outer space, and the series in fact relies quite heavily on science fiction motifs, even if it does not necessarily treat them seriously. Thus, in "From Venus with

Love" (January 14, 1967), a supposed invasion from Venus turns out to be a hoax perpetrated by dastardly earthlings, while the real invasion of Earth by a gigantic plant from outer space in "Man-Eater of Surrey Green" (December 11, 1965) is less a reflection of cold war invasion fears than a simple spoof of 1950s science fiction films.

The Avengers was far too cool to show real anxiety over the various threats it portrayed. On the contrary, the series seems precisely designed to allay cold war fears by showing the ease, self-confidence, and panache with which Steed and Mrs. Peel overcome these various threats. The series attained an additional level of coolness for its American audience, precisely because it was so British, along with such other imports of British popular culture as the Beatles and the Rolling Stones. In addition, the "England against the world" motif of *The Avengers* was not as tightly linked to the cold war as might first appear. It was, in fact, an old theme with obvious precedents in the imperial ideology of the nineteenth century. *The Avengers* contains numerous echoes of the British past, and dialogues between past and present are central to the series, most obviously in the main contrast between Steed, a man of tradition, who dresses impeccably but often in archaic styles, and Mrs. Peel, a most contemporary woman, whose clothing is always very much up-to-date, or even ahead of its time, the character herself eventually becoming an important fashion trendsetter for the world outside the series. Macnee was, after all, fifteen years older than Rigg, and Steed is clearly at least half a generation older than Mrs. Peel. Steed's preferences in clothing, cars, and domestic décor all clearly partake of the past, while Mrs. Peel prefers the clothes, cars, and décor of the 1960s. The comfortable, even warm (if restrainedly so) relationship between the two characters thus serves the function of reassuring viewers (perhaps especially British viewers) that the uncertain times of the present are not so disconnected from the seemingly more stable and dependable times of the past after all.

Then again, this ability of styles from different periods to mix freely and coexist peacefully also suggests a very postmodern disregard for historical specificity. As Brian Clemens, one of the show's creators, has noted in his foreword to Dave Rogers's *The Complete Avengers*, *The Avengers* achieved its effects through the creation of "a carefully contrived, *dateless* fantasy world depicting a Britain of bowlers and brollies, of charm and muffins for tea, a Britain long since gone—if it ever really existed!" Indeed, in *The Avengers*, the styles of different historical periods serve not as markers of genuine historical change, but as a sort of temporal cafeteria menu from which one can pick and choose at will. The series consciously strives to be hip and cool, and much of its appeal comes from the intense contemporaneity of its style. Yet the series also draws heavily upon British tradition for its images and motifs, and the hipness is often tempered by a certain wistful fascination with the past, even if the series also critiques those who live in the past or are unable to adjust to the changed realities of the present.

The interchangeability of past and present in *The Avengers* quite naturally lends itself to the science fiction theme of time travel, and several episodes explore this motif. Perhaps the most explicit of these episodes is "Escape in Time" (July 17, 1968). However, the time machine supposedly developed by the central villain of the episode, Thyssen (Peter Bowles), turns out to be a hoax that is part of a scheme in which Thyssen offers various villainous sorts, such as an exiled Latin American dictator, the opportunity to escape from justice in the contemporary world by fleeing into the past. In order to convince them to pay handsomely for his service, he offers his potential customers a sample trip into the past, though this trip consists simply of an elaborately staged visit to various parts of his mansion that have been decorated in the styles of different historical periods. After collecting their money, he does indeed help them disappear—by murdering them.

Even more telling than the frequent use in *The Avengers* of images from the past as mere decorations is the way in which the series treats images from the present in much the same manner. Thus, the engagement with serious issues such as the cold war becomes very much a matter of style rather than substance. For example, the series is intentionally vague in its treatment of the cold war about the nature of "the enemy," just as it is vague about so many details, including the exact nature of the relationship between Steed and Mrs. Peel. Quite often the two protagonists do battle directly with Soviet agents, though it is typical for these agents never to be identified specifically as Soviets, but rather simply to have vaguely Russian surnames and to speak in really bad Russian accents, somewhat along the lines of Boris and Natasha in the American *Rocky and Bullwinkle* cartoons. In any case, the Soviet spies of *The Avengers* are anything but terrifying. At times they are comically incompetent. At other times, they seem to be members of a sort of gentlemen's spy club, regarding Steed in particular almost as more of a colleague than a foe, and treating their battles with him as more of a sport than a life-or-death struggle for world supremacy. And Steed returns the favor, often regarding his Russian counterparts with warmth, even affection.

Perhaps the most telling Russian character to figure in *The Avengers* is Brodny, the comically Anglophilic Soviet ambassador to England (Warren Mitchell), who appears in two different episodes, "Two's a Crowd" (May 9, 1966) and "The See-Through Man" (February 3, 1967). The latter episode employs a science fiction motif that obviously draws upon Wells's *The Invisible Man*, as well as the films based on that novel. However, the high-tech device central to the episode again turns out to be a mere hoax. Soviet agent Major Vazin pretends to have obtained an invisibility formula from the British scientist Quilby (Roy Kinnear), a comic mad scientist type who routinely submits crackpot inventions to the "Ministry," the vaguely defined British governmental organization for which Steed apparently works. The idea is to force the British to divert precious scientific resources into an attempt to re-create the useless formula. However, Steed and Mrs. Peel see through the see-through man quite quickly and dispatch him rather easily. Even in this episode, in which actual Soviet agents attempt direct sabotage of British defense plans, the theme of cold war paranoia is treated with considerable tongue-in-cheek irony. Thus, Vazin originally obtains Quilby's formula under the guise of the "Eastern Drug Company," a ruse that easily fools the gullible Quilby, but one that Steed and Mrs. Peel recognize immediately. "We know 'you know who' lies behind *that* pseudonym," remarks Mrs. Peel, upon hearing of the transaction with Quilby. And this arch "you know who" is typical of the way in which the series plays with the idea of Soviet agents as natural foes, almost making a mockery of the automatic tendency to see Russians as evil and threatening. Similar circumlocution is frequently used in the series. In "Dead Man's Treasure" (March 13, 1968), for example, Steed and Mrs. Peel work to recover top-secret papers from "you know where," while opposed by enemy agents simply referred to as "the opposition."

In point of fact, most of the enemies faced by *The Avengers* are not Russians at all, but simply freelance supervillains, who become campier and wackier as the series proceeds, especially after the "zap-bam-pow" *Batman* influence began to show itself in the 1967 color season. The offbeat nature of these villains makes them seem less threatening, while the calm ease with which they are typically defeated by Steed and Mrs. Peel offers reassuring suggestions that

Mother England, even in the postcolonial era, is still more than capable of defending herself against any and all threats.

Reinforcing the science fictional aspects of *The Avengers*, these threats often came from mad scientists who, for one reason or another, have developed a grudge against English society, subsequently employing their scientific talents in a quest for revenge or retribution. These episodes, of course, reflect the anxieties of the general populace about science and scientists, neither of which they understood, but both of which were perceived as bearing earth-shattering power. And, given the centrality of the science race to the cold war, it is not surprising that the mad scientist episodes of *The Avengers* are quite often associated, directly or indirectly, with cold war concerns. In "The Cybernauts" (first broadcast in America on March 28, 1966, but in Britain on October 16, 1965, both predating the first appearance of the rather similar "Cybermen" in *Doctor Who*), Dr. Armstrong (Michael Gough), a top government scientist, becomes disgruntled by the refusal of the British authorities to support his efforts to use science as a weapon of peace, rather than war. In particular, instead of working to develop more powerful nuclear weapons, Armstrong hopes to develop robots that can be used to clean up nuclear contamination. Rebuffed by the authorities, Armstrong continues his research on his own, but with a sinister twist, seeking to develop an army of robots, or cybernauts, through which he can gain unlimited power and wealth.

Armstrong hopes eventually to provide his cybernauts with computer brains that can rival the human brain in their functioning, the only obstacle in his path being that such artificial brains would require greater miniaturization of the circuitry than is possible via current technology. Thus, in this episode, Armstrong seeks to gain control of a new Japanese electronic device that is supposed to replace the transistor and enable tremendous new advances in miniaturization. In particular, he employs his cybernauts to murder a series of top electronic executives who are negotiating for the British rights to the Japanese device, which brings Steed and Mrs. Peel onto the scene and leads, of course, to Armstrong's defeat.

"The Cybernauts" was one of the first Emma Peel episodes, made before the series turned more and more to camp and comedy. As such, it is a reasonably serious episode that treats some serious issues. Armstrong, for example, is only slightly over the top in the mad scientist role. He is, in fact, a somewhat sympathetic character, partly because of his initially humane impulses and partly because he is a cripple whose interest in automation arises from his desire to extend the capabilities of his own failing body. However, if *The Avengers* eschews jingoistic support for the British side in the cold war arms race, it is also far too cool and aloof to make any strong statements against nuclear armament. Indeed, if the episode does make a social statement, it is less a protest of the use of science in the interest of nuclear destruction than a general complaint about the dehumanizing tendencies of science and technology as a whole.

This statement is contained most clearly in a late exchange between Armstrong and Steed in which the former serves as the spokesman for coldhearted, inhumane science and the latter (as usual) represents humanity and tradition. In this exchange, Armstrong expresses his fears that the world's governments, headed by humans with their penchant for mistakes and bad decisions, are taking the world down the path to disaster and destruction. To prevent this, he envisions a world governed by his cybernauts, or "government by automation." Steed responds that, to him, this sounds like an "electronic dictatorship," suggesting that the choice of governments should be made not by Armstrong but by "the voters." What would Armstrong's plan bring about, he wonders: "A cybernetic police state? Push-button bobbies? Automated martinis, remote-controlled olives? No, I think I'll stick with good old flesh and blood."

The turn here from politics to mixed drinks indicates Steed's characteristic preoccupation, but also signals the unwillingness of the series to get too serious, veering away at the last moment from serious political commentary into jokery. Still, this speech indicates an underlying fear in *The Avengers* that modern technology may be leading to an increasingly dehumanizing automation. This fear is also expressed in the opening episode of the sixth season, a reprise of "The Cybernauts" entitled, simply enough, "The Return of the Cybernauts" (February 21, 1968). Here, Armstrong's brother, Paul Beresford (Peter Cushing), takes up his sibling's work, seeking to use the cybernauts to extract revenge for the death of Armstrong. Here the plot for world domination is dropped in favor of an entirely personal quest, indicating the way in which, by this season, the series had turned away from large-scale political plots and toward more and more offbeat and individualistic villains.

Cushing played Baron Victor Frankenstein in all three *Frankenstein* movies made by Britain's Hammer Films between 1957 and 1964, so he was perfect for the role of a mad scientist, which he plays to good

effect in "The Return of the Cybernauts," combining it with an ur-
bane charm and sophistication that he uses to help lure Mrs. Peel into
his clutches. In any case, the cybernauts themselves are actually quite
marginal to this episode, being used only to kidnap a group of top
scientists, from whom Beresford demands help in his scheme to
get revenge on Steed and Mrs. Peel by turning them into human
cybernauts. Worse, they will remain fully conscious of (and horrified
by) their plight but will simply be unable to resist Beresford's commands.

Similar themes also drive the action in "Never, Never Say Die"
(March 31, 1967), which links directly back to "The Cybernauts" by
opening with a teaser scene in which Mrs. Peel watches that episode
on television until she is interrupted when Steed somehow appears
on her screen with his trademark announcement, "Mrs. Peel, we're
needed." "Never, Never Say Die" features Christopher Lee, who, like
Cushing, had done a turn as a cinematic Sherlock Holmes, but was
best known for his roles in the same Hammer horror films as Cushing,
including roles as the monster opposite Cushing's Victor Frankenstein,
as Count Dracula opposite Cushing's Van Helsing, and as the mummy
opposite Cushing's John Banning. He had also appeared in numerous other horror films and as the villainous Fu Manchu, so he was
perfect for a role as one of the increasingly cartoonish *Avengers* villains. In "Never, Never Say Die," Lee plays Professor Stone, still another cybernautics expert, though one who seems considerably more
advanced than Armstrong or Beresford in that his cybernauts are virtually indistinguishable from human beings. Indeed, this episode revolves around a plot to gradually replace a series of prominent Britons
(mostly politicians) with look-alike doubles. Indeed, it turns out that
Stone himself has been replaced and that it is his own double who
is masterminding the plot. The motif of the runaway scientist whose
over-the-top creation gets out of control obviously recalls the *Frankenstein* tradition, though Steed suggests a different precedent from
British culture when he compares Stone's predicament to that of *Dr.
Jekyll and Mr. Hyde*.

This gradual replacement by nonhuman look-alike doubles also
recalls the cold war paranoia film *Invasion of the Body Snatchers* (1956),
and the motif clearly reflects the cold war fear of communist infil-
tration and slow takeover by ideological conversion. Such fears derive from the fact that communists could not be distinguished by the
traditional physical categories of otherness (particularly race and

gender) that had long informed Western thinking. In addition to fears of gradual communist ideological conquest from the East, this motif suggests a growing sense on the part of individuals that their lives were coming more and more under the control of an increasingly complex system of economics and technology that was threatening to strip them of their humanity, turning them essentially into machines.

Replacement by doubles was a favorite theme of *The Avengers*, though the theme was typically treated more with humor than with anxiety. For example, "Who's Who???" (May 19, 1967) spoofs the science fiction variation on the theme of replacement by doubles. Here, in a motif that would have been at home in *The Prisoner*, but with a comic twist, a former Nazi mad scientist, Krelmar (Arnold Diamond), invents a mind-exchange machine that allows enemy agents Basil and Lola (Freddie Jones and Patricia Haines) to switch bodies with Steed and Mrs. Peel so that they can assume their identities and then function as double agents, meanwhile enjoying the lifestyles of the original protagonists.

This far-fetched plot (which offers Macnee and Rigg the opportunity to play different characters) involves a series of murders of British agents, but, despite the carnage, it is played essentially as farce. For example, after each commercial break, a very British announcer comes on to explain the confusing goings-on, serving only to make them sound even more confusing than they really are. The scenario of this episode also offers the opportunity for the series to poke self-conscious fun at some of its own central devices, including the famous unresolved sexual tension between the protagonists. Here, Basil and Lola, in the bodies of Steed and Mrs. Peel, are sexually active indeed, allowing these bodies to experience each other at last, even if the usual occupants of the bodies are not at home at the time. Much comic uncertainty ensues, in a plot that anticipates the two-part *X-Files* episode, "Dreamland." However, the *X-Files* episode is actually much funnier, because Mulder switches bodies with a lecherous alter ego while Scully remains in her own body and is unaware of the reason Mulder is suddenly so amorous. In the *Avengers* episode, Steed and Mrs. Peel manage to recover their original mortal sheaths, and then head off for dinner in Paris after a final tag scene that reminds us how well they know each other.

Among other things, the coolness of the protagonists shows up here in their almost total lack of emotional response to the deaths of their fellow agents, which are treated in the episode essentially as comic events. Meanwhile, Steed seems less concerned with the national security implications of the identity-switch scheme than horrified by the undignified behavior of his alter ego. In the end, having recovered his body and his partner, he finds that Basil and Lola have drunk the last of his favorite champagne—without, of all things, having even chilled it. To make matters worse, the vulgar Basil, horror of horrors, has been smoking Steed's favorite cigars with the ends bitten, rather than clipped, off.

As a whole, *The Avengers* tends to treat its science fiction themes playfully and without any serious consideration of the sorts of speculative issues that inform the best science fiction. When it is not merely a hoax, most of the science in the series is either merely contemporary (lots of nuclear weaponry and surveillance devices) or preposterous and far-fetched. There is very little in the way of an attempt to imagine actual technological developments that might change the texture of life in the future. If anything, the series is vaguely antiscience and antitechnology. Virtually all scientific and technological breakthroughs threaten to have ominous consequences; they are consistently made by villainous scientists or are at least quickly appropriated by villains after being developed by well-meaning, but naïve, scientists.

In its uninterest in scientific developments that bring about a better world, *The Avengers* resembles much of the television science fiction of the 1960s, despite the widespread utopian rhetoric of the decade. On the other hand, partly because of its tongue-in-cheek tone and emphasis on style rather than content, *The Avengers* is also not particularly troubling in its cautions about advancing technology. The same, however, could not be said for *The Prisoner*, which could be troubling in this and many other ways as well—perhaps accounting for the fact that it lasted only seventeen episodes before being canceled.

The grim but weird tone of *The Prisoner*, a generic hybrid of science fiction and spy drama, is set in the first episode, when the nameless protagonist (played by Patrick McGoohan) resigns (apparently) from his position as a top British secret agent, then finds himself suddenly transported to a strange, surreal village, where he is trapped in the grip of powerful forces he can neither understand nor overcome. As such, of course, he is imprisoned in a literal version of the same predicament being experienced metaphorically by many in the world at large. The prisoner, meanwhile, is an almost stereotypical strong, individualist hero in the Western romantic tradition. Told that he is now to be referred to simply as "Number Six," he rejects this designation, declaring that he "will not be pushed, filed, stamped, indexed, briefed, debriefed, or numbered." He thus becomes a champion of individualism in an era when this principle was widely celebrated, but in which these celebrations clearly responded to an anxiety that true individuals were a thing of the past. This potential contradiction is central to the entire series, in which the defiant refusal of the prisoner to submit and conform can be taken either as heroic and inspirational or as romantic folly, depending on one's point of view. This undecidability was a key element of the program, leading David Buxton to declare it "undoubtedly the most enigmatic series of all time."[2]

Many episodes of *The Prisoner* contain strong elements of science fiction, as the authorities employ various high-tech methods in their attempts to overcome the protagonist's resistance and extract the secrets he accumulated in his earlier career as a British secret agent. Thus, while the prisoner is clearly the protagonist of the series, in this sense the audience was in very much the same situation as his captors, struggling to extract information that would help them to make sense of it all. That information is never revealed, however, and neither the authorities of the village nor the audience ever really learn much about the prisoner's previous career, though many felt they saw occasional hints that Number Six may actually be John Drake, the protagonist (also played by McGoohan) of the earlier British series *Danger Man* (broadcast in the United States as *Secret Agent* in 1965–66).

Perhaps the most striking of the high-tech tools of power employed by the village authorities is a large, surreal, white balloon (identified in later episodes as "Rover") that chases down and engulfs any individuals in the village who fail to conform to officially sanctioned rules of behavior. Indeed, Rover frequently foils the escape attempts of Number Six as the series proceeds, though the village authorities generally rely on subtler, psychologically based techniques of power. In this vein, their attempts at mind control and brainwashing address crucial concerns of the cold war, while their extensive capabilities for surveillance of individual behavior seem highly relevant to an audience growing increasingly concerned about loss of privacy in the modern era. In fact, *The Prisoner* was often quite overt in its suggestions that conditions within the village were merely special versions of conditions in the world at large. For example, in his first interview with Number Two, his chief interrogator and a leading village administrator (the identity of Number One, the ultimate village authority, is a closely guarded secret), Number Six learns that he has been under surveillance his entire life. Number Two shows him a number of photographs of various moments from his childhood onward. Number Six is shocked to learn that even his most private moments have been observed and recorded, even well before he had become a secret agent, and the implication is clear that all of us may be under similar forms of surveillance without our knowledge.

In the best tradition of the science fiction genre, futuristic technologies in *The Prisoner* are more important for what they tell us about the here and now than about far places and distant futures. Much of the technology employed in the series, in fact, is relatively contemporary, more science than fiction. On the other hand, the technologies envisioned in *The Prisoner* do sometimes look forward to later technological developments. In "A, B & C," for example, these technologies foreshadow the later development of computer simulations that are so effective that their "virtual reality" becomes essentially indistinguishable from the real world. In this episode, the authorities of the village produce just such a virtual reality, employing a combination of film, drugs, and electronics to produce a series of simulations that place Number Six in situations in which they hope he will reveal what they want to know. Six, however, discovers and foils the plan, scoring one of his few victories and turning the simulated tables on his real captors by projecting a countersimulated reality that implicates Number Two himself in Number Six's resignation from his former position as a secret agent.

Virtual reality is even more central to the unique "Living in Harmony," an episode so strange and potentially troubling that CBS refused to broadcast it in the original run of the series on American television. Viewers of this episode must have thought, initially, that they had tuned to the wrong channel, for it begins not as the protagonist drives his custom Lotus toward London to resign his job as a secret agent, but as a man rides his horse through the American West, reaching a frontier town where he resigns his job as the local sheriff. The man, however, is McGoohan, starring as a nameless laconic Western stranger of the type Clint Eastwood had perfected a few years earlier in *A Fistful of Dollars* (1964). In a quintessential case of postmodern genre mixing, the episode proceeds—for more than forty-three minutes of its forty-nine-minute running time—as a reasonably authentic television Western, though the plot of the episode (in which the ex-sheriff finds himself trapped in a strange town, unable to leave) cleverly parallels the typical plots of *The Prisoner*.

In the end, it turns out that the Western town and all of the events in it have been part of a virtual reality engineered by the village authorities, again using a combination of drugs and electronics. The virtual experience is designed, apparently, to put Number Six under so much stress that he will finally crack (he is even "killed" in the end of the Western part of the episode). Again, however, Number Six turns the tables on his captors. He survives the episode with his psyche intact, though the two assistants working with Number Two to carry out the plan are both unhinged (and eventually killed) by their involvement in this all-too-convincing simulation.

A similar attempt to extend the series beyond the claustrophobic bounds of the village occurs in "The Girl Who Was Death," one of the few basically comic episodes of the series. Here, through almost the entire episode, Number Six seems to be inexplicably back to work at his job as a secret agent, though in a decidedly offbeat way that causes Alain Carrazé and Hélène Oswald, in their book-length study of the series, to call the episode "a kind of surrealist *James Bond* made with the collaboration of the Marx Brothers."[3] The episode is also very much in the tradition of science fiction, as an oddly costumed Number Six races about in an (ultimately successful) attempt to foil the efforts of a mad scientist to destroy London with his new super-rocket. In the end, however, the entire episode turns out to have been a mere story that Number Six was telling to some of the village children, a situation the authorities had set up in the (unfulfilled) hope that he might drop his guard in the midst of this audience and reveal important information.

If technology is used in "A, B & C" and "Living in Harmony" to probe and manipulate the contents of Number Six's brain, a similar advanced technology is used in "The General" to place new contents in the brains of the entire village population, assuring their obedience to authority. In particular, the general of the title, as Number Six discovers at the end of the episode, is a giant supercomputer that is the key to a new brainwashing technology. This episode thus echoes the fears that some were already expressing about the potential use of computers as tools of an American national security apparatus that had, in the 1960s, turned its attention from the rooting out of Soviet agents to the surveillance and sabotage of antiwar and civil rights groups.

Perhaps even more important, the brainwashing that the general engineers involves the broadcast of special signals via the television screens that the inhabitants of the village spend so much of their time viewing. Thus, like *The Twilight Zone* and *The Outer Limits* before it (but with much less tongue-in-cheek irony), the episode explores fears about television itself—in this case, particularly anticipating similar motifs in later works such as David Cronenberg's 1982 film, *Videodrome*, in which sinister behavior-modifying signals are broadcast via television. In "The General," Number Six again spoils the plan and even destroys the general, but the implications of the episode are ominous, signaling the potentially negative consequences of a television medium that was rapidly expanding in scope and power.

The ability of the authorities of the village to manipulate perceptions of reality sometimes extends to fundamental questions of identity, posing the question of whether Number Six (or any of us) is really who he thinks he is, or whether he is simply whoever he has been told to be by larger powers. In "The Schizoid Man," the village authorities bring in an outside agent (Number Twelve) who looks exactly like Number Six and has been carefully trained to speak and act like him as well. Indeed, he is even more like Number Six than Number Six himself, who has meanwhile been conditioned to differ from his previous self in various ways. He is, for example, now left-handed, whereas before he had been right-handed. These changes have been made as part of an attempt by the authorities, led by Number Two, to convince Number Six that he is actually Number Twelve and that Number Twelve is the real Number Six, presumably unsettling the real Six and furthering his interrogation.

Aided by Alison (Jane Merrow), another woman who has been enlisted to win the trust of Six, only to betray him, Number Two nearly succeeds in convincing Number Six that he is not who he thinks he is. We observe, through the course of the episode, the gradual fragmentation of Number Six's confidence in his own identity, a process that he clearly finds terrifying. Meanwhile, there is a special irony in the way the prisoner begins to cling to the numeral six as a marker of his identity, even though he has staunchly refused, in previous episodes, to accept this designation. Eventually, Six discovers the plot and turns the tables on Number Twelve, who is subsequently killed by Rover in the confusion of identities. Number Six then impersonates Number Twelve and nearly succeeds in bluffing his way out of the village, but a telltale slip lands him right back where he started, as usual. The ultimate circularity of the plot leaves Number Six again trapped in the perpetual present that is the temporal fabric of the village, while the overall thrust of the episode suggests that individual identity might not be as stable and unambiguously defined as we would like to think.

Individual identity is also destabilized in "Do Not Forsake Me, Oh My Darling," in which a brilliant scientist has invented a machine that allows the minds of two different people to be interchanged, as in the "Who's Who???" episode of *The Avengers*. However, the scientist, Dr. Seltzman (Hugo Schuster), has disappeared before revealing his process for reversing the exchange. Feeling that Number Six is the only man who can locate Seltzman, the authorities devise a plan to transfer Six's mind into the body of the "Colonel" (Nigel Stock), a loyal agent. They then release the new Number Six (in the Colonel's body) and allow him to return to his home in London, knowing (especially after a little well-placed conditioning) he will do anything to track down Seltzman in an effort to get his own body back.

Ace agent that he is, Six succeeds, and the authorities follow him to Seltzman, then bring them both back to the village. There Number Six's mind is returned to his own body, but Seltzman manages to outwit the authorities, transferring his mind into the body of the Colonel and then escaping, leaving the Colonel's mind in Seltzman's own dying body. Once again, then, Six escapes to the outer world only to find that there, too, he remains under strict surveillance and is hardly free. Meanwhile, in *The Prisoner*, such high-tech methods of mind control and manipulation have almost entirely negative implications, due to their sinister use by official power in both the village and the world at large. The continuity of this usage reinforces the notion that the village is not fundamentally different from the world around it and that Number Six's dogged efforts to escape are essentially pointless. Thus, in the episode "Many Happy Returns," he actually succeeds in escaping back to London, only to have the British authorities promptly return him to the village. There are, in fact, signs that the entire escape was engineered by his captors as a way of breaking his spirits by raising his hopes, only to dash them.

Among other things, this episode again suggests that conditions in the village might not be much different from conditions in the world at large. Indeed, the true significance of the village throughout the series is its similarity to the world outside, even though Number Six doggedly persists in his attempts to return to that world. There is, however, a significant doubt in the series whether that return is even worthwhile. Indeed, in the series' final episode, "Fall Out," Six finally does escape and return home, seemingly to have gained nothing. This stunning final episode completes the final deconstruction not only of the opposition between the village and the world at large, but also between Number Six and his captors in the village. Bewildered audiences were left with no stable verities on which to depend, no solid interpretive ground on which to stand. They were also given nothing to nourish the individualist longings that had propelled them through their viewing of the earlier sixteen episodes, rooting for the virtuous, freethinking Number Six.

The episode begins with some of the strangest and most surreal scenes in the entire series, including a bizarre trial sequence in which Six's defiance of authority is applauded as a sign that he is the only true individual in the village. As a reward, he is declared free to go. First, however, he must learn the identity of Number One, who turns out, in a confusing sequence, apparently to be Number Six himself, or at least a dark aspect of Number Six, whose identity is thus fragmented in true postmodernist style. Then begins an apocalyptic sequence of violent revolution and total chaos, leading to the evacuation of the village to the strains of the Beatles song "All You Need Is Love," a musical choice the Brechtian irony of which tends to dismiss the sentiment expressed in the song, as well as the entire panoply of 1960s attitudes that it expresses.

Number Six at last escapes and returns to London. However, when he reaches his home, we discover that the door swings open automatically in the same telltale fashion as the door to his home in the village, suggesting that he is still in the grip of the diabolical forces of which he is himself a part. Six then hops in his Lotus and drives away—into the standard opening sequence of the series, which thus apparently completes the loop and returns him back to the beginning, presumably only to do it all over again. The notion of progressive narrative sequence is destroyed once and for all, as is the illusion that the world is really any different from the village or that Number Six is really independent of the forces that run the village and the world.

Roughly contemporaneous with the American runs of *The Avengers* and *The Prisoner* was the first major series devoted exclusively to space exploration to appear on American commercial television in the 1960s, Irwin Allen's rather silly *Lost in Space*, which lasted from 1965 to 1968 on CBS. Geared mainly toward a young audience and largely inspired by the science fiction serials of the 1930s (especially in the cliff-hanger endings of each episode), *Lost in Space* (set in the then-futuristic year of 1997) was essentially a family drama. The series detailed the efforts of the Robinson family to find their way home after their spacecraft, sent forth by the U.S. government on a mission to colonize a planet in Alpha Centauri, is thrown wildly off course by the presence of an accidental stowaway, the would-be saboteur Dr. Zachary Smith (Jonathan Harris). *Lost in Space* directly followed Allen's earlier successful series *Voyage to the Bottom of the Sea* (1964–68), extending the undersea adventures of that series into outer space. Generically, of course, *Lost in Space* is a castaway narrative, following in the footsteps of the now legendary *Gilligan's Island*, which had begun to air on CBS a year earlier. Meanwhile, the saga of the Robinson family is linked directly to *Swiss Family Robinson*, a film version of which had been a big hit for Disney in 1960, and which itself alluded to Daniel Defoe's classic eighteenth-century novel *Robinson Crusoe*, which, as *Lost in Space* began airing, had recently inspired the 1964 science fiction film *Robinson Crusoe on Mars* (1964).

The Robinsons' *Jupiter 2* spacecraft was a standard (though somewhat plain) flying-saucer design, thus linking the series to one of the most common images in the science fiction tradition. For most viewers, however, the most memorable image from *Lost in Space* was that of the excitable robot, frantically waving its mechanical arms and warning of various dangers, many of them triggered by the cowardly and nefarious actions of the ever-present Dr. Smith, a constant thorn in the side of the Robinson clan. This unnamed robot thus joined Robby the Robot from the 1956 film *Forbidden Planet* as the two most famous robots in the history of American popular culture. Indeed, both robots were created by the same man, Robert Kinoshita, and both even appeared together in several episodes of *Lost in Space* in which Robby "guest starred"—as he also did in several episodes of *The Twilight Zone*. *Lost in Space* was also linked to *The Twilight Zone* in that Billy Mumy played young Will Robinson, one of the central characters in the series. Mumy was known to American audiences for his earlier appearances in three episodes of *The Twilight Zone*, including the creepy classic "It's a Good Life" (November 3, 1961), in which adults must humor six-year-old Anthony Fremont, played by Mumy (then known as Bill), or risk disastrous consequences from his psychic powers. (This memorable episode was reprised on the UPN reincarnation of *The Twilight Zone* on February 19, 2003, featuring Mumy as a grown-up Fremont with a psychic six-year-old of his own. Mumy, by the way, had maintained his participation in the genre of SFTV with his ongoing role as the Minbari diplomat Lennier on *Babylon 5*, while he also popped up in 1998 in a guest appearance as Engineer Kellin on the *Star Trek: Deep Space Nine* episode, "The Siege of AR-558.")

As the seasons went by, the plots of the individual *Lost in Space* episodes tended to get more and more far-fetched, while the overall tone of the series drifted from drama to campy comedy, its monsters becoming more ridiculous than threatening. Eventually, the series was canceled without ever getting the Robinsons back home, though it continued to live a moderately successful life in syndication, gaining a minor cult following. A short-lived animated cartoon version of the series aired in 1973, while an updated theatrical film version of the series was released in 1998, roughly corresponding to the launch date of the *Jupiter 2* in the original series.

The second half of the 1960s also saw such Allen-produced science fiction series as *The Time Tunnel* (1966–67)—in which time travelers journey back to various hot spots in history—and the almost Swiftian *Land of the Giants* (1968–70). *The Invaders* (1967–69), in which alien invaders disguised as humans made life miserable for protagonist David Vincent (Roy Thinnes) was also a key SFTV series of the late 1960s. The alien invasion motif of *The Invaders* involved a paranoia that made it a clear predecessor to *The X-Files*, to such an extent that the success of the latter series in the early 1990s led to a miniseries sequel to *The Invaders* in 1995, while Thinnes himself became a recurring guest star on *The X-Files*. Still, neither *The Invaders* nor any of the four Allen-produced series was as imaginative as *The Twilight Zone* or as thought-provokingly scary as *The Outer Limits*. This did not mean, however, that American science fiction television had passed its peak by the middle of the 1960s. On the contrary, the most important SFTV series of the decade (and maybe *ever*) was broadcast near the end of the 1960s.

Airing on NBC from 1966 to 1969, Gene Roddenberry's *Star Trek* ran one year behind *Lost in Space* and achieved a similar modest success during its first network run, never, for example, breaking into the top fifty programs in annual viewership. The subsequent life of *Star Trek* was another thing altogether. It, too, spawned an animated series, but the cartoon version of *Star Trek*, running from 1973 to 1975 and featuring the voices of William Shatner, Leonard Nimoy, and other principals from the original series, was actually a modest success. Then, by the end of the 1970s, the popularity of *Star Trek* in syndication not only eclipsed that of the syndicated *Lost in Space*, but also easily outstripped that of its original network run. In fact, the syndicated run of *Star Trek* became one of the most spectacular phenomena of television history and made the series one of the most influential television programs of all time.

Star Trek, with its hordes of devoted Trekker fans—watching reruns, attending conventions, and consuming mass quantities of *Star Trek* books and merchandise—became the prototype for the cult series and made cultural icons of both its featured spaceship, the USS *Enterprise*, and its central characters (including William Shatner's Captain James T. Kirk, Leonard Nimoy's Mr. Spock, and DeForest Kelley's Dr. McCoy). The original series grew into a television franchise, spawning a succession of sequels, including *Star Trek: The Next Generation* (1987–94), *Star Trek: Deep Space Nine* (1993–99), *Star Trek: Voyager* (1995–2000), and *Enterprise* (beginning in 2001), that carried the *Star Trek* banner beyond the death of Roddenberry and into the new millennium. Because of such series, the original *Star Trek* is now commonly referred to as *Star Trek: The Original Series*, or simply as *TOS*. Meanwhile, the original series spilled over into theatrical film, becoming one of the most lucrative and successful franchises in movie history. At this writing, there have been ten *Star Trek* films, the first six of which are extensions of the original series, with the original cast, though the advancing age of this cast by the time of *Star Trek VI: The Undiscovered Country* in 1991 became an increasing source of comedy, as the rickety *Enterprise* crew dragged itself around the galaxy, thinning hair, thickening waistlines, and all. *Star Trek Generations* (1994) then served as a transition film that killed off Captain Kirk and handed the baton of the film franchise over to the cast and crew of *Star Trek: The Next Generation*, just coming to the end of its television run at that time.

The collective images that make up the universe of *Star Trek* have by now become a crucial part of the popular American imagination, while phrases such as "Beam me up, Scotty" have become part of the American vernacular. Meanwhile, the technological trappings of the *Star Trek* universe—with its warp drives, force fields, phasers, tricorders, communicators, transporters, and replicators—have become a central source of the popular notion of what the technology of the future might be like. The seemingly optimistic political vision of the franchise has been similarly powerful; in *Star Trek*, the political oppositions of twentieth-century Earth have seemingly been overcome, making the future Earth of the twenty-third and twenty-fourth centuries the capital of a vast, united, and benevolent "United Federation of Planets" that encompasses much of the galaxy, reaching out to new worlds with its message of tolerance, peace, and interplanetary cooperation.

Many of the ideas and images central to *Star Trek* evolve and change in important ways in the subsequent films and series, but the vision of the future put forth in the original series remains remarkably consistent throughout the franchise. This compelling (and heartening) future image is surely the most important reason for the ongoing popularity of the original series and of the entire franchise. Nevertheless, the original series was also rooted in its contemporary context in a number of important ways. Indeed, much of the attraction of the original series' optimistic vision of the future can be attributed to the way in which this vision was specifically linked to the solution of the sorts of specific social and political troubles that made the late 1960s a time of both great anxiety and great hope.

The extent to which *TOS* engaged such issues (despite the campy look and feel of the series, at least in syndicated retrospect) can perhaps be gauged by the staggering amount of serious academic criticism that has been devoted to the series, probably more than to any other series in television history. Dozens of scholarly essays have been devoted to the various incarnations of the series, some of them gathered in book-length collections such as *Enterprise Zones: Critical Positions on* Star Trek, edited by Taylor Harrison and others. There have also been numerous scholarly monographs on the *Star Trek* phenomenon, as well as unique studies such as *Star Trek: The Human Frontier*, a hybrid work of scholarly analysis and fan-oriented commentary, coauthored by the distinguished scholar Michèle Barrett and her teenage Trekker son, Duncan. Meanwhile, *Star Trek* has generated what is surely the most extensive and impressive body of fan-oriented commentaries, guides, and handbooks of any television series ever broadcast.

The *Star Trek* phenomenon thus goes far beyond the various series and films, but the original series is the beginning point of it all. Many episodes of the original *Star Trek* were classic space exploration tales in the tradition of the "space opera," a genre of action-adventure stories set in outer space that dates back to the 1920s but came of age in the 1940s and 1950s with the work of science fiction legends such as Isaac Asimov (who was, in fact, employed as a science consultant in the making of the first *Star Trek* film). Indeed, the Galactic Empire of Asimov's *Foundation* trilogy is clearly one of the most important predecessors of *Star Trek*'s Federation of Planets. The ability of the *Enterprise*, with its warp-drive technology, to zip about the galaxy with astonishing speed meant that the crew of the ship could encounter a wide range of interstellar phenomena, not to mention an amazing variety of "new life and new civilizations," the search for which was identified as central to its mission in the famous "to boldly go" opening narration, spoken by Shatner. Many of these new life forms were decidedly hostile, leading to significant amounts of danger and conflict and providing considerable plot material. Many episodes, for example, involve encounters with rival empires, including ongoing clashes with the fiercely warlike (but human-looking) Klingons and the cunning Romulans (offshoots of the Vulcan race who have opted for aggression rather than logic). Such clashes generate a number of different types of plot, including both out-and-out space battles and more subtle conflicts that are reminiscent of cold war spy dramas, as in the classic (and comic) Klingon episode "The Trouble with Tribbles" (December 29, 1967)[4] and "The Enterprise Incident" (September 27, 1968), an espionage thriller in which Kirk and Spock manage to steal a Romulan cloaking device.

Indeed, given the peaceful orientation of the Federation (and of the mission of the *Enterprise*), a surprising number of episodes involved such conflicts. It is also surprising that the *Enterprise* was so heavily armed in pursuit of its peaceful mission, but then the phasers, photon torpedoes, and force-field shields with which the ship was equipped certainly came in handy given the frequency with which the ship was attacked by alien aggressors. On the other hand, due no doubt to the very limited nature of the special effects available at the time, there were relatively few actual space battles in the original series. Instead, most of the combat occurred on the various planetary surfaces, involving relatively traditional weapons. A typical episode in this regard was "Arena" (January 19, 1967), in which a potential outer-space battle turns to hand-to-hand combat. Here, the *Enterprise* pursues an alien ship (belonging to a reptilian race called the Gorn) that is suspected of destroying a Starfleet base. In the course of the chase, both ships wander into uncharted territory that is claimed by an advanced race called the Metrons. Despite their high level of technology, the Metrons seem to have a rather primitive notion of justice; they capture both ships and decide to settle the dispute by placing Kirk in one-to-one combat with the captain of the Gorn ship, both of whom are transported to the surface of an uninhabited asteroid. The Metrons also declare that the ship commanded by the winner of the conflict will be set free, while the loser's ship and crew will be destroyed.

Kirk eventually gets the upper hand in the fight, leaving the Gorn in a defenseless position. However, Kirk refuses to kill his opponent, showing mercy even to an adversary so radically nonhuman and providing one of the series' many declarations (in the midst of the civil rights activism of the 1960s) in favor of the acceptance of racial difference. This decision impresses the Metrons, who conclude that the Federation may be more civilized than they had given it credit for being. Perhaps, they conclude, the Federation may someday even be worthy of dealing with the Metrons as equals. Thus, this episode also addresses another common *Star Trek* motif (continued in the later series as well), the testing of the crew of the *Enterprise* by advanced aliens to see if they are truly civilized—especially in cases where the aliens have heard reports of the gruesome violence that is such a central part of the earth history. Of course, Kirk and his crew continually pass the test, generally by eschewing violence against seemingly weaker foes or showing mercy to helpless opponents. Thus, even episodes that derived most of their energy from combat scenes often carried antiwar messages—at a time when controversy over the Vietnam War was threatening to tear American society apart.

In an acknowledgement of Earth's warlike past, the violence and aggression encountered by the crew of the *Enterprise* in the far reaches of space sometimes turns out to emanate from Earth. In "Space Seed" (February 16, 1967), for example, they discover a craft from Earth, vintage 1990s. In it, frozen in stasis, are a number of exiles from Earth's "eugenics wars," including the formidable Khan Noonien Singh (Ricardo Montalban), a genetically engineered superman who, once awakened, plans a program of conquest to recover the extensive political power he once held on Earth. The *Enterprise* crew is able to thwart Khan's efforts, exiling him and his followers to a barren, uninhabited planet, though he uses his considerable abilities to mount another plan of conquest from there, resulting in the action that will eventually lead to his death in *The Wrath of Khan* (1982), the second *Star Trek* film.

In "A Piece of the Action" (January 12, 1968), Kirk, Spock, and McCoy beam down to the planet Sigma Iotia II only to find themselves in the midst of a war between rival gangster groups whose culture is mysteriously similar to the gangster culture of Earth in the late 1920s. This coincidence seems startling until it is revealed that a much earlier Federation mission to the planet had inadvertently left behind a book entitled "Chicago Mobs of the Twenties," which the highly imitative Iotians had adopted as a model plan for their society. After several narrow escapes (and comic moments), the three Starfleet officers manage to engineer a peace in which the rival gangs are united in a single government that recognizes the Federation as its "Godfather." McCoy, meanwhile, accidentally leaves his communicator on the surface when they return to the *Enterprise*, leaving the crew—and the audience—to speculate on what the Iotians, with their penchant for imitation, might do with this piece of advanced technology.[5]

In "Bread and Circuses" (March 15, 1968), a sort of companion piece to "Arena," Spock and Kirk find themselves thrust into gladiatorial battles on the planet 892-IV in an arena modeled on the ancient Roman coliseum—with the added touch that the matches are televised in order to reach a wider audience. In this case, the similarity to cultural practices from Earth's past seems primarily to be a case of parallel development—a notion that frequently recurs in the *Star Trek* universe. However, outside interference has played a role as well, here in the form of a visit to the planet by the Federation ship the SS *Beagle*, whose captain, Merik, now serves as the First Citizen of the Empire. The rest of the crew, however, has already perished in gladiatorial contests, and the real power on the planet is held by Proconsul Claudius Marcus, who manipulates Merik (and the gladiatorial battles) for his own unscrupulous purposes.

Beamed down to the surface, Kirk, Spock, and McCoy become involved with an underground group of "sun worshippers" who are opposed to the planet's oppressive government. The heroes thus once again inadvertently become involved in a local conflict. They again escape, though Merik (showing a flash of his old honor and valor as a Starfleet captain) is killed in the process of aiding them. The events triggered by the visit of the *Enterprise* also give a boost to the sun worshippers, who now seem on the road to victory in their rebellion. Back aboard the *Enterprise*, Uhura (Nichelle Nichols) points out to Kirk and Spock that the "sun worshippers" are actually "son worshippers" and that their religion of brotherhood and love is in the process of re-creating the historical process through which Christianity supplanted the Roman Empire as the principal power in Europe.

In its portrayal of television as a key tool of power for the ruling order on 892-IV, this episode involves one of the few comments on the medium of television in *TOS*. About to send Kirk off for his televised execution, Claudius Marcus tells Kirk, "You may not understand because you're centuries beyond anything as crude as television." Kirk responds with a clear irony: "I've heard it was . . . similar," thus linking contemporary American television to the spectacles of violence that are central to the society of 892-IV.

The positive figuration of Christianity in "Bread and Circuses" is also a departure for *Star Trek*, in which the vision of the future is openly secular. The crew members of the *Enterprise* seem to practice no religion whatsoever, while the various religions they encounter on their travels are generally figured as artifacts of ignorance and super-stition that stand in the way of genuine progress.[6] Science, in some cases, is criticized as well. Khan, after all, is the product of genetic research, and the series occasionally features the stock science fic-tion character of the traditional mad scientist, such as Dr. Roger Korby (Michael Strong) who attempts to take over the *Enterprise* in "What Are Little Girls Made Of?" (October 20, 1966) with the aid of his an-droid creations, one of which is a perfect double for Kirk. In general, however, *TOS* treats science very positively and as the potential key to the solution of virtually all economic and social problems—in con-trast to the consistent warnings about the dangers of science that marked earlier series such as *The Twilight Zone* and *The Outer Limits*. In this sense, *Star Trek* reaches back to the eighteenth century, when the rise of Enlightenment science was often seen as the key to a uto-pian future. Indeed, in *TOS*, the twenty-third century is envisioned essentially as the culmination of the Enlightenment project of build-ing an ideal society based on knowledge, rationality, and science.

On the other hand, *TOS* consistently acknowledges the dangers inherent in overly rapid scientific advancement, frequently express-ing a concern that science and technology can be utilized positively only in societies in which social and ethical development keeps pace with scientific knowledge. As a result, all Starfleet missions to less-developed worlds are strictly forbidden from sharing technology or scientific knowledge that might lead to unnaturally rapid development. Indeed, such policies of noninterference are crucial to the ethos of the Federation. *TOS* is extremely careful to depict the Federation as benevolent and to avoid any suggestion that the organization is in-volved in an imperial project to colonize and subjugate the galaxy in the mode of the great nineteenth-century European colonial empires on Earth. Thus, all Starfleet missions are governed first and foremost by the famous "Prime Directive," which forbids interference in the development of societies that have yet to reach the level of sophisti-cation of the Federation itself—roughly measured by the development of warp-drive technology for interstellar travel. The use of this technological measure as a rule of thumb is not made entirely clear until the later *Voyager* series, but it is certainly consistent with the tendency of *Star Trek* to regard scientific and technological advancement as the central measure of a society.

This policy of noninterference is, significantly, shared by neither the Klingons nor the Romulans, both of whom seem to explore new worlds primarily with an eye toward conquest and imperial expansion. Then again, the Federation representatives aboard the *Enterprise* have a way of conveniently ignoring the Prime Directive as well, though Federation intervention is typically justified as a way of restoring the "normal" evolution of the societies involved. For example, the overt intervention that occurs in "A Piece of the Action" is intended to reverse the effects of the earlier Federation visit to Sigma Iota II, a visit that apparently took place before the adoption of the Prime Directive. Similarly, the *Enterprise* crew makes a crucial contribution to the literal overthrow of the planetary government (most planets in *Star Trek* seem to have only one or, at most, two governments) in "Bread and Circuses," but this intervention is presumably justified as a counter to the negative impact of the earlier visit of the *Beagle*.

In addition to the scenario of visits to exotic foreign planets for encounters with strange alien species, *TOS* employed other classic science fiction devices as well, one of the most important of which was the motif of time travel. Indeed, it is apparently the *Enterprise* crew that first discovers time travel (at least among members of the Federation), when the ship is momentarily thrust backward in time by reaching unprecedented high speeds at the end of the early episode "The Naked Time" (September 29, 1966). In "Tomorrow Is Yesterday" (January 26, 1967), a "black star" propels the *Enterprise* into a time warp that leaves the ship orbiting Earth in the late 1960s, essentially the time during which the episode was being viewed. This episode is the first in which *TOS* explores what has traditionally been a central concern of time-travel narratives, a temporal version of the Prime Directive in which the crew must carefully avoid any interference in the flow of history, thereby leading to unpredictable and potentially catastrophic results.

In "Assignment: Earth" (March 29, 1968), the *Enterprise* again travels back to a time period roughly contemporaneous with the first-run broadcasts of the series. This time, however, they do it on purpose in order to gather data on the cold war, seeking to determine how the earth managed to avoid destroying itself in a nuclear holocaust during that difficult time. In the process, they nearly stop the prevention of the holocaust when they become entangled in the efforts of an alien agent, Gary Seven (Robert Lansing), to intervene in the weapons race. Seven (apparently an earthling raised and trained by aliens) has returned to Earth to prevent the United States from launching an orbital atomic bomb, which would surely lead to a dangerous increase in cold war tensions. The highly efficient Seven (who was intended to be the protagonist of a spin-off series called *Assignment: Earth* that never materialized) succeeds in his mission despite the interference from the *Enterprise*, and disaster is averted.

"The City on the Edge of Forever" (April 6, 1967), one of the original series' most enduring episodes, is also a time-travel narrative. In this case, McCoy accidentally travels back to Earth's past through an alien time gate (a vague predecessor of the Stargate in the later series *Stargate SG-1*), and then changes history in a way that causes the *Enterprise* to cease to exist. Luckily, a landing party (including Kirk and Spock) is able to go after him and reverse his impact on history, restoring the future situation to its original state. Traveling back to Depression-era Chicago, they discover that McCoy's intervention involved saving a social worker, Edith Keeler (Joan Collins), who would otherwise have been killed in an automobile accident. Having been saved, she goes on to establish a pacifist movement so effective that it delays the entry of the United States into World War II long enough that Nazi Germany is able to develop nuclear weapons and conquer the planet. Reluctantly, Kirk and Spock are forced to prevent Keeler's salvation, allowing her to be killed. Meanwhile, along the way, Kirk has fallen in love with her, adding poignancy to the episode.

"The City on the Edge of Forever" has long been popular with fans for a number of reasons. For one thing, its main plot line involves a classic case of the alternate history genre, whose popularity has endured with science fiction fans. For example, probably the most respected novel of the legendary science fiction writer Philip K. Dick, *The Man in the High Castle* (1962), is precisely an alternate history tale in which the Nazis win World War II. One should not, however, dismiss the attraction of the heart-wrenching story of Kirk's tragic love for Edith Keeler. Indeed, while the series' dialogue with issues such as racism, sexism, and the cold war may account for some of the intellectual appeal of *Star Trek* to its fans, fan connection to the series over the years has typically been more emotional than intellectual. Much of this emotional appeal lies in the characters, with whom audiences established strong connections and identifications over the years. Connections among the characters are important as well, and much of the upbeat feel of *Star Trek* derives from its ability to project a genuine image of family and community through its portrayal of the affection and respect that the different members of the crew come to feel for each other over the years via their shared experiences aboard the *Enterprise* as it pursues its mission of galactic exploration.

Of the three most important characters, both Kirk and McCoy are, if anything, excessively emotional, given their professional positions, though Kirk manages to keep his emotions in check well enough to get the job done, while the crusty McCoy has a tendency to hide his true emotions with a gruff exterior. Oddly enough, though, the key to the emotional appeal of the series was surely the half-Vulcan Spock, self-characterized throughout the series as completely devoted to logic and to the suppression of all emotion. Of course, Spock is also half-human, so his struggle against emotions throughout the series is a difficult one, and he gradually develops powerful emotional attachments to both Kirk and McCoy, despite his general unwillingness to express his affection for his two longtime companions. Thus, when Spock sacrifices his life in the second film, he claims to do so not on the basis of love for his comrades, but on the entirely logical premise that "the needs of the many outweigh the needs of the few, or the one."

Of course, Spock's calculating attitude here is not shared by his crewmates, who all subsequently risk their lives and careers in the next film to save him, hijacking (and ultimately destroying) the antiquated *Enterprise* in order to undertake a seemingly illogical mission to rescue their resurrected friend. If this seems to be a contradiction, then it was one that was built into the portrayal of Spock from the very beginning. Though he may personally reject the illogical mathematics of an individualism that would endorse the sacrifice of the many in the interest of the few, much of the incredible popular appeal of his character derived from the fact that he himself was such a lone individual, the only Vulcan on the *Enterprise* (or any Starfleet ship, for that matter). No wonder so many lonely teenagers and young adults, feeling so misunderstood and alone in the world themselves, could identify with Spock's predicament. Indeed, Spock was the most beloved character in all of the *Star Trek* franchise, not in spite of being half-alien, but precisely because his alienness spoke to a sense of alienation that was central to the life experience of so many of the series' followers.

That Spock was a sort of science geek no doubt appealed to a particular demographic as well, but the fact remains that his greatest moments (in terms of fan appeal) were those in which he, for once, was forced to show emotion. For example, the raging hormones that drive Spock to the edge of sexual insanity in "Amok Time" (September 15, 1967) no doubt struck a very familiar chord in adolescent viewers. In this classic episode, Spock begins to display increasingly aberrant behavior, which turns out to be due to the onset of *pon farr*, a condition that all adult Vulcan males encounter every seven years. *Pon farr* requires Vulcan males to return to Vulcan to mate, and the drive to do so is so strong that their usual devotion to logic is stripped away by a chemical imbalance in the brain that puts the mating urge above all else. As a result, the logic-oriented Vulcans find the condition shameful, and Spock is reluctant to explain his condition to Kirk and his shipmates. Instead, he attempts to hijack the *Enterprise* to take it to his home planet, where he is to wed his betrothed, T'Pring (Arlene Martel).

Eventually, Kirk learns of the urgency of Spock's need to return to Vulcan. Placing his devotion to his friend above his duty to Starfleet, Kirk disobeys direct orders from Starfleet Command and takes the *Enterprise* to Vulcan. Kirk and McCoy then accompany Spock down to the planet to witness the wedding ceremony, which is to be conducted by T'Pau (Celia Lovsky), a near-legendary member of the Vulcan High Council and a personage whose presence signals the lofty position of Spock's family in Vulcan society. Unfortunately, when they arrive, they learn that T'Pring, separated from Spock for many years, now prefers a different mate, Stonn (Lawrence Montaigne). Stonn is a full-blooded Vulcan, though T'Pring makes it clear that Spock's human blood does not factor in her decision. Instead, she finds herself unable to envision Spock as a mate because his exploits with Starfleet have made him such a legendary figure on Vulcan.

T'Pring exercises her traditional right to appoint a champion to battle Spock for her hand. However, rather than choose Stonn, she chooses Kirk to fight for her, on the basis of a logical calculation that neither Spock nor Kirk will want to stay with her once he has killed his best friend in battle for her, leaving her free to be with Stonn, one way or another. And her calculation (on which Spock eventually congratulates her) proves correct. Spock (apparently) kills Kirk in hand-to-hand combat, but, due to the resultant emotional upheaval, he is freed from the *pon farr*. In turn, he frees T'Pring from their betrothal and returns to the *Enterprise* to face prosecution for killing Kirk. Then, back on the ship, he learns that Kirk has merely simulated death thanks to a drug administered by McCoy. The captain recovers, all is forgiven, and the *Enterprise* proceeds on its mission with Spock's usual logical demeanor restored.[7]

Spock also shows emotion (and libido) in "This Side of Paradise" (March 2, 1967), in which the *Enterprise* travels to the planet Omicron Ceti III, expecting to find the earth colonists there dead due to the effects of deadly Berthold radiation that has been bombarding the planet. Instead, they find the colonists alive and well, living, in fact, in unnaturally perfect health amid what seems to be a utopian paradise of peace, plenty, and tranquility. Meanwhile, Spock meets up with the botanist Leila Kalomi (Jill Ireland), a young woman with whom he had previously worked and who had obviously been attracted to him, though she had been unable at that time to overcome his rejection of emotion.

In turns out that the health of the colonists is due to the effects of strange plants that grow on the planet, spraying the colonists with spores that give them both perfect physical health and mental contentment. Even Spock is affected by the spores, which cause him to relax his usual logical exterior and settle into a life of romantic bliss with Leila. In fact, the entire crew of the *Enterprise* (with the exception of Kirk) is ultimately overcome by the spores, causing them to decide to abandon their ship and join the colonists in their seemingly idyllic life on the planetary surface. When even Kirk finally starts to succumb, he finds that his violent reaction to the thought of leaving the *Enterprise* negates the effect of the spores. He quickly employs this discovery to help Spock recover by triggering violent emotions in him. They then rig up a device that negates the effects of the spores on the others on the planet by subjecting them to subsonic waves. The crew returns to the ship, and the colonists agree to relocate to a new planet, where they can resume their struggle to build a better new world rather than simply living in passive tranquility.

This episode is typical of a general suspicion toward utopian ideals that is a crucial part of the *Star Trek* ethos, which tends to value struggle and strife as central to the very definition of what it means to be human. As Kirk (who usually voices the official attitude of the series) muses at the end of the episode, "Maybe we weren't meant for paradise. Maybe we were meant to fight our way through. Struggle. Claw our way up. Scratch for every inch of the way. Maybe we can't stroll to the music of the lute. We must march to the sound of drums." On the other hand, Spock, who quite often voices a dissenting opinion, is not so sure. Dismissing Kirk's speech as nonregulation "poetry," Spock points out that the situation on Omicron Ceti III was not unequivocally bad. "For the first time in my life," he notes, "I was happy."

Spock plays a similar role in the series' other central interrogation of utopian societies, "Return of the Archons" (February 9, 1967). In this episode, the *Enterprise* visits the planet Beta III to investigate the disappearance of a Federation ship there one hundred years earlier. They discover a culture that seems to live in complete tranquility, though this tranquility is once more portrayed in a negative light through the suggestion that it is achieved by a complete suppression of individuality and creativity. However, when Kirk, Spock, and others beam down to the planet, they quickly discover that the general air of tranquility on Beta III is partly maintained through an institution known as the "Red Hour," a sort of outer-space version of the medieval carnival, during which the inhabitants become an unruly mob, blowing off steam by acting out precisely the violent and passionate tendencies that are otherwise kept entirely in check.

The inhabitants of the society are governed by a group of "lawgivers" known as "The Body," which in turns takes its directions from a mysterious omniscient entity known as Landru. The landing party from the *Enterprise* soon joins forces with an underground movement dedicated to subversion of the power of Landru and the lawgivers, then discovers that Landru is actually a powerful supercomputer built six thousand years earlier by a scientist who had hoped to guide his increasingly violent society toward peace. This notion is highly reminiscent of the suggestion in the classic science fiction film *The Day the Earth Stood Still* (1951) that an intergalactic police force of super robots might be required to enforce peace on Earth. However, while the film was a warning against violence, the *Star Trek* episode is largely a warning against the forced suppression of violence. Kirk manages to cause the computer to destroy itself, thus "liberating" the Betans and allowing them to pursue the evolution of their culture without computerized interference.

That evolution will not, however, proceed without Federation interference. As the *Enterprise* prepares to leave orbit, we learn that they are leaving behind a sociologist, Lindstrom (Christopher Held), and a "team of experts" to "help restore the planet's culture to a human form." Of course, "human form" here means a form that suits the values of the Federation and twenty-third-century Earth. Once again, then, *Star Trek* becomes the culmination of the values of the

Enlightenment, in this case of the tendency of Enlightenment thought to interpret the specific values of Western European civilization as absolute and universal "human" values. So much for the Prime Directive. Indeed, at one point in the episode, Spock even points out that to destroy Landru would itself constitute a violation of the Prime Directive. Kirk, whose interpretation of the directive seems to be very liberal (less strict, for example, than the later Jean-Luc Picard), dismisses Spock's concerns, arguing that the Prime Directive does not apply here because this is not a "living, growing culture." Apparently, for Kirk, the Prime Directive only forbids interference in the development of planets that are not already developing in directions of which he approves.

As the episode ends, Lindstrom reports that the society of Beta III is already becoming more human: without the intervention of Landru, various quarrels and even physical assaults have begun to occur. As Lindstrom puts it, reporting the violence to the *Enterprise*, "It may not be paradise, but it's certainly human." Once again, Spock is the only member of the crew who questions whether they have done the right thing. Indeed, he clearly wonders if it is really an improvement to allow the inhabitants of the planet to pursue their individuality if it means they will often resort to violence, achieving their individual goals at the expense of others. After all, we have been told in the episode that, with Landru in charge on Beta III, there had been "no war, no disease, no crime" and that Landru has been programmed to seek "tranquility, peace for all, the universal good." Spock, in fact, declares Landru a wonderful feat of engineering and dismisses Kirk's complaint that the computer lacked "soul" as "predictably metaphysical," whereas Spock says he prefers "the concrete, the graspable, the provable." He then notes "how often mankind has wished for a world as peaceful and secure as the one Landru provided." Kirk, however, has the last word: "Yes, and we never got it. Just lucky, I guess."

Such suspicion of literal utopias aside, *Star Trek* depicts the future society on Earth as rather utopian in orientation, just as the *Enterprise*, with its close-knit crew, is a utopian community of sorts. While we get few real details in the original series, it seems clear that we are supposed to infer that most traditional social inequities on Earth, especially those based on race and gender, have been eradicated in the world of the twenty-third century. That the series itself often repeats 1960s-era stereotypes concerning race and (especially) gender simply serves as a reminder that the series was produced in the twentieth century, when such inequities have not been erased. Roddenberry and the show's writers certainly looked toward what they saw as a better future, even if their vision was thoroughly Western and even if they were not always able to see beyond their own context.

Hunger and poverty seem to have been eliminated in the *Star Trek* future as well, though this aspect of the series' vision would be explored much more thoroughly in the later incarnations of the series than in the original version. Presumably, the elimination of economic inequities has been made possible through the productive power of advanced technology. In particular, the same technology that allows the crew of the *Enterprise* to produce various objects (especially food) seemingly out of thin air, through the use of devices known as "replicators," can also be used to replace traditional manufacturing and farming processes on Earth. However, these replicators (based on the same technology as the famous transporters[8]) merely rearrange the molecules of matter. Therefore, they still require raw materials for their operation, and it is not entirely clear where most of these raw materials are obtained.

In a nod toward the importance of raw materials, virtually the only actual workers who ever appear in *Star Trek* are miners, though these miners are typically depicted not as an oppressed working class but as a rough and rugged band of individuals who travel to distant planets in order to work very much on their own. Often, the materials they mine (such as the dilithium crystals that are crucial to the operation of the *Enterprise*'s engines) are extremely rare and valuable, which means that mining can be extremely lucrative. Moreover, rather than work as employees of mining corporations, most of the miners in *Star Trek* seem to be largely self-employed, which means that they are able to keep most of the profits for themselves. Thus, the dilithium miners of "Mudd's Women" (October 13, 1966) may be a bit uncouth, but they are also quite wealthy. The pergium miners of "The Devil in the Dark" (March 9, 1967) also seem headed for great wealth, once the *Enterprise* crew has solved a problem they have been having with a crystalline creature that lives in the mines. Indeed, they are able to strike a deal with the creature to do most of the digging for them; all they have to do is collect the pergium—and the profits.

The only episode in which miners are presented as the victims of exploitation is "The Cloud Minders" (February 28, 1969), in which the *Enterprise* travels to a planet in which society is marked by extreme class divisions of the kind that once existed on Earth. In this episode, the *Enterprise* comes to the planet Ardana, where the principal industry is the mining of a rare mineral called zienite that the *Enterprise* needs to help stop a deadly plague on the planet Merak II. Unfortunately, when they arrive they discover that labor troubles have shut down the zienite mines. In particular, the animalistic miners (known as "Troglytes," with clear hints toward "Troglodyte"), who live their lives in the mines beneath the planetary surface, are rebelling against their rulers, who live in the cloud-city of Stratos, suspended high in the air above the planetary surface.

Stratos, as Spock notes with approval, is a "totally intellectual society" where "all forms of violence have been eliminated." It is, in fact, famed for the achievements of its inhabitants, who, supported by the income from the zienite mines, have no need to work and are free to pursue their intellectual and cultural potential. Its inhabitants, in short, recall the Luminoids of *The Outer Limits*. As with the Luminoids, however, someone still needs to do the work. Initially, the contrast between the refined cloud-dwellers and the brutish miners seems to resemble that between the ultracivilized Eloi and the vicious, cannibalistic Morlocks of H. G. Wells's *The Time Machine*. The miners thus seem to be the villains in their conflict with Stratos, especially when their rebellion threatens to prevent the *Enterprise* from bringing the much-needed zienite to Merak II. However, it soon becomes clear that the miners are being exploited by the cloud-dwellers, who justify this exploitation on the basis of racial stereotypes that depict the miners as members of an inherently violent inferior race with no capacity for intellectual or cultural development. It turns out, however, that the miners and cloud-dwellers are actually members of the same race and that the development of the Troglytes has simply been stunted by the effects of poisonous gases inhaled while working in the mines.

This situation, of course, is precisely the one that has informed capitalism on Earth for centuries, with the exploitation of workers being justified by their basic intellectual inferiority. Spock, as usual, employs his logic to get to the heart of the situation. Droxine (Diana Ewing), the daughter of Plasus (Jeff Corey), the ruler of Stratos, explains to Spock (with whom she shares a few amorous sparks) that the Troglytes have no use for culture or education because they are simply "workers." Spock calmly responds, "In other words, they perform all the physical toil necessary to maintain Stratos." Droxine, apparently missing his point, simply agrees. "That is their function in our society," she says, but the anticapitalist point about class-based exploitation has been made.

Kirk manages to demonstrate that it is, in fact, the gases that are making the Troglytes violent and backward, just as gruesome working conditions on Earth have often interfered with the development of working-class humans. Plasus, realizing the situation, promises to work to rectify the situation. In return, the miners supply the needed zienite, and the *Enterprise* is able to come to the rescue of Merak II. Of course, in the meantime, Kirk and his crew have once again blatantly violated the Prime Directive, in this case to overcome a form of class-based exploitation that had once plagued the earth but has presumably long been extinct by the twenty-third century.

This confident assumption that the social and economic problems of twentieth-century Earth will have been solved within the next few centuries is the most important example of the famed optimism of *Star Trek*, despite the lack of details about how these solutions will have been achieved. This optimism sets the series strongly apart from most of the other science fiction television of the 1960s, which tends to deal either with threatening alien invasions or with the potential negative impact of technology gone awry. Moreover, despite the historic importance of *Star Trek* as a watershed in television history, it seemed to have relatively little influence in this regard. Most of the science fiction series that followed *TOS* continued the focus on problems rather than solutions that marked the series that came before it—presumably because problems generate drama and lend themselves to more compelling narratives. Indeed, after *Star Trek*, the next major series to be truly optimistic about the future was, well, *Star Trek*, in its second incarnation as *The Next Generation*. Nevertheless, what came between the first two *Star Trek* series is an interesting story in itself.

CHAPTER 3

Lean Years to *Star Trek: The Next Generation*: Science Fiction Television Is Reborn

The cancellation of the original *Star Trek* series marked the beginning of a relatively slack period in the production of SFTV, even as Stanley Kubrick's *2001: A Space Odyssey* (1968), with its unprecedented special effects, had just demonstrated as never before the capabilities of visual-media science fiction to produce astonishment and wonder in its audiences. Indeed, the production of new series was so slow that, if *Star Trek* was ultimately the most important science fiction series of the 1960s, it was probably also the most important series of the 1970s, reemerging in syndication with a popularity it had never experienced in its first broadcast run. Otherwise, the most successful American science fiction series of the 1970s were *The Six Million Dollar Man* (1974–79) and its spin-off, *The Bionic Woman* (1976–78), though these series were only vaguely science fictional, relying more on action-adventure plots typically derived from international rivalries related to the cold war. Meanwhile, seemingly promising SFTV series such as *Planet of the Apes* (canceled after only fourteen episodes on CBS beginning in 1974) went nowhere.

In the 1970s, cold war fears were on the wane, even as the culmination of the race to the moon in 1969 lessened America's fascination with the space race. The possibilities (and threats) offered by science were thus much less in the public imagination than they had been earlier. The lack of American SFTV production in the early 1970s can be attributed to other factors as well. In the meantime, events such as the baleful U.S. misadventure in Vietnam, the energy crisis, and Watergate combined with growing fears of overpopulation and environmental contamination to make Americans skeptical and cynical about the future. In science fiction film, the result was a flurry of pessimistic, dystopian visions of the future, including *A Clockwork Orange* (1971), *The Omega Man* (1971), *Silent Running* (1972), *Soylent Green* (1973), and *Zardoz* (1974). In American television, less given to such dark depictions, the result was a near withdrawal from science fiction altogether.

The situation was a bit better in British science fiction in the 1970s, though the most important series of that decade might have been *Doctor Who*, a holdover from the 1960s. New series of the 1970s included *UFO* (1970–71) and *Space: 1999* (1975–77), while the decade was topped off with the superb *Blake's 7* (1978–81). American SFTV picked up at the end of the decade as well, spurred largely by the huge commercial (and technical) success of the first *Star Wars* film in 1977. *Battlestar Galactica* (1978–79), for example, was so much like *Star Wars* that it triggered a lawsuit, while *Buck Rogers in the 25th Century* (1979–81) resurrected an old science fiction classic but with a clear *Star Wars* influence. The phenomenon of *Star Wars*–inspired series was short-lived, however, and SFTV seemed to have reached an all-time low by 1987. In that year, however, the production of *Star Trek: The Next Generation* propelled American SFTV into a rich new age.

On balance, British science fiction television of the 1970s fared better than its American counterpart. The decade opened as Jon Pertwee assumed the title role of *Doctor Who*, bringing that series into an interesting new phase. If the eccentric and wisecracking Patrick Troughton had been a bit rumpled, Pertwee, the third doctor, was probably the most dapper of them all. Sporting ruffled shirts and Edwardian coats and cloaks, he sped about in high style in his bright yellow roadster, Bessie. Indeed, the entire series stepped up a notch in style, as Pertwee's first appearance at the beginning of Season Seven coincided with a switch from black-and-white to color transmission. For example, Pertwee's first sequence, "Spearhead from Space" (January 2–24, 1970), looked more like something out of *The Avengers* than it did previous *Doctor Who* episodes. The plot of this sequence was very *Avengers*-esque as well, featuring the Nestenes, a collective alien intelligence that schemes to take over the earth by replacing key government and military officials with plastic replicas made in a doll factory that they have taken over.

The doctor himself, still getting accustomed to his new regeneration (imposed on him by his own people as punishment for interfering in the affairs of others), is a bit dazed and confused through much of this first sequence. However, he soon regains his balance and proceeds with a savoir-faire that would come to mark Pertwee's years in the role. Meanwhile, the doctor's scope of action would remain limited for some time—part of his exile involves a crippling of the TARDIS that leaves him largely stranded on present-day Earth, where, rather than traveling to exotic times and planets, he works to repel invasions from a variety of exotic foes. The series thus became a sort of cold war alien-invasion drama, reflecting the fears of the era. Nevertheless, despite this reduced scope, the doctor himself became more dashing and action-oriented than ever. Moreover, the alien-threat theme allowed him to get into even more trouble with preposterous monsters, as when, in the "Inferno" sequence from the 1970 season, a project to drill through the earth's crust releases green goo that turns the project workers into homicidal werewolf creatures. This sequence thus addresses the issue of unrestrained and irresponsible development and its effects on the environment, extending the scope of these episodes beyond the normal alien-invasion theme of this period. Indeed, this drilling, spearheaded by project head Professor Stahlman (Olaf Pooley) with a Frankensteinian fanaticism and blindness to potential consequences, not only creates werewolves but also threatens to release uncontrollable forces that would destroy the planet. Much of this episode is spent on an alternate-universe Earth (to which the doctor inadvertently travels due to a malfunction in the TARDIS, which he is still attempting to repair), where this destruction proves inevitable, though the doctor manages to get back to our Earth just in time to prevent a similar disaster here. Meanwhile, this alternate Earth, which shows Britain in the grip of a dystopian fascist regime, also provides a bit of interesting political commentary.

The introduction of Pertwee as the doctor coincided with the introduction of Caroline John as Liz Shaw, his new sidekick. Still attractive, but much brainier than most of the doctor's previous female companions, Shaw, a scientist, is brought in by Brigadier Lethbridge-Stewart to aid in the battle of his United Nations Intelligence Taskforce (UNIT) against alien invasion, though at first she expresses extreme skepticism that such an invasion is a real threat or that UNIT may be aided in its work by an eccentric time lord who travels about space and time in a vehicle that looks like a police box. In this sense, Shaw clearly anticipates the skepticism of the scientist Dana Scully in *The X-Files*, while her subsequent pairing with Doctor Who in the next several sequences provides one of many precedents for *The X-Files'* pairing of Scully with Fox Mulder.

The pairing of the fourth Doctor Who, played by Tom Baker, with his female associate, Romana, was also such a precedent, especially in the remarkable sixteenth season (1978–79), when Romana was played by Mary Tamm. Tamm was certainly a great beauty, but she also brought a great deal of wit and spunk to the role. Her ongoing banter with the doctor was a highlight of the season, foreshadowing not so much the team of Mulder and Scully as that of David Addison and Maddy Hayes in *Moonlighting*, except that *Doctor Who*, always a bit reticent on the representation of sexuality, did little or nothing to suggest a romantic spark between the two. Instead, their spark was intellectual, sometimes recalling the relationship between Steed and Mrs. Peel in *The Avengers*. Tamm's Romana, herself a time lord, was very much the doctor's intellectual equal or even better, though he always had the edge in experience and wiliness.

Unfortunately, Romana, while recalling the earlier Emma Peel in many ways, may in other ways have been a bit ahead of her time, and many fans were irritated by her lack of submission to the near-sacred figure of Doctor Who. In any case, perhaps partly because of such complaints, the considerable promise offered by the character of Romana never quite developed, and she was reduced all too often to the role of damsel in distress, waiting for her rescue by Baker's gallant, if somewhat comical, doctor. As a result, Tamm left the series after this, her first season, being replaced in the role of Romana by the more submissive Lalla Ward through the usual expedient of time lord regeneration. Baker, however, lasted seven seasons over the period 1974–81, giving him the most longevity of any of the doctors. He was also by far the most popular with American audiences, partly because he was the first to be seen extensively in America, but very much because he was a particularly youthful doctor, a figure of individualist rebellion against the normally conservative practices of the powers that be among the time lords of Gallifrey. Sporting a copious mop of woolly hair and wearing a long coat and flowing scarf, Baker looked a bit like Harpo Marx and often brought a touch of anarchic comedy to the role. However, he was also one of the most obviously superhuman of the doctors, remaining fearless, unflappable, and good-humored in all sorts of dire circumstances, from which he generally extracted himself rather easily, though sometimes requiring the help of Romana and K-9, his loyal and lovable, but definitely silly-looking, mechanical dog.

In the twenty-six-episode sixteenth season, the doctor and Romana are charged by the White Guardian with retrieving the six segments of the Key to Time, which, when reassembled, will allow the guardian to stop time momentarily so he can restore the balance of the universe, which is veering dangerously toward permanent and total chaos. The only problem is that the segments are not only scattered about the universe but also hidden and disguised, each having taken on the appearance of a completely different object—or even living being. Luckily, the guardian supplies them with a "tracer" that allows them to locate the key segments and to convert them back into their true form, though they encounter numerous obstacles along this seemingly straightforward path. This quest plot did indeed take the entire season, but it essentially consists of six different quests, one for each segment of the key. Each of these subquests is, in fact, quite different, taking the doctor and Romana into very different environments and essentially plunging them into a variety of different genres.

The first sequence of the season, the rather lackluster "The Ribos Operation," introduces both Romana and the entire quest, as the two time lords travel to the primitive planet of Ribos (most of the planets visited during this season are relatively primitive), where they encounter a medieval culture and a harsh long-term winter but still manage to recover the first segment of the key (disguised as a chunk of the incredibly valuable mineral "jethrick"), despite also running afoul of the formidable Graff Vynda-K (Paul Seed), a deposed tyrant seeking to recover his crown by military conquest. The next sequence, "The Pirate Planet," was written by Douglas Adams of *The Hitchhiker's Guide to the Galaxy* fame. As such, it has occasional moments of the kind of zany humor that marked Adams's most famous creation, but in general this story suffers greatly from a preposterous premise and general silliness.

The third story in the "Key to Time" saga is "The Stones of Blood," in which the doctor and Romana travel to present-day Earth, identified in this sequence as the doctor's favorite planet. There they encounter a strange cult revolving around a Stonehenge-like circle of rock monoliths, some of the stones of which actually turn out to be Ogri, blood-sucking, silicon-based life forms from another galaxy. In the course of overcoming these life forms, the doctor and Romana also encounter the Megara, strange computerized energy creatures who are charged with enforcing the law of the Galactic Federation. The depiction of these creatures as being so focused on the letter of the law that they violate its clear intent makes for some interesting satire, and, on the whole, this sequence is quite charming despite its far-fetched premises.

In "The Androids of Tara," the doctor and Romana once again travel to a medieval planet, though one that still has traces of high technology, apparently left over from a formerly advanced civilization now destroyed by some sort of "plague" (which might have been a nuclear war). In this case, the segment of the key is recovered quite quickly, Romana having used the tracer to identify it as part of a local statue. Unfortunately, both Romana and the doctor then become embroiled in local political intrigues (partly because Romana turns out to be a dead ringer for an important local princess), thus making it difficult for them to get off the planet alive. In this civilization, however, the ruling aristocrats have nothing but disdain for technology, which is strictly the domain of "peasants," the only class that is allowed to have technological expertise and to tinker with high-tech machinery, in this case mostly having to do with androids so advanced that they can easily pass for human beings. Indeed, much of the plot of this amusing sequence revolves around political intrigues involving such doublings, which are further complicated by Romana's exact resemblance to the Princess Strilla. In any case, the time lords (with considerable assistance from K-9) ultimately help to foil the efforts of the evil Grendel (Peter Jeffrey) to usurp the throne of Tara (once again illustrating the doctor's refusal to adhere to the *Star Trek*–like official noninterference policy of the time lord hierarchy); they then make off with the fourth segment of the key.

Of all the sequences in Season Sixteen, "The Power of Kroll" is the one that is most heavily informed by political commentary. Here, the doctor and Romana travel to one of the moons of the planet Delta Magna, a marshy moon to which the indigenous tribesmen of the planet, the green-skinned "Swampies," have been banished in a motif that obviously recalls the relocation of Native American tribes onto reservations in the United States. Moreover, just as those tribes were sometimes again displaced when valuable mineral deposits were located on the reservations, these Swampies are in danger of extermination because the moon has been found to be an incredibly rich source of methane, which can be converted via high-tech (by local standards, anyway) refineries into protein for use in feeding the ruling race back on Delta Magna.

In a motif reminiscent of the early scenes of the classic film *King Kong* (1933), the Swampies worship a huge and formidable beast (the "Kroll" of the title) that turns out to be a gargantuan squid, made huge, as we discover, by ingesting the fifth segment of the Key to Time and absorbing its colossal energies. The doctor and Romana ultimately use the tracer to convert Kroll back into the segment, which they then add to their growing collection. In this case, however, the quest for the segment is almost beside the point. The most interesting moments in this sequence have to do with the depiction of the cultural clash between the Swampies and the technicians at the refinery, many of whom regard the Swampies with a racial hatred bordering on the genocidal.

The sixth sequence of Season Sixteen, "The Armageddon Factor," also contains a certain amount of political commentary, this time mostly contained in a critique of militarism. The time lords land on the planet of Atrios, which has for years been locked in a bitter nuclear war with the rival planet Zeos. In a motif that clearly comments on the cold war arms race, these planets seem headed for mutual destruction, a situation the doctor finds unsurprising. "That's the way these military minds work," he explains, calling it "the Armageddon Factor." Meanwhile, it turns out that the war has actually been engineered by the Black Guardian, the evil twin of the White Guardian, and his nefarious minion, the Shadow. This story thus seems to depict the universe as being in the throes of a Manichean struggle of good versus evil, although, in a somewhat confusing final sequence, it appears that the White Guardian had been the Black Guardian in disguise all along. In any event, the time lords manage to save Atrios, while it turns out that Zeos has long been depopulated, its side of the war carried on by robots. The doctor and Romana also retrieve the final key segment, which this time is disguised as Princess Astra of Atreos, played by Lalla Ward, Tamm's subsequent replacement as Romana. As they assemble the entire key, the Black Guardian appears to claim this prize, which he hopes to use to destroy the entire universe. Realizing the danger, the doctor quickly orders the key to disassemble, and the segments once again scatter across the cosmos. Thus, the entire season is, in a sense, negated, as the long, tortuous process of assembling the key ends by reversing itself, restoring the cosmic situation to what it had been at the beginning of the season.

While *Doctor Who* chugged merrily along throughout the decade, the first important new British science fiction television series of the 1970s was *UFO*, the look of which was clearly influenced by the then-recent *2001: A Space Odyssey*. The first fully live action series to have been created by puppet-meister Gerry Anderson (creator of the earlier "Supermarionated" puppet series such as *Stingray* and *Thunderbirds*), *UFO* centered on the activities of SHADO (Supreme Headquarters Alien Defence Organization), a top-secret, high-level international organization dedicated to both repelling an alien invasion of the earth and keeping all knowledge of this invasion from the general public. As such, it anticipated many of the central motifs of later science fiction series, especially *The X-Files* and *Stargate SG-1*. On the other hand, there are no sinister government conspiracies in *UFO*: the operations of SHADO are simply kept secret to avoid the creation of public hysteria. *UFO* ran for a single season of twenty-six hour-long episodes on Britain's ITC, beginning in 1970. However, it was in many ways the direct predecessor to Anderson's next series, *Space: 1999*.

Set in 1980 (and thus only ten years in the future relative to the original broadcast), *UFO* nevertheless projected a great deal of technological advancement. Indeed, the technology deployed by SHADO is so advanced as to be a bit unbelievable, though the series and its creators probably deserve some credit for their technological optimism, even if the series itself often had a rather dark tone due to the sense of alien threat that pervades it. Heavily funded through the United Nations, SHADO sports an impressive array of high-tech defenses in its battle against UFOs, though it also seems to have an amazingly skimpy supply of each weapon. For example, important as an early line of defense is a well-equipped moon base that launches interceptors equipped with missiles that seem to destroy approaching UFOs rather easily. Yet the base has only three interceptors, each of which carries only one missile. SHADO's defenses also include a high-tech observation satellite known as SID (Space Intruder Detector) that is especially good at detecting UFOs as they approach Earth.

Once the UFOs (which, by the way, are themselves rather small and cheesy looking compared to the impressive craft deployed by SHADO) enter Earth's atmosphere, they are opposed principally by fighter jets that are launched from a fleet of several futuristic submarines known as Skydivers. There is also a collection of tanklike mobile units that pursue aliens on the ground, as well as a full infrastructure of communications and transportation equipment, including craft that routinely fly between the earth and the moon. SHADO's headquarters itself is a top-secret facility located underground beneath London's Harlington-Straker movie studio, which serves as the organization's cover.

Indeed, the putative head of the studio, Ed Straker (Ed Bishop), is actually the head of SHADO: his elevator-office is able to move up and down between the two facilities, allowing him to run both. Straker and the other major characters are, in fact, the heart of the series, which, despite its premise and its high-tech gimmickry, is very much character driven, in this sense following in the footsteps of *Star Trek*. At times, in fact, the UFO threat seems almost beside the point, merely providing a framework within which the personal dramas of the characters can play out. This is especially true of Straker, whose devotion to SHADO continually wreaks havoc in his personal life. For example, in the episode "Confetti Check A-OK," an extended flashback reveals how the founding of SHADO interrupted Straker's honeymoon, while his subsequent top-secret work (which he is not able to discuss even with his wife) sets his marriage on a doomed course that will eventually end in divorce. The Strakers do have a son in this episode, but we already know from the earlier episode "A Question of Priorities" that this son will die from injuries suffered in an automobile accident because Straker's devotion to the cause of fighting UFOs prevents him from diverting SHADO resources that might have saved his son's life.

Through it all, Straker (a former colonel in the U.S. Air Force) keeps a stiff upper lip, hiding his personal troubles behind a stoic exterior. That exterior is so stoic, in fact, that the other characters sometimes criticize him for being too cool and rational. One of his top aides, Colonel Alec Freeman (George Sewell), is particularly critical of Straker in this regard. Meanwhile, Straker's administrative duties keep him out of much of the actual fighting, leading to the addition, several episodes into the series, of Colonel Paul Foster (Michael Billington) to his staff. The young, handsome, and somewhat emotional Foster is the central action character of the series from that point forward, though he himself experiences significant complications in his personal life due to his work for SHADO. *UFO* features several prominent female characters as well, including Lieutenant Gay Ellis (Gabrielle Drake), who, in some episodes at least, is the commander of the SHADO moon base. We do not, however, see much into the private lives of the female characters, personal angst apparently being, in this future world, the realm of males only.

Despite the occasional placement of female characters in positions of authority, UFO was even more blatant than Star Trek about the use of its female characters as eye candy and of the female form as an audience catcher. The future world of the series is one in which virtually all women seem to have terrific bodies, set off by extremely tight-fitting futuristic costumes. Indeed, the costuming of the series was crucial to its futuristic look. Thus, in addition to the high-tech sets and prominent gimmicks and gadgets, the characters are given space-age wardrobes and hairstyles. Some of the uniforms worn by SHADO personnel, especially among technicians in the London headquarters, are vaguely unisex in design, though the bodysuits worn by such personnel tend to fit a bit more snugly when worn by the female characters. Even important figures (pun intended) such as Lieutenant Ellis wear highly provocative clothing, the purple wigs worn by female personnel on the moon base only serving to set off their shiny, shape-fitting uniforms.

While the exact nature and motivation of the alien invaders in UFO are never made entirely clear, viewers learn early on in the series that these invaders are apparently very bad news for earthlings. In particular, it seems that they come from a dying planet and are members of a dying race so similar to humans that they are able to use humans for spare parts, replacing their own failing organs with transplanted ones harvested from abducted earthlings. On the other hand, anticipating the twists and turns in the alien-invasion plot of The X-Files, there are occasional hints that the aliens are not similar to humans at all but have simply donned stolen human bodies for use in their operations on Earth. In any case, it is clear that the aliens intend at least to continue harvesting human abductees and probably even to colonize the entire planet.

This premise allowed the series to engage a number of highly topical issues of the late 1960s and early 1970s. For example, the organ harvesting motif addressed widespread public fascination with the possibilities (both positive and negative) opened up by transplant technology, a fascination that had grown mostly from the work of South Africa's Doctor Christian Barnard, who had performed his first successful human heart transplant in December 1967. Most obviously, of course, UFO was very much a cold war drama, and its depiction of a sinister alien threat was a rather transparent reflection of Western cold war fears of communism and the Soviet Union. The top-secret nature of SHADO allowed some episodes essentially to become cold war spy dramas. The episode "Exposed," in which Foster is recruited to join SHADO, is one such drama, focusing on the elaborate surveillance and information-gathering capabilities of SHADO. "Court Martial" is an espionage/courtroom drama in which Foster narrowly escapes execution when he is accused of leaking top-secret information that is in fact being obtained by an industrial spy seeking the secrets not of SHADO but of the Harlington-Straker Studios.

SHADO's ability to pry into the lives of private citizens has potentially ominous implications, and *UFO* was often somewhat dark in its depiction of such issues, which were highly topical in the cold war context of the show. Also sometimes featured were the battles of Straker (the strong individual) against the forces of bureaucracy that often hamper his operations. Central here are his occasionally heated disagreements with General James Henderson (Grant Taylor), head of the International Astrophysical Commission (IAC), which the UN has given oversight authority over SHADO. Thus, in addition to worrying about his private problems and the alien invasion, Straker must continually struggle against a complex, multilayered bureaucracy that includes the UN, the IAC, and SHADO itself.

All in all, the individual episodes of *UFO* often made for compelling drama, while the series' treatment of topical issues could be quite thought provoking. Surprisingly, given its seemingly pivotal role, the alien invasion was the least compelling aspect of the series. In addition to the fact that the actual UFOs are so simplistic, the battles shown between the SHADO craft and the UFOs are never very exciting. The aliens themselves are not very interesting, either, partly because we see little of them and learn little about them. When we do see them, they look exactly like humans, except with green-tinted skin (an effect, we learn, of the chemicals used to allow them to survive the long space journey to Earth). Ultimately, *UFO* was more effective as cold war drama than as science fiction, doing little to explore genuinely provocative ideas about the future, but often succeeding in producing entertaining television.

Anderson's next series, *Space: 1999*, was highly entertaining as well, though it relied more on traditional science fiction motifs for its success. Produced and broadcast by British ITV and broadcast in syndication in the United States for two seasons spanning the period 1975–77, *Space: 1999* was, for its time, a stylish series with impressive sets and special effects. The look of the show no doubt had much to do with the vision of executive producer and cocreator Anderson, but the effects were largely due to the creative genius of Brian Johnson, who would go on to become the special effects supervisor for Ridley Scott's *Alien* (1979). Johnson had also worked on the special effects for *2001: A Space Odyssey*, a film that exercised an especially clear influence on the sets and effects for *Space: 1999*.

The cast for the series, headed up by the American husband-and-wife team of Martin Landau (as John Koenig, commander of Moonbase Alpha) and Barbara Bain (as research doctor Helena Russell), was also impressive; however, the acting is a bit sensational, but then Landau and Bain had largely made their reputations with melodramatic acting in *Mission: Impossible*. Still, *Space: 1999* often created a strong sense that the actors felt a bit ridiculous in the situations in which they had been placed by the script. An additional problem is that the future science projected in the series is far too advanced for 1999. However, by far the biggest difficulty with the series is its entirely implausible premise, in which an explosion in a nuclear waste dump on the moon sends the entire planet and its more than three hundred inhabitants (the crew of Moonbase Alpha) hurtling out of Earth's orbit and then out of the solar system on the road to deep-space adventure. Unable to steer the escaped satellite, the Alphans simply go along for the ride, encountering come what may—which turns out, given the vastness of space, to be a surprisingly large amount. Indeed, the plots of the individual episodes became increasingly far-fetched as the series went along, leading to its relatively quick demise, despite some surprising initial ratings successes, especially in the American syndication market.

That being said, individual episodes of *Space: 1999* can be highly entertaining. A typical episode begins with a series of strange and enigmatic events (often declared "impossible" by Koenig or others), leading to a sort of detective-story sequence in which the events are gradually investigated and explained. Along the way, the very existence of Moonbase Alpha and its inhabitants is frequently threatened, creating, at least in some cases, genuine suspense, despite the fact that audiences pretty much know all along that the Alphans (or at least the major characters) will survive. In the process, the series engages a compendium of standard science fiction motifs, both in the depiction of the high-tech trappings of Moonbase Alpha and in the various adventures of the Alphans. These motifs include encounters with both hostile and benevolent alien civilizations, strange outer space physical phenomena (time warps, black holes, and the like), time travel, alternate universes, and so on.

Space: 1999 has often been compared to *Star Trek* in the way its characters wander the universe, encountering strange, mysterious, and often dangerous phenomena, at the same time thoughtfully exploring issues and ideas relevant to the lives of their real-life television audience. Individual episodes of *Space: 1999* are sometimes especially reminiscent of *Star Trek*. A good case in point would be "Guardian of Piri," the eighth episode of the first season, which combines elements of *Star Trek* episodes "Return of the Archons" and "This Side of Paradise." Here, the Alphans discover a depopulated planet, Piri, ruled by a guardian supercomputer programmed to produce and maintain an environment of perfect peace and happiness for its creators. The computer attempts to carry out its programming by luring the Alphans into this perfect existence as well, and only Koenig, here at his most Kirk-like, seems to understand that the druglike tranquility produced by this existence will lead to sure death for his human crew, who needs struggles and challenges in order to survive. As he says at one point, "Leave me with my pain. It reminds me I'm human." It turns out that Koenig is right; in fact, perfection has already led to the extinction of the original Pirians. He is, of course, successful in rescuing his crew and getting them back aboard the moon, inexplicably destroying the guardian by eliminating its alluring robot servant (played by former Bond girl Catherine Schell in a skimpy costume that would have looked very much at home on *UFO* or the original *Star Trek*), who has apparently been engineered to help seduce the Alphans, though the episode demurely downplays the potential implication that she has been designed as a sex machine.

This vision of humanity as a combative species, itself a science fiction cliché, is often repeated in various forms in *Space: 1999*. For example, in the episode "Missing Link," Koenig is captured for use as a sort of zoo animal by a superior being who regards him as perhaps occupying a more primitive position in the evolution of his own species. This being, Raan (the indomitable Peter Cushing), is shocked by Koenig's violent tendencies—and even more shocked when Koenig and Raan's daughter, Vana (Joanna Durham), fall in love. Eventually, to break up the relationship, Raan convinces Koening to return to Moonbase Alpha, leaving Vana behind. Finally, the episode endorses the notion that the emotionalism of humanity, while having its

drawbacks, is ultimately an asset, one of the principal characteristics that make the human species a special one in the cosmos.

This endorsement of emotion, of course, is also found in numerous *Star Trek* episodes. *Space: 1999* also resembles *Star Trek* in its attempt to build interest in its characters rather than merely in its plots
and situations. However, the ensemble of characters—Koenig, Russell,
senior scientist Victor Bergman (Barry Morse), astronaut Alan Carter
(Nick Tate), and computer officer David Kano (Clifton Jones)—was
never quite able to generate the interest and audience identification
of *Star Trek* characters Kirk, Spock, and McCoy. Indeed, *Space: 1999*
has a reputation as the series that *Star Trek* fans, feeling that it unsuccessfully mimics their favorite program, love to hate. Koenig,
clearly the central figure in *Space: 1999*, comes off as particularly
unsympathetic, partly because Landau (a sometimes fine actor who
would eventually win an Academy Award) seems ill-fitted for the part,
making his sometimes histrionic performance seem especially uncon-
vincing. Koenig's behavior also lacks the camp value of William
Shatner's Kirk, perhaps because it is not effectively set off against a
Spock figure, Morse's Bergman never quite attaining that status.

There are other similarities between *Space: 1999* and *Star Trek* as
well, especially in the way the multiracial, international crew of the
moon base projects a potential future of global cooperation. In the
second season, the crew gained even more in *Trek*-like diversity with
the addition of Schell as the shape-shifting alien, Maya, Moonbase
Alpha's new science officer. Koening sums up the series' rather pe-
destrian call for racial tolerance by reassuring Maya when she first
joins the crew (having been rescued from her exploding planet) that
"we're all aliens until we get to know one another." With Maya as
the science officer, Russell as the chief physician, and Zienia Merton
as Sandra Benes, a key data analyst, *Space: 1999* featured a number
of women in responsible positions. In that sense, the series went
beyond *Star Trek*, as well as in the way its crew wore unisex uniforms,
as opposed to the miniskirts sported by the female crew members of
the starship *Enterprise*—or the outrageously sexist costumes of the
female characters in *UFO*. All in all, however, the desultory nature of
the travels of the crew of Moonbase Alpha (at least the *Enterprise* could
be pointed in a chosen direction) left them without any real mission
and left the series without any real point. Perhaps the wandering
moon was meant to be taken as an allegory for human life as a whole,
suggesting that we all must move through life come what may, but

the lessons of this allegory remained unclear, if there were any lessons at all.

Although the special effects of *Space: 1999* suggested developing visual possibilities in science fiction television, the next important British series used relatively crude effects (reminiscent of *Doctor Who*). *Blake's 7*, which achieved cult status in both Britain and the United States, ran for four seasons, each consisting of thirteen hour-long episodes, from 1978 to 1981. It was thus a post–*Star Wars* series, but it showed little influence of the dazzling special effects that distinguished that landmark film. Instead, *Blake's 7* depended on ideas and concepts largely emanating from the brain of series creator Terry Nation, a key writer in the early seasons of *Doctor Who*. *Blake's 7* was, in many ways, the ultimate counter to *Star Trek*, depicting a dark dystopian future dominated by an oppressive galactic Federation that is brutal, corrupt, and unremittingly imperialistic. It is, in short, the virtual opposite of the benevolent United Federation of Planets in *Star Trek*. Meanwhile, the principal characters of the series, far from being a loyal band of Federation officers as in *Star Trek*, are a ragtag band of rebels, battling heroically against the overwhelming power of the Federation.

These protagonists are, however, anything but conventional heroes. In the beginning they are led by Roj Blake (Gareth Thomas), a charismatic rebel leader who had earlier led a large-scale uprising on Earth, only to be captured and made into an obedient citizen through administration of the mind-numbing drugs (a metaphor for television?) through which the Federation keeps its oppressed population in line. When Blake resumes his involvement with the ongoing resistance movement, he is again captured, then publicly discredited through fabricated evidence that identifies him as a child molester. He is then put aboard a transport vessel along with other convicted felons who are being exiled for life to the prison planet Cygnus Alpha. On the way there, however, Blake leads a revolt among the prisoners that ultimately finds several of them in possession of an abandoned high-tech alien spaceship that they happen across in deep space.

Renaming this ship the *Liberator*, Blake and his crew use its advanced capabilities to begin a campaign of subversion and sabotage against the Federation, which in return mounts an extensive effort to track down and destroy the rebels. These capabilities include such devices as a *Star Trek*–style transporter, a technology not available to the Federation. Most important, however, is Zen, an advanced computer that controls the ship and that, more or less, responds to the commands of Blake and the crew, though it also continues to have an agenda of its own. This crew originally includes Kerr Avon (Paul Darrow), a misanthropic computer genius; Jenna Stannis (Sally Knyvette), a beautiful smuggler and expert space pilot; Vila Restal (Michael Keating), a cowardly but gifted thief; and Olag Gan (David Jackson), a gentle giant who has been fitted with a device in his brain that limits his former tendencies toward violence. They are soon joined by Cally (Jan Chappell), an Auron telepath, thus completing the group of seven (including Zen).

In contrast to the air of community and esprit de corps that prevails on the *Enterprise*, the crew members of the *Liberator* constantly squabble among themselves. Blake himself has a definite dark side, sometimes seeming more fanatical than idealistic. The crew as a whole is thrown together essentially by accident rather than through any common mission. However, as the series proceeds, they do develop a sort of grudging mutual commitment to their battle against the Federation. Thus, when Blake himself is lost in space after a cataclysmic battle at the end of the second season (because Thomas left the series to join the Royal Shakespeare Company), the crew holds together and continues their mission of subversion, now under the unlikely leadership of the seemingly self-interested Avon. Knyvette left the series after the second season as well, complaining of a lack of development in her character. Blake and Jenna were replaced in the crew, respectively, by the mercenary Del Tarrant (Steven Pacey) and the beautiful blonde gunslinger Soolin (Glynis Barber), though Tarrant was a particularly unexciting character, leaving Avon the main task of keeping the series interesting.

In addition to its cast of complex and flawed heroes, *Blake's 7* also featured extremely interesting villains, led by Servalan (Jacqueline Pearce), the supreme high commander of the Federation, and Travis (played in Season One by Stephen Grief and in Season Two by Brian Croucher). At first, the black-clad Travis is Blake's main antagonist, a role that is made more interesting by the way in which his single-minded devotion to tracking down and eliminating Blake mirrors Blake's own obsessive tendencies. Travis, as the pursuer of Blake, is something of a stock character, described by John Kenneth Muir in *A History and Critical Analysis of* Blake's 7 as the "Hapless Pursuer." As such, Blake looks back to characters like the Master in *Doctor Who* and, outside the realm of science fiction, to Barry Morse's Lieutenant Gerard in *The Fugitive*. He also looks forward to such figures as Captain Bailar Crais and Scorpius in *Farscape*. However, Travis's obsession makes him particularly one-dimensional, while his repeated failures to defeat Blake (despite his devotion to the task and the vastly superior resources at his command) eventually wear thin, leaving the deliciously evil (and ultimately much more interesting) Servalan to carry the Federation banner in the final two seasons.

Blake's mysterious disappearance at the end of Season Two very clearly anticipates the later disappearance of Fox Mulder in *The X-Files*. *Blake's 7* also anticipated *The X-Files* in other ways, perhaps the most important of which was its dark tone. The groundbreaking *Blake's 7* also served as an important structural predecessor to *The X-Files* (and other series, such as *Babylon 5*) by linking its individual episodes into a sequential "myth arc" plot, though many episodes stand alone and do not really contribute to the overall plot development. *Blake's 7* draws upon a virtual catalog of standard science fiction motifs in the course of its four seasons, but it manages nevertheless to remain innovative and surprising—up to its shocking (if, in retrospect, inevitable) conclusion. In the final episode, Blake returns as a somewhat seedy bounty hunter and is killed by Avon. Avon and his entire crew are then killed by the Federation, which emerges unchallenged and triumphant. (Actually, the series ends with a freeze-frame, in which a surrounded Avon seems about to be gunned down by the overwhelming forces of the Federation, somewhat in the mold of the final shot of *Butch Cassidy and the Sundance Kid*.)

Blake's 7 was thus ultimately one of the darkest science fiction series ever to appear on television. However, the most notable British productions in the years immediately following it turned to comedy. The six-episode television miniseries of *The Hitchhiker's Guide to the Galaxy*, which aired on BBC in early 1981, was an adaptation of Douglas Adams's earlier radio serial of the same title (which had begun airing in 1978). The radio version also inspired a series of novels by Adams, making *The Hitchhiker's Guide* a true multimedia event. In all media, it was a work of high silliness, featuring a heavy dose of toilet humor. However, it also contained a great deal of social satire, though the completely unserious way in which it lampooned various human foibles made it almost a parody of social satire rather than social satire proper. It was also more a parody of science fiction than science fiction proper, with various staples of the genre (space travel, time travel, galactic empires, dangers of arrant technological development, planetary catastrophes, and so on) being treated with anything but respect and seriousness.

The television version (which basically adapts the first six episodes of the radio program) begins as protagonist Arthur Dent (played by Simon Jones, who had also voiced the role on radio) learns that the earth is about to be demolished because it is in the path of a new hyperspace expressway currently under construction. However, this cataclysm turns out to be no big deal, as Earth is an insignificant planet in the larger scheme of things. Indeed, the way in which the series begins with the end of Earth makes a major contribution to what seems to be the main point of the series: that earthlings take themselves far too seriously.

Adams and the producers of the series did not make the same mistake. The program veers zanily from one nonsensical motif to another. Dent is saved from the destruction of Earth by the good offices of his friend Ford Prefect (David Dixon), who turns out to be an alien visiting Earth to do research for a new edition of *The Hitchhiker's Guide to the Galaxy*, an encyclopedic electronic reference book intended to provide useful information to travelers as they move about the galaxy. It also provides a great deal of general advice for daily living (its central pointer: "Don't panic"), making it the ultimate source of information on "life, the universe, and everything." Of course, much of this information is comical and satiric. For example, the entire entry under "Earth" simply reads "Harmless."

The plot of the miniseries is triggered when Prefect uses a matter transference beam to transport himself and Dent onto a ship in the Volgon construction fleet, escaping the impending destruction of Earth. The hostile Volgons (whose motto, like that of the Borg of the later *Star Trek* series, is "resistance is useless") soon eject the two into space. Fortunately, they are rescued by a passing ship, which just happens to be equipped with an "infinite improbability drive," which allows it to travel about space almost instantaneously. The ship is captained by the two-headed, three-armed Zaphod Beeblebrox (Mark Wing-Davey, another holdover from the radio series), formerly the president of the galaxy, but now a fugitive. Its crew comprises Trillian (Sandra Dickinson), an apparent blonde bimbo who is actually devastatingly intelligent, and Marvin, a robot who has been programmed to have a human personality and is thus always depressed. This group then wanders about the galaxy, seeking the meaning of life but encountering only one comic misadventure after another, in a mode that can be taken partly as a parody of the cosmic explorations of the starship *Enterprise*. Indeed, the third episode of the series openly refers to the famous opening voice-over of *Star Trek*, when it tells us of an earlier heroic age of Galactic Empire when men "boldly split infinitives that no man had split before."

If *The Hitchhiker's Guide* opened British SFTV of the 1980s with a comic turn, it ended that way as well. *Red Dwarf*, the brainchild of Rob Grant and Doug Naylor (former head writers of the satirical British puppet series *Spitting Image*), was a sitcom (broadcast on BBC2) set on a mining ship in outer space. This unlikely scenario proved surprisingly successful, and the series gained a cult following as it cruised through its first six seasons from 1988 to 1993, though each season was short, typically consisting of twelve half-hour episodes. A seventh season was then broadcast in 1997 and an eighth in 1999. At the time of this writing, there is still talk of a possible ninth season, while a feature film version for theatrical release (featuring the cast from the television series) is in production.

In the course of its long run (it is the longest-running sitcom in the history of BBC2), *Red Dwarf* has addressed virtually every stock motif of science fiction television. In addition to its basic outer-space setting and space-exploration theme, it features a variety of robots, nanobots, androids, mutants, holographic humans, and intelligent (sort of) computers. Various plot episodes involve time travel, mind exchange, parallel universes, and strange natural phenomena. They also involve specific allusions to various science fiction classics, as when the android Kryten approaches his expiry date in Season Three's "The Last Day," echoing a central motif of the 1982 film *Blade Runner*. However, the series is first and foremost a character-based sitcom, depending for its effects not on the investigation of strange new worlds and experiences, but on snappy dialogue and other comic interactions among its relatively small cast.

The premise of the series is quite simple. As it begins, the mining ship *Red Dwarf* cruises through space in search of ores to mine. Unfortunately, a radiation leak (caused by a botched repair job) kills off all the crew except one Dave Lister (Craig Charles), the lowest-ranking member of the entire crew. Lister, it turns out, has been placed in "stasis" (suspended animation) for refusing to reveal the whereabouts of the contraband pet cat he has smuggled on board. When Lister awakes, he finds that it is three million years later and that he is the only human remaining on the ship—and perhaps in the universe. He finds, however, that he is accompanied by Holly (Norman Lovett), the ship's somewhat daft onboard computer, which claims to have an IQ of 6,000 but which seems oddly lacking in intellect. Lister is also accompanied by a hologram simulation of Arnold Rimmer (Chris Barrie), the officious technician whose incompetent work led to the original radiation leak. The fastidious Rimmer had been the slovenly Lister's tormentor when they were both alive, and he continues that role three million years later, though the two gradually develop a strange sort of bond, vaguely along the lines of Felix Unger and Oscar Madison in *The Odd Couple*. Meanwhile, they are also joined on the ship by "Cat" (Danny John-Jules), the descendant of Lister's original feline pet, who has now evolved into near-human form. However, the dapper and ebullient Cat still retains a number of feline characteristics (such as wandering about the ship marking his territory with an aerosol spray), while otherwise seeming a bit like a cross between James Brown and Morris Day.

Among other things, the characters find that their ship has been headed away from Earth during the past three million years, so that they are now an incredible distance from home. Thus, in a motif that anticipates *Star Trek: Voyager* while reaching back to predecessors such as *Lost in Space*, the basic plot of the series involves the efforts of the surviving crew to get back home to Earth, encountering various strange experiences along the way. The difference, of course, is that these experiences are generally comic in nature. Typical is the last episode of the second season, "Parallel Universe," in which Holly invents the "Holly Hop Drive," apparently something like the trans-warp drives that appear in the later *Star Treks*—or the infinite improbability drive of *The Hitchhiker's Guide*. With this drive, they expect to be able to return to Earth almost instantaneously via a single leap through space. Instead, however, they find that they leap into a parallel universe where they encounter a duplicate version of *Red Dwarf*, with one minor difference—the genders of all the crew members have been reversed. Cat is the one exception: his opposite/double is not a female cat but a male dog.

The interactions between the two crews lead to considerable comic mayhem, much of which satirizes various gender conventions. For example, the chauvinistic Rimmer finds that the new female Rimmer regards men as sex objects much as he had previously regarded women (despite his almost total inability to attain such objects). Perhaps predictably, the two Listers get drunk together and then have sex. In this season-ending episode, we are presented with a cliff-hanger that parodies the tendency toward such finales in other science fiction series: the characters get back to their own universe only to find that, while in the parallel universe (where all gender roles were reversed), Lister had gotten pregnant during his encounter with his female double.

Red Dwarf remains unique in its combination of sitcom and science fiction, and its comedy has a distinctively British tone, which perhaps explains why the American networks passed on a proposal to produce an American version of the series. Of course, it didn't help that American networks had also tried science fiction comedy (such as NBC's *Quark* in 1978) without much success, though the sitcom *ALF* (about a suburban family that adopts a furry alien who accidentally crashes his spacecraft into their garage) had a successful run on NBC from 1986 to 1990. However, *Red Dwarf*, along with *ALF*, may have helped to pave the way for the later highly successful American sitcom *3rd Rock from the Sun* (NBC, 1996–2001). Described by its creators as "Carl Sagan meets the Marx Brothers," *3rd Rock* explored the comic exploits of a group of aliens on Earth, vaguely in the mode of the successful "Coneheads" skits from *Saturday Night Live*. It was, however, much more of a conventional sitcom than *Red Dwarf*, the science fiction elements being used simply to create additional comic situations. *Red Dwarf*'s comedy probably also influenced the later *Lexx*, though the highly satirical *Lexx* was not a sitcom, despite its strong emphasis on comedy.

The major American series of the late 1970s, *Battlestar Galactica* and *Buck Rogers in the 25th Century*, also threw in healthy doses of humor, perhaps trying to make the seemingly tired SFTV genre seem a bit more hip to contemporary audiences. More than humor, though, these series relied on slick special effects and on ensemble casts of characters that audiences could identify with and root for, partly because they were mostly recognizable types from the audience's own time period, simply transposed into the future without modification. Thus, by following the adventures of these characters, audiences could almost imagine themselves in that future environment.

Battlestar Galactica, like *Red Dwarf*, is another story of space travelers struggling to get back home. Homer's *Odyssey*, of course, is the prototype of all such sagas, and this heritage calls attention to the fact that science fiction stories of space travel have always tended to draw upon earlier narratives of adventures at sea. In the case of

Battlestar Galactica, however, there is a twist on the *Odyssey* story. For one thing, certain elements of the series clearly derive from the Western, linking the trek across space to the exploration of the American West, just as Gene Roddenberry had once pitched *Star Trek* as "*Wagon Train* in Space." There are also numerous biblical links, with Earth playing the role of the Promised Land of the Old Testament. In *Battlestar Galactica*, the humans who are struggling to get to Earth have never actually been there. They are the remnants of a far-flung interstellar empire populated by colonists for whom Earth is a semimythical ancestral homeland. As the series opens (five thousand years in the future), this empire has been shattered in a war against a relentless race of robot warriors known as the Cylons, who are obviously reminiscent of the Cybermen of *Doctor Who* but look suspiciously similar to the storm troopers of the then recent *Star Wars*.

In fact, lots of things about *Battlestar Galactica* seemed suspiciously similar to *Star Wars*, including the overall look of the series, its technology, and its special effects. Given the recent success of *Star Wars*, these similarities were no doubt intentional, especially given that the series hired John Dykstra, who had done the special effects in the film, to do the effects in the series as well. These effects were impressive, the best seen on television to that point. Other aspects of the series were less successful, however, perhaps because they were overshadowed by the special effects. The basic plot is never all that scintillating and quickly grows repetitive, as the defeated colonists band together in an eclectic convoy of ships and head in what they hope is the direction of Earth, dogged by the Cylons all the way.

Every episode is built basically on this same plot, with spice (sometimes not very effectively) added by the effects and by the attempts to build an impressive cast of characters. These were led by the wise and kindly Adama, the paternalistic commander of the *Galactica* itself and of the whole convoy. A sort of combination of Moses and Ben Cartwright (just as the series itself combined elements from the Bible and Westerns), Adama was played by Lorne Greene, who had played the patron of the Cartwright clan in *Bonanza* and was thus one of the most recognizable father figures in television history. Given Adama's dignified elderliness, the action roles in the series had to be played by Adama's virtuous and Luke Skywalker-esque son, Apollo (Richard Hatch), and Apollo's sidekick, the wisecracking nonconformist Starbuck (Dirk Benedict), whose name recalled *Moby Dick* but whose character clearly recalled *Star Wars*' Han Solo.

Battlestar Galactica seems pretty much uninterested in the ethnic diversity for which *Star Trek* has become famous. Given the far-flung backgrounds of the various members of the convoy, there is, in fact, surprisingly little such diversity in *Battlestar Galactica*. The human race does not seem to have evolved or changed at all, and all of the characters that matter are humans, though aliens do occasionally appear here and there, including, at one point, a variety of them in a virtual re-creation of the famous bar scene from *Star Wars*. Virtually all of the humans are white and most of them are male if they occupy a responsible position. Adama's second in command, Colonel Tigh (Terry Carter) is black, but there are very few blacks in the convoy. Meanwhile, women in the series seem designed primarily as decorations, all of the major feminine roles being played by beautiful young actresses. Granted, Athena (Maren Jensen) is the *Galactica*'s communications officer (in the tradition of Uhura), but her position on the ship smacks of nepotism more than equal opportunity for the sexes. The other major female character, Cassiopea (Laurette Spang), seems to have little to do other than serve as the dashing Starbuck's love interest.

Despite the flat characters and lack of imaginative plot, the sheer impressiveness of the special effects (especially in comparison to most previous SFTV) won *Battlestar Galactica* a fairly large audience, at least early on. But the effects worked less well on the small television screen than the large screens of movie theaters, and the series quickly diminished in popularity. Ultimately, it ran for only twenty-four episodes in a single season (with a two-month break in the middle.) It was then retooled and brought back for a brief run as *Galactica 1980*, with only Greene remaining from the original cast. In the sequel, which becomes a sort of alien-invasion series, the convoy reaches Earth, only to find that this planet, too, is now threatened by the Cylons. The Galacticans struggle to boost Earth's technology to the point where the planet can defend itself, meanwhile fending off suspicions that they themselves are alien invaders. *Galactica 1980* never really hit its stride and lasted only ten episodes. It was regarded by many critics as one of the worst SFTV series in history.

The initial success of *Battlestar Galactica* on ABC helped encourage NBC to revive one of the all-time science fiction classics in 1979 with the premier of *Buck Rogers in the 25th Century*. While the use of the Buck Rogers franchise may have had a certain nostalgia value, this version was a definite update, replacing the serious tone of the original serials with a definite turn toward hip comedy, heavily spiced with a dose of sex. Unlike the virtuous, gee-whiz original, this Buck, played by Gil Gerard, is another in the line of the lovable rogue Han Solo characters. Brave but irreverent, virtuous but horny, the new Buck is an astronaut from the twentieth century who arrives (after a stint in frozen suspended animation in outer space) on the earth of five hundred years in the future just in time to help ward off various alien threats, especially from the nefarious Draconians, led by the evil Princess Ardala (Pamela Hensley), whose skimpy costumes almost made Buck (and numerous male viewers) forgive her for the fact that she was seeking to destroy the human race. Luckily, the earthlings had plenty of sex appeal on their side as well, in the form of Colonel Wilma Deering (played by model Erin Gray), whose sophisticated charm and skintight bodysuits made her the closest thing to Emma Peel ever to appear in an American television series.

Like *Battlestar Galactica*, *Buck Rogers* made extensive use of the new computerized special effects techniques that had been pioneered in *Star Wars*. Unlike *Galactica*, which tried to see itself as a sort of grand epic in the tradition of the *Odyssey* and the Bible, *Buck Rogers* was pure pop culture, never taking itself too seriously. If anything, it was sometimes a bit *too* silly, as in its excessive use of the comic chattering robot, Twiki, clearly modeled on C-3PO from *Star Wars*. Meanwhile, its reliance on humor that was derived from the gap between Buck's twentieth-century background and his new twenty-fifth-century environment could only work for so long. Thus, when the series returned for its second season in spring 1981 (an actors' strike had delayed the 1980 fall season), it was significantly modified. Buck and Wilma were still the main characters, but now they were members of the crew of the *Searcher*, exploring the galaxy to look for the scattered survivors of those who abandoned Earth to escape a "great holocaust" that had occurred shortly after Buck's original departure.

The series thus reversed the trajectory of *Battlestar Galactica*, shifting its emphasis from alien invasion to space exploration, this time with a dose of cold war cautionary tale thrown in for good measure. In an homage to science fiction master Isaac Asimov, the *Searcher* was commanded by Admiral Asimov (Jay Garner), who was, in fact, identified as a descendant of the writer. Other members of the crew included Dr. Goodfellow (Wilfred Hyde-White), an eccentric elderly scientist, and the unlikely Hawk (Thom Christopher), who was half man and half bird. Twiki was also on board, although now perhaps the most important computer character was Crichton, a computer so sophisticated that it looked down on humans and couldn't believe it had been created by them. Despite being set in outer space, this new version of the series never really got off the ground and was canceled after an abbreviated thirteen-episode season.

The next several years constituted a lean period for American science fiction television. Indeed, through much of the 1980s, the most important SFTV series was *still* the original *Star Trek*, which continued to draw loyal audiences in syndication. The most important new science fiction program on American television in the early 1980s was not a conventional series, but a four-hour miniseries—Kenneth Johnson's 1983 alien-invasion epic *V*, which was so successful that it was followed in 1984 by a six-hour sequel, *V: The Final Battle*. In *V*, a virtual compendium of previous alien-invasion motifs, huge flying saucers suddenly appear over major cities around the globe. The aliens, who appear to look exactly like humans, then make contact, declaring themselves friendly. In a move that nods toward contemporary environmental concerns on Earth, the aliens explain that they have come to Earth because their planet (in the Sirius system) has serious environmental problems that can be solved only with the use of a chemical that they hope to manufacture on Earth, using the refuse of Earth's cities as raw materials. In return, they promise to share all of their vast knowledge with the people of Earth.

The people of Earth naturally jump at this deal, and soon many of the people of Earth are working in plants to manufacture the chemical needed by the aliens, now widely referred to as "the Visitors." Meanwhile, the aliens slowly consolidate their power, gaining control of the media and virtual control of all government agencies, including the police, supplemented by jackbooted alien storm troopers. In addition, they foster widespread suspicion and paranoia toward those who might be able to resist their power. These potential enemies (central among whom are scientists of various kinds) are soon being arrested and taken away en masse in ways that are clearly meant to echo the Nazi roundup of Jews prior to World War II. Indeed, the link between the aliens and Nazis is made clear in a number of ways, including the fact that the aliens employ an official logo that is quite similar to a swastika. The series even includes an elderly Jewish concentration camp survivor who openly compares the aliens to his former Nazi tormentors.

Just as few Germans resisted the Nazis, only a few brave souls question the Visitors' motives, even as these arrests become more and more widespread. Chief among those who doubt the aliens is Mike

Donovan (Marc Singer), a crusading telejournalist who has spent his career filming in hot spots around the world, including Cambodia and El Salvador. When he turns his investigative talents toward the Visitors, he quickly discovers that they are not quite what they appear to be. In particular, their human appearance is a ruse: they are reptilian creatures that have only assumed a human disguise in order to facilitate their contact with the people of Earth.

Of course, this disguise strategy is in itself understandable given the xenophobia of earthlings, which is demonstrated in the very telling way in which audiences were supposed to conclude immediately that the aliens were evil simply because they looked different from humans, especially because they had lied about the difference. Of course, by this time there was a whole science fiction tradition in which aliens disguised as humans turned out to be evil invaders seeking to conquer Earth, so audience reactions were also conditioned to some extent by generic expectations. Meanwhile, we learn that these particular aliens are even more sinister than we might have imagined. The chemical being manufactured by the aliens on Earth is a pure hoax. In fact, they have come to Earth to spirit away the planet's water and its people, some of whom will be converted into soldiers for use in further conquests, but most of whom will simply be consumed as food.

Led by Donovan and beautiful young biochemist Dr. Julie Parrish (Faye Grant), those who question the aliens gradually build an effective underground resistance movement. Indeed, the title of the series comes from the large red "V" that the rebels defiantly emblazon as graffiti in various locations as a reminder that the resistance exists. The second half of the first miniseries is the story of this resistance as it battles the superior resources of the aliens. The battle against the Visitors goes on as the series ends: in fact, we are told as the final episode concludes that the fight is only beginning.

This ending sets up the sequel miniseries, in which the fight against the Visitors (now repeatedly referred to as fascists) continues. The same characters continue to lead the fight as well, now increasingly aided by sympathetic "Fifth Columnist" aliens and by covert military operations expert Ham Tyler (Michael Ironside). Another plot twist involves a sexual encounter between Earth girl Robin Maxwell (Blair Tefkin) and one of the aliens, leading to the birth of a half-human, half-alien girl—and to the development of a biological agent that is devastatingly toxic to the aliens. This agent, distributed as red dust via a vast armada of hot-air balloons, proves the undoing of the aliens, leading to a victory for the earthlings that seemed heroic at the time of the initial broadcast. From the post-9/11 perspective of the early twenty-first century, however, this seems a bit more problematic, given the implied endorsement of the terrorist tactics and biological warfare that are practiced by the earthlings in their defense against the aliens.

This second *V* miniseries was followed a few months later by a weekly series also entitled *V* and featuring much of the original cast. However, the series was never a ratings success and lasted only through nineteen hour-long episodes from October 1984 to March 1985, though reruns were shown from May until July 1985. At the end of the series, a peace accord is reached between the Visitors and Earth, and all seems well. However, with the quick demise of *V* as a series, the outlook was not quite as rosy for American science fiction television, which was still struggling to find its first hit series of the 1980s.

Yet, even as all seemed bleak, Gene Roddenberry was working behind the scenes, planning a comeback. Actually, Roddenberry had initially envisioned a resurrection of *Star Trek* (with the original cast) in the 1970s, but that project was abandoned in favor of the development of the *Star Trek* feature film series. In 1987, after the release of four successful feature films, Roddenberry and his associates took the bold step of launching a second *Star Trek* television series with an entirely new cast, set in the twenty-fourth century, nearly a century later than the original series. Given the emotional attachment of many fans to the original series, the chances that the new series, entitled *Star Trek: The Next Generation* (hereafter referred to as *TNG*), would be able to move beyond the shadow of its illustrious predecessor seemed dim indeed. In an additional risky move, the new series (at Roddenberry's insistence, because it gave him greater creative control) was not broadcast on a network but distributed in syndication.

The original series, however, had already proven the potential of syndication as a format for science fiction television, with its special appeal to niche audiences. Moreover, it had been twenty years since the first broadcast of the original series, so *TNG* involved not only a new generation of characters, but also a new generation of fans. For some fans (especially younger ones), the first four *Star Trek* films, with their glossy look and state-of-the-art special effects, were beginning to make the original series look almost comical, if still lovable. *TNG*, on the other hand, had extremely high production values (and budgets) from the very beginning. Indeed, in terms of the look of the series, *TNG* follows more closely in the footsteps of the first four films than of the original series. Partly because of its impressive effects and high-budget look, *TNG* not only survived the initial scrutiny of some skeptical fans but went on to become the most successful American science fiction television series in history, lasting for seven years and scoring some of the highest ratings ever recorded for a syndicated program. The series also became highly influential, establishing (or at least solidifying) conventions for science fiction television that numerous later series would follow.

However, despite its high production values, the real secrets to the success of *TNG* were its sunny view of the future of mankind and its ability to establish a cast of characters who developed strong bonds not only among themselves but also with audiences. In this sense, *TNG* is very much in the spirit of the original *Star Trek* series, in spite of the very different look. *TNG* (partly because of its longer run) was able to fill in far more details about the "future history" of mankind; in some cases, the new series even modified the original series' version of future events. In general, however, the vision of the future in *TNG* is absolutely consistent with that of the original series. Earth once again is the center of the United Federation of Planets (which continues to expand, adding new planets), humanity is again at the center of the universe, and high technology has combined with the enlightenment gained from contact with other species to produce a time of peace and prosperity on Earth.

TNG includes a cast of characters that is, as in *TOS*, composed of the crew members of a Federation starship, in this case again the *Enterprise*, but now the *Enterprise-D* (Starfleet registry number NCC-1701-D), indicating that it is the fifth (the ship of the original series had no alphabetic suffix) starship to bear that name, each also carrying the Starfleet registry number NCC-1701.[1] The *Enterprise-D*, clearly identified as the Federation flagship, is much larger than the *Enterprise* of the original series and carries a far larger crew, including (due to the long duration of some of their missions) the families of many of the crew members. In all, more than one thousand people are on board at any given time. The presence of these families opens the possibility for a wider range of characters and of relationships among characters. Nevertheless, the important positions on board correspond almost directly to those on the original *Enterprise*, so that many of the characters of the two series can be matched up almost on a one-to-one basis. However, Roddenberry was clever enough not to make this correspondence too close, usually filling the same positions with characters whose personalities and other attributes are dramatically different from those of their counterparts in the original series.

At the head of the crew, of course, is the captain, in this case Frenchman Jean-Luc Picard (played by British actor Patrick Stewart), an older, wiser, less impetuous, and more aloof leader than James T. Kirk had been. Picard, aided by Stewart's stentorian voice, is a more imposing figure of authority than Kirk, but his crew is still devoted to him (and he to them), though he tends to avoid mingling socially even with the senior officers. The stern Picard does have a sentimental side, and he is strongly nostalgic about certain elements of Earth's past culture; for example, he prefers to read antique bound books rather than employ the electronic readers through which text is usually accessed on the *Enterprise*. He is particularly fond of Shakespeare, which provides a tie-in with Stewart's experience as a Shakespearean actor, while also helping to lend an air of culture to the series itself.

The first officer of the *Enterprise-D* is Will Riker (Jonathan Frakes). Younger, more emotional, and more action oriented than Picard, Riker has many of the characteristics of Shatner's Kirk. Indeed, Riker often fills roles in *TNG* that Kirk would have filled in the original series. Meanwhile, Riker himself is definite captain material and, in the course of the series, turns down multiple offers to command a ship of his own so that he can stay aboard the *Enterprise* (which, as the Starfleet flagship, gets all the choice missions) and learn from his mentor, Picard.

The "Spock" role in *TNG* is filled by Data (Brent Spiner), an android so sophisticated that he is able to function as a Starfleet officer, even as his advanced positronic brain also functions as a high-tech computer that often supplements the main computer system on the *Enterprise*. Data was created by the brilliant but eccentric cybernetic scientist Dr. Noonien Soong, who built the android (and an evil twin android, Lore) in his own image, using technological breakthroughs known only to him. In *TNG*, Starfleet's scientists have yet to understand fully the principles upon which Data operates. As a result, they are unable to make more such androids, leaving Data alone in the universe, much as Spock, as a human-Vulcan hybrid, often felt alone. Totally logical in his thinking, Data is incapable of emotion or irrationality; he is, in this sense, what Spock had always aspired to be. Data, on the other hand, wants more than anything (like Pinocchio) to be human and to be able to experience emotion, a project he struggles with throughout the run of the series, eventually acquiring an "emotion chip" that aids in the task. Among other things, this quest blurs the line between human and machine, and *TNG* includes several episodes in which Data is used to explore the question of just what it takes to be regarded as human (which remains the universal norm in *TNG*), a question that is also obviously at stake in the various encounters with alien species that are so central to all of the *Star Trek* series.

Data often finds himself fighting for rights he has been denied because he is perceived as different. In the episode "Measure of a Man" (February 13, 1989), for example, Data must fight to be recognized as a person in order to avoid being disassembled for scientific study. In such episodes, Data clearly functions as a figure of oppressed and misunderstood minorities of all kinds. He is also a principal focus of the considerable sentimentalism that informs *TNG*, and his struggles to become human are sometimes presented with great pathos. In "The Offspring" (March 12, 1990), Data attempts to build another android, which becomes his "daughter." Her eventual "death" in the episode is then treated with great sentimentalism, even though Data himself claims to be emotionally unaffected. And, of course, the ultimate death of Data (who sacrifices himself to save Picard) in the film *Star Trek: Nemesis* (2002) is one of the most sentimental moments in the entire *Star Trek* oeuvre.

The ship's medical officer (a position that, in Starfleet, apparently also makes one a key advisor to the captain) in *TNG* is Dr. Beverly Crusher (Gates McFadden), a much gentler and more nurturing physician than McCoy had been.[2] Dr. Crusher is the widow of Picard's friend Jack Crusher, who has been dead for some years as the series opens, having been killed in action under Picard's command. Picard, it turns out, had always been strongly attracted to Beverly, and romantic sparks continue to fly between the two of them throughout the series, though they never really pursue their mutual attraction. Jack and Beverly Crusher are the parents of teenage whiz kid Wesley Crusher (Wil Wheaton), who serves on the *Enterprise* through the first four seasons of *TNG*, leaving afterward to attend Starfleet Academy, though still making occasional appearances in the series.

The chief engineer of the *Enterprise* through most of *TNG* is Geordi La Forge (LeVar Burton), though La Forge spends the first season as the ship's flight controller (essentially, the pilot). Blind from birth, La Forge is distinctive for the metallic VISOR (Visual Instrument and Sensory Organ Replacement) that he wears across his eyes, allowing him to sense a far greater portion of the electromagnetic spectrum than can ordinary human eyes. A very prominent character in *TNG*, La Forge plays a much larger role in *TNG* than had Uhura in the original series, thus making him *Star Trek*'s first truly prominent African-American character. Younger and more emotionally vulnerable than Montgomery "Scotty" Scott, his predecessor in the original series, La Forge is a brilliant engineer, a fact that also helps to make him Data's best friend among the crew, though his affinity for machinery sometimes interferes with his interpersonal skills. Indeed, a major plot element in the series involves the ongoing difficulties of Geordi's hapless love life.

The other two principal characters in *TNG* have no counterparts among the crew of the original *Enterprise*. One of these, Worf (Michael Dorn), is played by an African-American actor, but the character himself is a Klingon (though he was raised by human foster parents), marking one of the major changes in the galactic political structure between the twenty-third and twenty-fourth centuries. In the original series, the warlike Klingons had been among the Federation's chief antagonists in the galaxy. Now (in a political turn begun in the film *Star Trek VI: The Undiscovered Country*), the Federation and the Klingon Empire are allies, if uneasily so. For reasons that are never explained, the Klingons of *TNG*, like those of the films, sport prominent forehead ridges that clearly distinguish them from humans, even though the Klingons of the original series had looked essentially like (vaguely Russian) humans.[3]

The final major crew member aboard the *Enterprise-D* is the beautiful Deanna Troi (Marina Sirtis), the ship's counselor. Half human and half Betazoid (a race of telepaths), Troi has empathic abilities that let her sense the emotions of others, which comes in handy in her job but is also often used for tactical purposes in sensing the intentions of potential enemies. Troi and Riker had earlier been romantically involved, but his devotion to his career had ultimately taken precedence. A clear attraction remains between the two characters throughout the series, though they do not resume their former relationship. Late in the series, in fact, there are numerous hints of a budding romance between Troi and Worf, though in the still later *Star Trek: Nemesis*, Riker and Troi are finally married, while Worf also marries in *Deep Space Nine*.

Such romances are indicative of the way relationships among the various characters of *TNG* are the crux of the series, with the mutual caring and cooperation of the *Enterprise* crew serving even more clearly than in the original series as a sort of microcosm of the cooperative ethos of the Federation as a whole. Moreover, to add a bit of variety, in *TNG* these relationships extend beyond the major characters to include numerous recurring characters who are not quite regular members of the cast—or even crew members of the *Enterprise*. One frequently recurring character in *TNG* is Q (John DeLancie), a superbeing with virtually unlimited powers who torments the *Enterprise* and its crew in numerous episodes, including the two-hour inaugural "Encounter at Farpoint" (September 28, 1987). In this episode (an installment in the ongoing series of *Star Trek* episodes in which the *Enterprise* crew and humanity in general are placed on trial by advanced alien species), Q labels humans as barbarians and challenges Picard and his crew to prove otherwise—under penalty of death if they fail. They succeed, of course (otherwise there would have been no series), though Q himself is not entirely convinced. Nevertheless, over the course of his next several appearances in *TNG* (later, he also appears in *Star Trek: Voyager*), Q develops a grudging admiration for humans and especially for Picard and his crew. Another recurring character is the enigmatic Guinan (Whoopi Goldberg), one of several civilian employees aboard the *Enterprise*. Guinan runs "Ten Forward," a lounge/bar where the various crew members can relax after a hard day of exploring the galaxy. The wise Guinan is a sort of superbartender, listening to the troubles of her customers and offering sage advice. A member of an extremely long-lived species, the El-Aurians, Guinan is herself hundreds of years old. We never really learn much about her background, though we do learn that she apparently has an unusual bond with Picard (who greatly respects her wisdom) and that her people, the El-Aurians, have been virtually wiped out by the Borg.

Among other things, the longer life of *TNG* compared to the original series meant that it was able to explore the backgrounds and personalities of its major characters in far more depth than the original had been able to do. In *TNG*, in fact, we get numerous peeks into the family backgrounds of all the major characters. For example, Deanna Troi's Betazoid mother, Lwaxana Troi, is a recurring character in *TNG*. A boisterous and outrageous woman with a particularly active libido (often aimed at Picard, much to his discomfort), Lwaxana also provides one of the many links back to the original series in that she is played by Roddenberry's widow, Majel Barrett, who had played Nurse Christine Chapel in *TOS*. Though largely a comic character, Lwaxana can provide drama as well, as in the episode "Dark Page" (November 1, 1993), in which she is tormented by memories of the drowning death of her other daughter, Kestra, at age seven. Lwaxana has been so overcome with guilt over this death that she has kept all knowledge of the existence of Kestra from the younger Deanna until this episode.

Most of the other crew members have dark episodes, or at least troubled family relationships, in their past as well. In the episode "Sins of the Father" (March 19, 1990), Worf attempts to defend his late father, Mogh, from charges that he was a traitor who sold out to the Romulans, enabling the "Khitomer Massacre," in which Romulan forces destroyed a Klingon outpost, leaving the young Worf as one of only two survivors. In this episode, Worf also meets Kurn (Tony Todd), the brother he never knew he had. Worf and Kurn (aided by Picard, who functions in the episode as a sort of honorary Klingon) discover that Mogh was innocent of treachery and that the real traitor was the father of Duras (Patrick Massett), now a powerful Klingon political figure. Convinced that the revelation of the truth about Khitomer will result in a devastating Klingon civil war, Worf drops his defense of Mogh and allows the truth to stay hidden. In the course of the series, we also meet Worf's human foster parents (who raised him after his rescue from Khitomer). Worf also discovers that he has a son of his own (from a previous relationship), extending the generational treatment of his family.

Like Troi and Worf, Riker has a problematic parent who appears in the series. In "The Icarus Factor" (April 24, 1989), the *Enterprise* travels to Starbase Montgomery, where Riker is to be briefed on his new assignment as the captain of the starship *Aries*. There Riker is surprised to discover that the civilian strategist who is to brief him is none other than his father, Kyle (Mitchell Ryan), from whom he has long been estranged, having left home at age fifteen. Riker's refusal to accept Kyle's overtures toward reconciliation eventually lead the two to a confrontation in a martial arts match, after which they finally resolve their differences. Riker, however, then decides to refuse his new command and stay aboard the *Enterprise* instead. Indeed, it would only be in *Nemesis* that Riker would finally accept his own command as the captain of the starship *Titan*, and then only after one last Federation-saving adventure aboard the *Enterprise*.

Picard experiences family complications in "Bloodlines" (May 2, 1994), when he encounters a young man who appears to be (but actually isn't) his son.[4] In the episode "Family" (October 1, 1990), Picard travels to his old village in France (after a twenty-year absence) as part of his recuperation from the trauma of having been assimilated by the Borg. Unfortunately, despite the idyllic setting of his family vineyards, Picard discovers another trauma in a confrontation with his brother, Robert (Jeremy Kemp), who still runs the family vineyards and who thinks Picard regards himself as superior because he is a Starfleet captain. However, the two brothers resolve their differences (though not before literally coming to blows), and Picard even begins to consider accepting a job that will keep him on Earth, his confidence having been shaken in the encounter with the Borg. Ultimately, of course, Picard decides to stay on the *Enterprise*, which is, we are assured, where he truly belongs.

The Borg themselves represent by far the most compelling enemies encountered by the Federation in *TNG*—and probably in any of the *Star Trek* series. A nightmare race with numerous precedents in dystopian and horror fiction, the Borg, as their name indicates, are cyborgs, composites of the organic and the mechanical/electronic. They are composed of individuals from various humanoid races who have been "assimilated" into the Borg collective through the addition of numerous implants that give them powerful destructive capabilities while also stripping them of free will and the ability to think as individuals. There is, in fact, only one collective Borg mind, shared by all of the various "drones," whose only mission is to sweep across the galaxy, assimilating any individuals who might be useful as drones and any technology that might be useful to them in increasing their own capabilities.

The Borg drones are descended from a number of specific predecessors, ranging from Frankenstein's monster to the zombies of *Night of the Living Dead* (1968). As their appearances on *Star Trek* continue, they tend to get darker and creepier, looking less like robots and more like high-tech zombies. In many ways, the Borg are modeled on insects, such as bees and ants, and in the later *Voyager* series they even have a queen, analogous to queen bees. They are, however, complex and clearly derive from a number of sources. At an obvious level, they represent contemporary fears that human beings are gradually becoming slaves to their own technology. In their suppression of individualism, the Borg recall Western cold war depictions of communism. Moreover, given that individualism is one of the central values informing all of the *Star Trek* series, this trait alone makes them the virtual antithesis of the Federation. On the other hand, in their insatiable drive to accumulate, the Borg evoke Marxist descriptions of capitalism. This trait again sets them in direct opposition to the ideology of the Federation and *Star Trek* as a whole, both of which are quite devoted to the notion that capitalist greed and competition for wealth will be swept away in the future.

Emanating from the "Delta Quadrant" of the galaxy (Earth and the Federation are in the "Alpha Quadrant"), the Borg first appear when they attack and obliterate several Federation outposts near the Neutral Zone that separates the Federation from Romulan space at the end of *TNG*'s Season One. Actually, in this episode, the Romulans are suspected of the attack, and the Borg do not actually appear in *TNG* until a year later, in the episode "Q Who?" (May 8, 1989), in which the *Enterprise* does direct battle with a Borg cube (Borg vessels are generally either cubes or spheres), escaping only when Q intervenes to propel the *Enterprise* to a safe part of the galaxy. In the first part of the rousing two-part episode "The Best of Both Worlds" (June 18, 1990), the Borg end Season Three with another cliff-hanger, assimilating Picard himself. Season Four then opens with the second part of this episode (September 24, 1990), in which Picard is recovered and a Borg invasion of Earth is thwarted, though with great losses on the part of a Federation fleet sent to repel the invasion.

In a subsequent episode, the *Enterprise* crew captures a Borg drone, which they name Hugh (Jonathan Del Arco), then (with only limited success) attempt to restore his humanity. This episode, "I, Borg" (May 11, 1992), sets the stage for one of the major plot arcs in the later *Voyager*, in which the drone Seven of Nine is retrieved from the Borg, launching an extended effort to restore her humanity and her ability to function as an individual. In the two-part episode "Descent" (June 21 and September 20, 1993), Data's evil twin, Lore, also surfaces at one point as the leader of a dissident Borg group (whose drones are more able to function as individuals) that may be even more evil than the main collective. Lore and his minions once again threaten the Federation—and once again supply *TNG* with a tense two-part, season-spanning episode, this time encompassing the end of Season Six and the beginning of Season Seven. All is well, however, as Data (who had, for a time, sided with Lore) and Hugh help defeat Lore, leaving Hugh in command of the new Borg group, hoping to lead them in positive directions.

The Borg, far more ominous and terrifying than anything in the original series, represented a genuine new direction for *Star Trek*. Nevertheless, despite such innovations, *TNG* was quite open and self-conscious about its status as a sequel to the original series. *TNG* even featured occasional guest appearances by cast members of *TOS*, despite the fact that it is set roughly seventy-five years further in the future. The most important of these appearances is the one made by Spock in the episode "Redemption" (June 17 and September 23, 1991), one of many two-part episodes that end one season with a cliffhanger, then start the next with a resolution. Thanks to the miracles of Vulcan physiology (Vulcans have a life span of two hundred years or more), Spock is still alive and well in the second half of the twenty-fourth century, though now he serves as a distinguished diplomat rather than a Starfleet officer. In this episode, Ambassador Spock joins the Romulan underground, which hopes to reunite the Romulans with their former Vulcan brethren, meanwhile ending the long Romulan legacy of militarism and aggression.

"Scotty" (James Doohan), the chief engineer of the original *Enterprise*, is able to appear in the episode "Relic" (October 12, 1992) through the expedient of having been trapped in a transporter beam for seventy-five years. Already aging and headed for retirement even in his own day, Scotty seems out of place indeed in the world of the *Enterprise-D*. He still knows a thing or two about engineering, however, and is instrumental in this episode in saving the new *Enterprise* from certain destruction. Later, in *Star Trek: Generations* (1984), the first of the *Star Trek* films to feature the cast of *TNG*, a time-travel oddity allows Kirk to join Picard, fighting side by side to defeat the mad scientist villain Soran (Malcolm McDowell). Meanwhile, in this film, the *Enterprise* is again destroyed, paving the way for the appearance of the *Enterprise-E* in subsequent films.

Several episodes of *TNG* directly echo episodes of the original series, such as the first-season episode "The Naked Now" (October 5, 1987), which is essentially a remake of the original series episode "The Naked Time" (September 29, 1966). In "The Naked Now" an alien contagion strips away the inhibitions of crew members, allowing their most basic desires and motivations to be revealed—but also rendering them incapable of operating the ship and nearly leading to disaster. Thus, this episode (the very first, after the two-hour opener) allowed the makers of the new series a quick start in introducing the new characters to their audience at an intimate level. This episode also made it clear that *TNG* would be unapologetic about following in the footsteps of its illustrious predecessor. Indeed, the *TNG* episode directly references the *TOS* episode as the new crew members realize that this same contagion had struck the original *Enterprise* and they seek (unsuccessfully, as it turns out) to draw upon that earlier experience to cure the current contagion.

Not only is the cosmopolitical situation in *TNG* consistent with that in the original series, but also the *Enterprise-D* is in many ways surprisingly similar to the original *Enterprise*, despite the later setting. The ship is larger and has fancier, all-digital controls (as opposed to the occasional old-fashioned analog dials and switches that, by 1987, made the original ship look very dated), but most of its basic technology is roughly similar to (if more advanced than) that of the original. The most important innovation, in fact, involves not weaponry or propulsion systems but recreation. The new ship is equipped with "holodecks" that provide virtual reality simulations of any number of environments so that the crew can get away from it all from time to time. Of course, these holodecks (like the change to digital controls) really represent a change in technology between 1969 and 1987, rather than between 2290 and 2365. After all, *TNG* began after years of development in computer technology and video gaming had made audiences widely aware of the possibilities offered by virtual reality. It also began one year after William Gibson's novel *Neuromancer* had launched the whole new genre of "cyberpunk" science fiction, with its central focus on virtual reality.

Nevertheless, however based in the technological concerns of the 1980s, the holodecks bring a whole new postmodern dimension to the 2360s of *TNG*. For one thing, the holodecks (which seem to malfunction in serious ways suspiciously often) provide a new source of danger and conflict that adds variety to the plots of individual episodes. For another, the virtual reality capabilities of the holodecks allow the exploration of a nearly unlimited variety of situations and genres, including overt references to individual classics of those genres. "A Fistful of Datas" (November 9, 1992), for example, is set in a simulated Old West environment that allows the episode to become a high-tech Western, just as one might expect from the titular homage to the Clint Eastwood classic *A Fistful of Dollars*. Many holodeck simulations are based on literature from Earth's past, such as various plays of Shakespeare and the Sherlock Holmes stories of Sir Arthur Conan Doyle. Perhaps the most prominent of the holodeck genre explorations involves hard-boiled detective fiction, such as that practiced by real-life writers Dashiell Hammett and Raymond Chandler. Picard, in particular, turns out to be an aficionado of the detective genre, and several episodes allow him to act out the role of Dixon Hill, protagonist of a (fictional) series of detective novels from the 1930s and 1940s that were set in the San Francisco of that time.

TNG carefully avoids any real exploration of the obvious sexual possibilities of the holodeck, which provides completely realistic simulated stimuli for all five senses. Indeed, TNG is much more demure in its treatment of sexuality in general than was TOS. Granted, the holodeck is often the site of romance. For one thing, it's the perfect place for a date between real crew members. For another, it allows one to generate a simulation of the perfect mate. In the episode "11001001" (February 1, 1988), aliens are able to take over the Enterprise when both Picard and Riker are distracted in the holodeck by a beautiful computer-generated woman, Minuet (Carolyn McCormick). In "We'll Always Have Paris" (May 2, 1988), an open homage to the classic 1942 film Casablanca, Picard uses the holodeck to reenact an earlier encounter with his first love. And in "Booby Trap" (October 30, 1989), Geordi generates a holographic image of the beautiful Dr. Leah Brahms (Susan Gibney), an engineering expert who designed the warp engines of the Enterprise-D, to help him solve an engineering crisis. But he also falls in love with the image, much to the disgust of the real Dr. Brahms when she learns of the simulation in the later "Galaxy's Child" (March 11, 1991). However, despite Dr. Brahms's strong reaction, there is no hint of simulated sexual contact in this or any of the other holodeck episodes.

Of course, the holodecks really do on the Enterprise precisely what Star Trek as a series (and, for that matter, most science fiction) has always done: provide new and unusual settings in which the characters can experience various situations and negotiate a variety of conflicts. In the case of TNG, despite the various encounters with "new life and new civilizations" around the galaxy, the most important of these new situations is the future of Earth itself and of humanity in general. In 1987, TNG began broadcasting in the late years of the cold war and was thus able, even more than the original series, to look beyond the antagonistic global political situation of the cold war and toward a future time of a world united in peace and tranquility under a single global government. Presumably, this monolithic government is extremely tolerant of diversity, though it partakes of the potential dystopian ramifications of all visions of world government, which leaves room for only one basic political philosophy on the entire planet. This is no problem for *TNG*, though. In a continuation of a strong tradition of celebrating global governments in the utopian fiction of such modern authors as H. G. Wells, we even learn in the episode "Attached" (November 8, 1993) that the Federation is extremely hesitant to admit any planets that do not have a unified world government, the existence of such a government being taken as a necessary sign of an advanced state of civilization.

In its depiction of the future history that leads from global antagonism to planetary peace and unity, *TNG* differs somewhat from the original series, which indicates that this movement occurred without a global nuclear holocaust, though the "Eugenics Wars" of the 1990s were apparently quite widespread. In *TNG*, however, we learn in the very first episode that the second half of the twenty-first century had been marked by global nuclear destruction that virtually drove humanity back into barbarism. When Picard and his crew members are placed on trial by Q in a primitive-looking courtroom with a savage-looking gallery, we learn that this court is like something from the "mid-21st century. The post-atomic horror."

This difference between the two series was probably enabled by the later setting of *TNG*: with cold war tensions easing, it was less disturbing to audiences to envision a nuclear holocaust than it might have been back in the 1960s. On the other hand, partly because of the lessons learned in this holocaust (and also, we eventually learn, because of lessons learned from the Vulcans after first contact with them), such global conflict would be unthinkable in the twenty-fourth century. Thus, when Q impersonates a cold war–era military officer in "Encounter at Farpoint," exhorting the *Enterprise* to return immediately to Earth to fight "commies," Picard responds, "What? That nonsense is centuries behind us!" Q responds that this may be the case, but that humanity is "still a dangerous, savage, child race."

Picard, of course, is able (at least partly) to convince him otherwise, and we learn in *TNG* that the human race has indeed come a long way since the antagonisms of the cold war. For example, the high level of technology and the low level of political tensions on Earth have produced a sort of material paradise in which all needs are met virtually without the use of human labor, thus freeing up humans for more fulfilling activities, such as exploring the galaxy on a starship. With all material needs met at the touch of a replicator button, there is no need for such things as money, and the series even occasionally jokes about the quaintness of the very concept of currency. In "The Perfect Mate" (April 27, 1992), for example, Dr. Crusher offers Picard a penny for his thoughts. When Picard asks if she actually has one of these obscure artifacts, she replies, "I'm sure the replicator will have one on file."

In "The Neutral Zone" (May 16, 1988), the *Enterprise* discovers a derelict ship containing the frozen bodies of three humans from the twentieth century. When they are thawed out, the difference between their attitudes and those of the twenty-fourth century provides a telling commentary on human advancement in the past four hundred years. For example, one of them is an investor who wonders about business conditions in this (to him) future world. Picard responds, speaking to him almost as if he were a child, "People are no longer obsessed with the accumulation of *things*. We've eliminated hunger, want, the need for possessions. We've grown out of our infancy." When the investor, who can imagine only profit as a motive, wonders what challenges and motivates people under such circumstances, Picard replies that people are now motivated by the desire to fulfill their potential as human beings. "The challenge," he says, "is to improve yourself, to enrich yourself."

The Federation, then, is a sort of economic utopia, abundantly affluent but free of greed and competition for profits, yet still able to provide challenges and opportunities for individual growth and development. Set against these idealized conditions are the occasional alien cultures that still place an emphasis on competitive profit making. Chief among these are the buffoonish Ferengi, who live only for the pursuit of profit and the accumulation of wealth. Totally unscrupulous and entirely self-serving, the huge-eared Ferengi serve as a sort of caricature of twentieth-century capitalists. They are willing to lie, cheat, deceive, and even kill in order to increase their profits, and their characterization in *TNG* makes the pursuit of profit seem simultaneously silly and sinister. Furthermore, though the Ferengi can be quite dangerous, they are never really a match for the *Enterprise* and its crew, whose nonprofit ideology is thus presented as superior in both the moral and practical sense.

Despite the sometimes idealized presentation of the Federation, *TNG* continues the argument made in the original series that humanity, in order to achieve its full potential, must struggle against obstacles and constantly strive for more. Thus, *TNG* continues, though perhaps in a slightly muted form, the suspicion toward utopian societies that had been so central to the earlier series. In the early episode "Justice" (November 9, 1987), the *Enterprise* crew encounters an alien race, the Edo, who seem to live in a perfect sensual paradise of abundant food, perfect health, and fulfilling, guilt-free sexuality. Unfortunately, as in the "Return of the Archons" episode of the original series, the Edo must obey a higher power, in this case an advanced being whom the Edo regard as a god and who demands total, unwavering obedience to a seemingly arbitrary set of rules. Indeed, when Wesley inadvertently violates one of these rules by wandering into a forbidden area, he is immediately condemned to death. Luckily, in another example of humanity on trial, Picard manages to convince the godlike being of his crew's good intentions and the injustice of Wesley's punishment, so the boy is allowed to go free.

"When the Bough Breaks" (February 15, 1988) echoes "The Return of the Archons" as well. Here, a technological utopia on the planet Aldea is ruled over by a supercomputer custodian. Due to the high level of their technological advancement, the Aldeans have all their needs automatically met, freeing them to pursue their individual potentials—as long as these pursuits do not threaten the status quo. In short, Aldea is a version of what the Federation might be if its citizens were to lose their desire to meet new challenges and to strive for more. Predictably, however, the Aldean technology has a downside. In one of several comments on environmental concerns in *TNG*, this technology has destroyed the planet's ozone layer, leading to radiation poisoning (and sterilization) of the entire population.[5] This episode thus makes literal the figurative concern throughout the first two *Star Trek* series about the ultimate sterility of any utopian society that does not accept the necessity of ongoing change, no matter how ideal that society might appear on the surface.

This notion is also central to "The Masterpiece Society" (February 10, 1992), perhaps the most nuanced treatment of utopianism in the first two *Star Trek* series. Here, the *Enterprise* discovers a utopian colony of genetically engineered humans, each of whom has been selectively bred to play precisely the role that he or she is supposed to fill in the society. The society seems to run quite smoothly until their entire planet is threatened with destruction by the approaching core fragment of a neutron star. Reluctantly, the colonists agree to accept the help of the *Enterprise* crew to avert the disaster, even though they feel that any contact with flawed outsiders might damage the delicate balance of their perfect society. Of course, it is these very outsiders who save the colony, with Geordi playing the key role, even though someone blind from birth like him would not have been allowed to exist in this eugenically pure society. However, the colony is seriously unbalanced by the encounter with the *Enterprise*, especially after two dozen of the colonists decide to leave with the visitors so that they can explore experiences beyond those available in their small, isolated community. Once again, the Federation, with all its flaws, comes out looking better than a utopian alternative, which is unable to handle any kind of change. In this case, however, the judgment is a bit more ambivalent than is usually the case in *Star Trek*, perhaps because the colonists at least choose their own course rather than having it determined by a master computer or superior being. At the end of the episode, Picard, who is consistently more respectful of the Prime Directive than Kirk had ever been, expresses a certain regret that the perfect colony has been destabilized and forever changed by the intervention of himself and his crew. Indeed, he wonders whether the aid offered by the *Enterprise* might ultimately have been as damaging to the colony as the core fragment would otherwise have been.

The continual endorsement of change that informs so many *Star Trek* episodes is also built into the history of the franchise itself. In 1994, *TNG* was terminated by its producers (Roddenberry had died in the meantime) so that it and its cast could move into feature films, even though the series was at the height of its popularity at the time of its cancellation. The end of *TNG* also cleared the way for the ongoing growth of the *Star Trek: Deep Space Nine* series that had begun running in syndication in 1993 and for the new *Star Trek: Voyager* series that was slated to begin broadcasting in 1995. These two latest *Star Trek* series moved in significant new directions that brought them well beyond the scope and tone of the first two series. In the meantime, science fiction television as a whole experienced an unprecedented period of richness and innovation in the 1990s. Much of this phenomenon can be attributed to material considerations such as the growth of cable television channels (especially the Sci Fi Network), which presented significantly expanded opportunities for syndication and provided homes for programs (such as most science fiction series) that attract a strong niche market but may not be a strong draw for the kinds of general audiences needed by the major broadcast networks. Nevertheless, the Golden Nineties of science fiction television could not have occurred without a ground-breaking predecessor like *TNG*, which did so much to reinvigorate the genre, proving that SFTV still had both ideas and audience appeal.

CHAPTER 4

The Golden Nineties: Science Fiction Television in an Age of Plenty

The success of *Star Trek: The Next Generation* provided little in the way of an immediate boost to the production of science fiction series on television. Indeed, many programmers still regarded SFTV as a proven loser, with *TNG* simply serving as the exception that proved the rule. As the 1990s proceeded, the subsequent success of both *Star Trek: Deep Space Nine* and *Star Trek: Voyager* did little to change this situation, their membership in the *Star Trek* franchise making them special cases as well. However, by the time *TNG* ended in spring 1994, two of the most successful and important non–*Star Trek* SFTV series ever produced had already begun to air. Indeed, *The X-Files*, appearing on the Fox broadcast network, drew audiences at its peak that were bigger than any that the *Star Trek* series had ever drawn. And the critically acclaimed *Babylon 5* drew enough viewers to complete its initially projected run as a five-year science fiction epic. These series, combined with the ongoing *Star Trek* franchise and with the growth of the Sci Fi Channel on cable, ultimately made the 1990s perhaps the richest decade in the history of SFTV.

Of course, the 1990s were also perhaps the richest decade in the history of American capitalism, marked by falling government budget deficits and an unprecedented stock market boom that ran through most of the decade. With this boom underway and with the cold war now over, one might expect a corresponding boom in science fiction, with its long history of predictions of a golden future. Interestingly enough, however, science fiction in the decade was marked by a retreat from such projections. Science fiction novels, films, and television series of the 1990s either said little or nothing about the future (as in *The X-Files*) or projected a troubled future that was significantly darker than envisioned in earlier works, especially in the first two highly optimistic *Star Trek* series.

As the 1990s began, the optimistic *TNG* was still riding high, while NBC's *Quantum Leap*, which ultimately ran from 1989 to 1993, was already becoming one of the most successful network SFTV series ever, even if it was light on the science and heavy on the fiction. *Quantum Leap* had an optimistic spin, as protagonist Sam Beckett (Scott Bakula) traveled through time into the past, materializing in the bodies of various troubled personages during crises in their lives. Ignoring the usual science fiction time-travel convention of avoiding any interference in history, Beckett invariably helped his hosts overcome their various personal dilemmas in various heartwarming ways. Add in the nostalgia effect gained by allowing audiences to visit times from their own childhoods (Beckett could only travel back to times within his own lifetime, which began in 1953), and the program became one of the warmest and fuzziest series in SFTV history.

By May 1993, *Quantum Leap* was nearing the end of its run and *TNG* was approaching its last season. SFTV was beginning its dark turn with the broadcast of the miniseries *Wild Palms*, one of the most high-profile SFTV programs of the decade. Executive-produced by filmmaker Oliver Stone and featuring a brief appearance by cyberpunk science fiction writer William Gibson, *Wild Palms* drew significantly on science fiction concepts like Gibson's cyberspace. Set in Los Angeles in 2007, *Wild Palms* depicts a future America in danger of falling completely under the oppressive control of the sinister forces represented by a right-wing quasi-religious political group known as the "Fathers" and their public front, the "Wild Palms" media group and "Mimecom" television empire, both headed by the evil senator Anton Kreutzer (Robert Loggia). These Fathers are willing to go to any extremes to further their power; for example, they have for some time engaged in an extensive program of bloody terrorism (such as exploding a nuclear bomb in Florida, killing ninety thousand people) so they can blame these acts on and thus justify the suppression of their political opponents.

The Fathers also engage in an extensive program of high-tech brainwashing. Kreutzer is the founder of a philosophy known as "synthiotics," which forms the basis of a new cult religion called the

"New Realism." This religion is based on the postmodern notion that reality is relative and provisional. Recognizing that what we normally think of as "reality" is to a certain extent an artificial construct, the New Realists take the next step and decide to attempt literally to generate an alternative reality that is more to their liking. In particular, Kreutzer and his cronies are heavily involved in researching computer-generated virtual reality, a technology that, as Kreutzer's bride-to-be, Paige Katz, puts it, will allow the creation of a "new improved reality controlled by Mimecom and sold straight out of 7-11."

As *Wild Palms* opens, in fact, Mimecom is about to release a new broadcast technology that allows normal television sets (with the use of a special adaptor) to generate highly realistic holograms reminiscent of those in Ray Bradbury's *Fahrenheit 451*. This new technology is initially used in a seemingly innocuous sitcom entitled *Church Windows*, but this program is only the first step in a plan to use the power of this new medium to gain Kreutzer the presidency and to gain the Fathers absolute control of the United States. Indeed, *Church Windows* is merely the beginning of a massive program of psychological manipulation intended to infuse the minds of the American populace with their substitute reality. The realism of the broadcast holograms is significantly enhanced through the use of a drug known as "Mimezine," which turns out to be addictive; part of Kreutzer's plan to take control of America involves a program of addicting the entire population to this drug. The satirical implication seems clear, if not very original: television acts like an addictive drug, numbing the minds of the American populace.

The principal opposition to the Fathers consists of the anti-authoritarian "Friends," who have by 2007 been driven entirely underground by physical attacks from Kreutzer's storm troopers and by public opinion that has been aroused by the many terrorist acts perpetrated by the Fathers but attributed to the Friends. But these Friends remain numerous, resourceful, and well organized. For example (in one of the more far-fetched motifs in the series), the Friends maintain an extensive network of underground tunnels, accessed through trap doors in the bottoms of swimming pools.

The plot of *Wild Palms* is further complicated by the fact that Kreutzer's dream of the presidency is secondary to his real dream of attaining immortality by converting himself into a computer simulation, again recalling cyberpunk fiction. Eventually, he succeeds in storing his identity in a computer chip, but only after the Friends have

modified the chip so that it erases him, leaving him to fade into noth-
ingness while quoting the ending lines of T. S. Eliot's "The Hollow
Men." Such literary allusions are used at several points in an attempt
to invest *Wild Palms* with a certain sophistication. The individualist
Friends, for example, are fond of chanting Walt Whitman's "O Captain, My Captain," while W. B. Yeats's "Running to Paradise" serves
as a sort of anthem for the Fathers.

Wild Palms has its interesting moments. For example, the focus on
the Fathers in general suggests the presence in American society of
huge conspiratorial forces—a motif reminiscent of the films of Stone,
especially *JFK*. This link is then reinforced in the series when Stone
appears on a 2007 talk show to discuss the fact that his theory of
the Kennedy assassination has just been proved true by newly released evidence. All in all, however, the soap-opera-style plot complications of *Wild Palms* are often in serious danger of descending into
farce, even though the series does attempt to make a number of
serious social and political points. Cultist religions are an obvious
target of the satire of the series, but the suggestion that one should
not seek happiness in the alternative world envisioned by such religions also resonates with the reality-manipulation motif, which functions as part of an extensive interrogation of the electronic media's
power. Advanced technology in general is interrogated as a potentially powerful social force that might produce either good or ill, depending upon how it is used. Control of such technology by groups
like Kreutzer and his associates is shown as particularly dangerous,
and indeed the advanced technology shown in the 2007 setting of the
series (like the capitalist boom of the 1990s) improves the standard
of living only of an elite segment of the populace.

For most citizens, conditions in much of this future society are
actually considerably worse than those in 1993, particularly in the
"Wilderzone," an outlaw area of Los Angeles reminiscent of Gibson's
"Sprawl." Indeed, conditions seem to have deteriorated dramatically,
given that the series takes place only fourteen years in the future. Of
course, such exaggeration is typical of satire, but the dark and cynical
vision of *Wild Palms* was definitely a new departure for American
SFTV, heralding a trend that would continue through the decade.

With the advent of *Deep Space Nine* (*DS9*) in 1993, even the *Star
Trek* franchise began to move in darker directions, albeit gradually and,
at first, only slightly. The series is continuous with *TNG*, picking up
in the year 2369, where *TNG* was at that point. Perhaps the most

notable change from the early *Star Trek*s to *DS9* is that the principal setting of the latter is on a stationary space station rather than a highly mobile starship. Even more striking, however, is that the Deep Space Nine station is not a product of Federation technology, but was originally built by the Cardassians, who have recently abandoned it after suddenly pulling out of Bajor, the nearby planet that they had been brutally occupying as a mining colony. As a result, though the station is still very high-tech, it lacks the sleek lines and bright lighting typical of Federation craft and is instead rather dark and ugly, in keeping with the general figuration of Cardassians in the series as something like outer space Nazis.

With the station now in Bajoran hands (but with the relatively poor and undeveloped Bajor unable to defend itself without outside help), the Federation agrees to send Starfleet personnel to help maintain the space station—and to help ensure that the Cardassians will not return. This move then becomes all the more critical when the station suddenly gains immense strategic importance with the nearby discovery of the first known stable wormhole, which allows passage into the Gamma Quadrant, previously unexplored by Starfleet. During the first seasons of the series, much work is devoted to attempts at converting the station to Federation technology under the leadership of Chief of Operations Miles O'Brien (Colm Meaney), newly transferred from the starship *Enterprise* (and from *TNG*). O'Brien (whose Irishness echoes the Scottishness of Montgomery Scott) spends much of his time simply repairing constant malfunctions (especially in the station's replicators), but he also puts considerable effort into reprogramming the station's computerized systems to match Starfleet, rather than Cardassian protocols.

Still, the personnel aboard the station never seem fully in control of its technology, as when O'Brien's efforts trigger an automatic program that almost leads to the self-destruction of the station in the episode "Civil Defense" (November 11, 1994). Even the *Defiant*, the advanced Federation starship that is assigned to the station in Season Two (thus giving the series more mobility) is merely a prototype in which many of the bugs have yet to be worked out. Moreover, originally developed for use against the Borg, the *Defiant* represents the first class of Federation starships to have been developed specifically for use as warships rather than for exploration and diplomacy, indicating another dark turn in the *Star Trek* universe. Even when technology on the station works well, as with the "holosuites" that resemble the holodecks of *TNG*, it is sometimes put to less-pristine uses. All of the holosuites on the station belong to a bar run by the Ferengi Quark, where they are often used for precisely the kind of sexual simulations that *TNG* so primly avoided.

Quark's bar itself adds a new dimension to the series. Not only does it signal the presence of private enterprise aboard the station, but in this case the business is a somewhat shady casino and bar run by Ferengi entrepreneurs who are willing to do virtually anything for a quick buck (or, in this case, bar of latinum). The Ferengi material in *DS9* is still used largely for comic relief, and Quark (Armin Shimerman) is as greedy and conniving as the next Ferengi, yet his character lends a new dimension to an alien race usually presented only in caricature in *TNG*. If you prick Quark, he bleeds—though he would certainly not be above selling his blood (or, preferably, someone else's) for a profit. Still, he can behave decently and even nobly. In the episode "Family Business" (May 15, 1995), we even learn that he loves his mother, despite the fact that she is an eccentric female who commits such outrages as engaging in business, going out in public, speaking to strangers, and even (horror of horrors!) wearing clothes—all activities strictly forbidden to Ferengi females.[1] Meanwhile, in "The Jem'Hadar" (June 13, 1994), Quark reminds viewers that the Ferengi are not that different from the patriarchal human capitalists of their own day, eloquently arguing that the human distaste for Ferengi in the twenty-fourth century is simply due to the fact that "we're a constant reminder of something in your past you'd like to forget." The only difference, he adds, is that humans of the past were even worse: the Ferengi, however venal, have never reached the level of outrage attained by human slavery, wars, and concentration camps.[2]

Quark is not only the first major Ferengi character in *Star Trek*, he is also the first major character not to be a member of the central ship or station crew. If the nefarious Quark turns out to have a lovable side, it is also the case that even the truly villainous Gul Dukat (Marc Alaimo), the Cardassian leader, who functions throughout the series as a dangerous thorn in the side of the *DS9* crew, has facets and depths achieved by none of the villains in the other *Star Trek* series. Dukat is a brutal racist, a totally unscrupulous political manipulator, and a man willing to go to any extremes, including torture and mass murder, to achieve his own ambitions. Yet he is a loyal family man who actually sometimes comes to the rescue of the major characters,

and there are occasional hints that he himself is a victim of circumstances. Elim Garak (Andrew Robinson), the former Cardassian intelligence agent who runs a tailor's shop aboard the station, is treated
even more sympathetically, despite his constant maneuvers to try to
get back in the good graces of the Cardassian powers that be.

In *DS9*, the crew itself is also somewhat more complex and diverse
than in other *Star Trek* series, partly because they are not all Starfleet
personnel. Since the station is run as a cooperative venture between
the Federation and Bajor, the first officer of the station is a Bajoran,
Major Kira Nerys (Nana Visitor). A former resistance fighter against
the Cardassian occupation of her planet, Kira maintains a deep hatred
of the Cardassians (though, as the series proceeds, she becomes less
bitter), while at the same time entertaining doubts that the terrorist
tactics she employed against the Cardassians were always justified.
Kira also initially opposes the Bajoran decision to ask the Federation
to help operate Deep Space Nine, so she begins the series in a mode
of hostility toward the Starfleet officers that come aboard to help
manage the station, though she soon learns to respect them and they
her. Kira's strength and courage (not to mention her expertise with
weapons and hand-to-hand combat) certainly go beyond conventional feminine stereotypes, making her among the most interesting
female characters to appear on *Star Trek*.

The chief security officer aboard the station, Odo (Rene
Auberjonois), is also not a member of Starfleet. Odo had been the
chief of security for the station when it was under Cardassian control, and he stays on in that role after the Cardassian withdrawal. Odo
grew up on Bajor, but he is not Bajoran, or even humanoid. In fact,
he is a shape-shifter, able to assume virtually any shape at will, which
makes him the most versatile—and most alien—of any of the main
characters of the various *Star Trek* series. On the other hand, not having grown up around other shape-shifters, he has not quite perfected
his skills. In particular, he has problems with the human face, and
the humanoid form he generally assumes includes a face that looks
somewhat like a plastic mask.

This appearance only furthers his outsider status—and his effec-
tiveness as an outside observer of the foibles of the humanoid characters aboard the station. Odo comments on his observations in a
grouchy and grumpy mode, which he often intentionally utilizes to
hide his own growing humanity (especially his love for Kira). Having
lived his life in the Alpha Quadrant as the only known shape-shifter,

Odo is somewhat in the same situation as *TNG*'s one-of-a-kind android, Data, and even more of an outsider among humans than Spock or Worf had been. Still, when he finally discovers his own people in Gamma Quadrant in the two-part episode "The Search" (September 26 and October 3, 1994), he realizes that he now feels more at home among his humanoid companions. He even joins the humans in their later war against the Dominion, the powerful Gamma Quadrant empire of which his people (known in the Gamma Quadrant as Changelings) are the founders and rulers.

In *DS9*, even the Starfleet personnel in the crew are unconventional by *Star Trek* standards. O'Brien is a relatively straightforward addition to the line of *Star Trek* chief engineers, but brash, young Julian Bashir (Saddig el Fadil, who changed his name to Alexander Siddig in the fourth season) is a decided departure from the traditional chief medical officer. He comes to the station fresh out of Starfleet Academy, where he graduated second in his medical-school class. He is a gifted physician (and a talented athlete), but he has a great deal to learn, and much of his story in the series involves a gradual maturation under fire. In "Doctor Bashir, I Presume?" (February 24, 1997), we learn that he is unusual in another way as well: he had been genetically modified as a child via illegal DNA resequencing that left him with enhanced vision, intelligence, reflexes, and hand-eye coordination. By the beginning of the sixth season, with his secret out at last, Bashir is able to display his superhuman abilities, deftly performing computerlike (or perhaps Spock-like) computations that lead Garak to remark, "You're not genetically engineered—you're a Vulcan!"

The station's science officer, Jadzia Dax (Terry Farrell) is also unusually young—in a sense. The brilliant, beautiful, and free-spirited Jadzia, fresh from her doctoral studies in physics, is only twenty-eight when the series begins, and Deep Space Nine is her first major assignment. However, she is also a Trill, a hybrid species that involves a combination of a humanoid host and a small "symbiont" that lives within its abdomen. As explained during the introduction of the species in the *TNG* episode "The Host" (May 13, 1991), the symbionts are extremely long-lived and are transferred to a new host when the old one dies. Jadzia's symbiont (the "Dax" portion of her identity) is over three hundred years old, and she is the eighth host, maintaining the memories of all the former ones, who have been both male and female.[3]

Jadzia's most recent predecessor, Curzon, was a male. In fact, he had been the best friend of Commander (later Captain) Benjamin Sisko

(Avery Brooks), who comes to the station in the initial episode with deep reservations about the assignment and even about continuing his career in Starfleet. Because his wife, Jennifer, has been killed during the battle with the Borg described in the *TNG* episode "Best of Both Worlds," Sisko wonders if it would be best to take his son, Jake (Cirroc Lofton), back to Earth to live a more conventional life than that offered by Starfleet. He decides to stay on (and even ultimately remarries) but remains something of a rebel, sometimes pursuing what he believes is right even if it flies directly in the face of Starfleet directives. Thus, in "The Die Is Cast" (May 10, 1995), Sisko defies a direct order from Starfleet headquarters and takes the *Defiant* into the Gamma Quadrant on a mission to rescue Odo, who has been kidnapped by a joint force of Romulans and Cardassians seeking to launch a preemptive strike against the Dominion.

Sisko's nostalgic love of baseball and his taste for fine cooking (gained growing up in New Orleans, where his father owns a restaurant) are sometimes reminiscent of Picard's antiquarian love of Shakespeare and old books, but Picard is much more of an organization man, Sisko much more of an outsider. As the first African-American to play the captain of a *Star Trek* crew, Brooks adds a new dimension to the traditional *Star Trek* penchant for ethnic diversity. But Sisko brings other dimensions as well. In addition to being a husband and father, he maintains a tragic side and a depth of character that other *Star Trek* captains lack. Moreover, he is not merely a Starfleet officer but also a religious icon to the Bajoran people, who come to view him (rightly, as it turns out) as the Emissary, sent to serve as a liaison between them and the mysterious "prophets," whom they worship as gods. These prophets turn out to be hyper-advanced aliens who live inside the wormhole, and Sisko's ability, as Emissary, to secure their help, is crucial to the ultimate victory over the Dominion. In the end, Sisko himself leaves the human realm and goes to join the prophets (though promising someday to return), topping off the motif of Bajoran spirituality that runs through the series.

Spirituality as a whole is treated more seriously and respectfully in *DS9* than in its *Star Trek* predecessors, perhaps suggesting a decline in the earlier confidence that science and technology held the solutions to all human problems. *DS9* also differs from the other *Star Trek* series in that the war with the Dominion provides a strong continuous plot arc that spans several seasons, breaking the *Star Trek* tradition of strictly episodic presentations. A growing air of threat looms in the background of Season Two, which is peppered with vague allusions to the mysterious Dominion, culminating in "The Jem'Hadar," a season-ending cliff-hanger in which the Dominion issues an ultimatum, insisting that all traffic through the wormhole into their quadrant be halted. Encounters with the Dominion become more serious in Season Three, including the discovery that the Changelings are the rulers of the Dominion. Meanwhile, by the end of the third season, we learn that the Changelings, using their shape-shifting abilities to impersonate various Alpha Quadrant races, are engaging in subversive activities designed to weaken the Alpha Quadrant and to encourage animosity among its various powers. Ultimately, however, the Federation, the Klingon Empire, and the Romulan Empire join forces to inflict heavy losses on the Dominion (with the help of biological weapons) in subsequent seasons, and peace is finally restored in the final two episodes of the series when Odo (who eventually goes back to live among his people after the end of the war) manages to convince the Changeling leader that the Dominion can peacefully coexist with the "solids" (non-shape-shifters) of the Alpha Quadrant.

Despite (or maybe because of) these differences, *DS9* is careful to establish numerous links to previous *Star Treks*. The very first episode of *DS9* opens with a guest appearance by Patrick Stewart as Jean-Luc Picard to brief Sisko on the Bajoran situation—and to begin passing the baton from *TNG* to *DS9*. Jonathan Frakes appeared in the *DS9* episode "Defiant" (November 21, 1994) as Tom Riker, the double of Will Riker (created in a transporter mishap as revealed in the *TNG* episode "Second Chances"). Frakes also directed several episodes of *DS9*, as did LeVar Burton, who had played Geordi La Forge on *TNG*.

In the episode "Trials and Tribble-ations" (November 4, 1996), the *Defiant* even travels back in time, allowing the cast of *DS9* to interact (in vintage Starfleet uniforms) with the original *Star Trek* cast, returning to its own time with a cute but troublesome extra passenger (obtained by Odo, who falls for its charms): one of the tribbles from the classic original series episode "The Trouble with Tribbles." In the past, the miracles of modern computer imaging technology allow the *DS9* crew to participate in that original episode, including an encounter with the old-style, human-looking Klingons of that episode. Asked about the difference between them and the brow-ridged Klingons of later *Star Trek* productions, Worf (having by this time joined the *DS9* crew) uncomfortably responds, "It is a long story. We do not discuss it with outsiders."

The addition to *DS9* of *TNG*'s Worf (still played by Michael Dorn) at the beginning of the fourth season provided a strong link between those two series. Worf remains a key member of the crew from that point forward, eventually becoming romantically involved with (and marrying) Jadzia Dax. Worf, though providing a strong link to *TNG*, also highlights the differences between life on Deep Space Nine and on the *Enterprise*. For example, in the episode "Hippocratic Oath" (October 16, 1995), when Worf complains of his difficulty adjusting to the more complex conditions aboard the space station, Sisko counsels him that Starfleet officers often have trouble adapting to a situation in which "there's no manual" and "unofficial rules" are paramount. Worf replies that, on the *Enterprise*, he could at least always distinguish his friends from his enemies, to which Sisko notes, "Let's just say DS9 has more shades of gray."

Still, many episodes of *DS9* are directly reminiscent of specific earlier *Star Trek* episodes. For example, the mirror universe of the classic original series episode "Mirror, Mirror" is revisited in episodes such as "Crossover" (May 16, 1994), "Through the Looking Glass" (April 17, 1995), and "Shattered Mirror" (April 22, 1996). In the original series episode, the characters in the mirror universe were almost all virtual opposites of their selves in the original universe. The "gray areas" of *DS9* come to the fore here, as well, though, and the relationship between the characters and their doubles in the mirror universe is much more complex than in the original series. The mirror versions of Kira and Bashir seem suitably evil, but Jennifer Sisko and O'Brien seem virtually unchanged in the mirror universe, and Jadzia seems similar, though perhaps more sexualized. Even Tuvok (the Vulcan security officer from *Voyager*, played by Tim Russ), makes an appearance in the mirror universe and seems little changed from the original Tuvok. On the other hand, the mirror Sisko is a womanizing scoundrel, though he still has a courageous streak that helps him to lead a rebellion against the dystopian alliance that reigns in the Alpha Quadrant of the mirror universe.

Some of the most memorable episodes of *DS9*, as with *TOS* and *TNG*, involved trips to Earth's past. In "Far Beyond the Stars" (February 9, 1998), Sisko experiences one of the visions that increasingly come to him late in the run of the series, this time finding himself living as Benny Russell, an African-American science fiction writer struggling to make a living in early 1950s Manhattan. The other cast members appear in that setting as well, giving Shimerman, Dorn, and

Auberjonois, who usually appear in heavy alien makeup, a chance to play human characters. Russell is a talented writer (who, among other things, begins the SF world of *Deep Space Nine*), but he must fight to overcome the racial prejudice that makes it almost impossible for a black science fiction writer to break into print. The episode thus engages in an interesting dialog with *Star Trek*'s science fiction predecessors, while joining a long line of *Star Trek* episodes devoted to social commentary. In this case, however, the commentary is considerable stronger than usual, including such graphic images as Russell being savagely beaten by two white policemen.

Similarly, in the excellent Season Three two-parter "Past Tense" (January 2 and 9, 1995), Sisko, Dax, and Bashir attempt to beam down to Starfleet headquarters in San Francisco, only to find themselves propelled, via a transporter aberration, backward in time to the year 2024. There, they find themselves in the difficult situation of attempting to get back to their own time while simultaneously struggling to avoid changing history even in the face of grim conditions that seem to demand action. This situation is very reminiscent of that of Kirk and Spock in the original series episode "The City on the Edge of Forever." In this case, the time travelers arrive in a dystopian America in which the problem of homelessness has been dealt with by the brutal expedient of herding the homeless into "sanctuary districts," where they can be kept out of sight but where the conditions make the districts little more than concentration camps.

Dax meets up with a wealthy entrepreneur who is immediately taken by her beauty and invites her into his privileged world. Sisko and Bashir, however, are not so fortunate and are quickly picked up as vagrants and interned in one of the sanctuary districts. There, they realize they have arrived on the verge of bloody riots that will eventually call attention to the plight of the homeless in these districts and thus lead to needed reform. Then, when they find that their arrival nearly prevents the riots, they are placed in the difficult position of working to ensure that the riots occur after all. The very different Americas encountered by Dax and by Sisko and Bashir in this episode call attention to the vast gap between the wealthy and the poor, and the intense drama of this episode takes the *Star Trek* tradition of social commentary to a new level of seriousness.

In particular, the dire social conditions of 2026 are obviously extensions of the social problems of the 1990s, and the episode's engagement with these problems provides a stark reminder that the

boom years of that decade also had a dark side in the growing proliferation of homelessness and social outcasts abandoned by a profit-
oriented system relatively uninterested in the sufferings of such
"unproductive" individuals. An era of unprecedented wealth for some
was an era of extreme hardship for many.

DS9 still assures us that these problems will eventually be solved,
at least on Earth, but the series frequently questions whether such
solutions are as absolute or as perfect as suggested in *TOS* or *TNG*.
In "Paradise" (February 14, 1994) *DS9* takes up the old *Star Trek* theme
of a flawed utopia, though in a much more complex and nuanced
mode than its predecessors. Here, Sisko and O'Brien, off in a runabout
on a mission of exploration, beam down to the surface of a planet
only to discover that, once they are there, a "duonetic field" that blan-
kets the planet renders all electromechanical devices (including
phasers, communicators, and transporters) inoperative. They are
quickly discovered by a group of colonists from Earth who made an
emergency landing on the planet more than ten years earlier and have
managed to get by without high-tech devices ever since. In fact, they
have not merely survived but have prospered, at least in nonmaterial
ways, and the community they have founded on the planet, led by
the charismatic Alixus (Gail Strickland), seems to be a sort of agrarian
utopia.

At first, all seems well, as Alixus and the colonists welcome the
newcomers to join them while they wait for Starfleet to locate their
orbiting runabout and come to rescue them. Sisko and O'Brien join
the community, working side by side with the colonists in the fields.
Meanwhile, the colonists (and especially Alixus) insist that life without advanced technology has not been so bad and has, in fact, offered a number of advantages. Working in the fields and growing their
own food puts them in touch with their environment, while sharing
the load makes them feel that they all belong to a genuine community. One of the colonists, Joseph (Steve Vinovich), is a former engineer who has come to appreciate the advantages of this new life
despite his technical background. As he tells Sisko, "We are more
committed to each other; we are truly a part of each other's lives.
We've renewed a sense of community that man left behind centuries
ago."

Despite this devotion to community, the colonists also feel that their
experience on the planet has helped them better to realize their own
individual identities. Indeed, when Sisko resists the attempts of Alixus

to recruit him to her cause, she tells him that his life in technological society has caused him to become "disconnected from your core identity." When Sisko ignores her and directs O'Brien to continue to seek a way to overcome the duonetic field so that they can get off the planet, she orders him locked up in a metal box, a punishment typically used to enforce the rules of the colony. Sisko refuses to give in, preferring to stay in the hot metal box rather than abandon his own beliefs. In the meantime, O'Brien manages secretly to locate the source of the field: a machine set up by Alixus herself—in other words, a high-tech machine set up to force the colonists to live without high-tech machines.

O'Brien deactivates the machine and returns to the colony with his phaser now working. He releases Sisko from the box and they confront Alixus, who admits that she secretly engineered the original emergency landing on the planet in order to pursue her own dream of an agrarian community freed of the dehumanizing effects of modern technology. Sisko and O'Brien prepare to take Alixus back with them to face justice for having hijacked the colonial expedition but are surprised to learn that the other colonists, despite all that has been revealed, prefer to stay on the planet and continue their community. They even consider reactivating the duonetic field to avoid a disruption in their established way of life, but field or no field, they plan to continue that way, believing that its benefits are genuine, even if they were lured into it under false pretenses. Thus, while Alixus is depicted as a dangerous fanatic and Sisko and O'Brien stand as entirely virtuous representatives of the technology-based lifestyle of the Federation, the episode stops far short of the earlier *Star Trek* tendency to view technology as a social panacea, admitting that the lifestyle of the colonists appears to be restoring something that they had lost in the modern world.

In the two-part episode "The Maquis" (April 25 and May 2, 1994), the moral stance of even the Federation comes into question. Actually, this episode builds on the late *TNG* episode "Journey's End" (March 28, 1994), in which a treaty between the Federation and the sinister Cardassians leaves several Federation colonies in Cardassian space. The colonists refuse to vacate their homes, which places them in constant danger, especially after the Cardassian Central Command begins to smuggle weapons to their own colonists in the area, hoping that they will drive away those who are with the Federation. These colonists, however, frustrated at the lack of support from the Federation, form their own guerrilla movement, the Maquis, to fight the Cardassians. Because their activities violate the treaty, the Federation regards the Maquis as outlaws. They are, in fact, a bit inflexible, but they are also depicted as genuine freedom fighters, who have, to some extent, been abandoned by the Federation because to support them would be politically inconvenient. Indeed, in "The Maquis," we learn that Starfleet Commander Calvin Hudson (Bernie Casey), one of Sisko's oldest and most trusted friends, has joined the Maquis. That Sisko allows Hudson to escape in a Maquis ship when he has the opportunity to shoot it down demonstrates both his loyalty to his friend and his understanding that the line between right and wrong is far from clear in this case.[4]

As Sisko himself explains during the episode, Earth in the twenty-fourth century is a paradise with no social or economic problems, which simplifies many moral judgments. But life for the Maquis (and many others in the galaxy) is much more complex and difficult, something the Starfleet commanders back on Earth do not always seem to understand. Later, the Dominion war would threaten even these idyllic conditions on Earth, as Changeling infiltrators invade the planet in a mode reminiscent of paranoid cold war science fiction films such as *Invasion of the Body Snatchers* (1956). However, even in this war there continue to be gray areas. While the Changelings are ultimately depicted as dangerous and ruthless foes, the fact remains that the war began because the Federation initially invaded Dominion space (and refused to vacate when asked to do so), not the other way around.

The crew members of *Star Trek: Voyager* (which began broadcasting on January 16, 1995) were also invaders in an alien space, though inadvertently so. For the next several years, *Voyager* and *DS9* were broadcast in tandem—just as *DS9* had been broadcast along with the final seasons of *TNG* in its first two seasons. *Voyager*, like *TNG* and the original *Star Trek*, is set aboard a Federation starship, and in that sense it represents a return to *Star Trek* convention. It also continues the *Star Trek* timeline, beginning in the year 2371. However, the advent of *Voyager* brought about many changes in the *Star Trek* universe. For one thing, it was broadcast on the fledgling United Paramount Network (UPN) (partly owned by Paramount, which had long owned the distribution rights to *Star Trek*), breaking the then-established tradition of broadcasting *Star Trek* series in syndication. For another, it is set in a new environment, Starship *Voyager* and its crew having been suddenly propelled, in the first episode, into the distant Delta Quadrant of the galaxy as they move through a region of space known as the "Badlands" in search of a ship of Maquis rebels. In this quadrant, *Voyager* initially has no contact whatsoever with the Federation (though contact is eventually established), and it is the case throughout the series that they remain very much on their own, unable to count on support from Starfleet as they struggle to make their way back home.

Because of this "us against the galaxy" scenario, the *Voyager* crew in many ways develops even tighter bonds than those that had characterized the crew of *TNG*. On the other hand, the crew does have certain special tensions due to the fact that it is made up of both Starfleet personnel and Maquis rebels, whose ship has also been propelled into the Delta Quadrant. The two groups, finding themselves together in this alien space, decide in the initial episode to join forces and form a hybrid crew, with Chakotay (Robert Beltran), a former Starfleet officer in command of the Maquis vessel, becoming the new first officer of *Voyager*. Chakotay, whose Native American descent adds ethnic and cultural diversity to the show, also adds a traditional element of masculine heroism to a crew commanded by Kathryn Janeway (Kate Mulgrew), the first woman to captain the central crew of a *Star Trek* series.

In addition to such innovations as a prominent Native American crew member and a female captain, the fact that *Voyager* literally travels where no one from Starfleet has gone before adds a refreshing sense of discovery to the show. The absence of the Federation's civilizing effect makes the Delta Quadrant a far darker and more dangerous place than the Alpha Quadrant, giving *Voyager* as a series a darker tone than the original series or *TNG*, though generally not as dark as *DS9*. However, *Voyager* has its comic moments as well, several of them having to do with the fascination of pilot Tom Paris (Robert Duncan McNeill) with twentieth-century American popular culture. The holodeck episode "Bride of Chaotica" (January 27, 1999), in which Paris interacts with a world reminiscent of the science fiction serials of the 1930s, is typical of this phenomenon. The holodecks as a whole play a far more prominent role in *Voyager* than in *TNG* or *DS9*. For example, in "Fair Haven" (January 12, 2000), the residents of a simulated Irish town seem so real that Janeway falls in love with one of them.

Much of the darkness of *Voyager* comes from encounters with dangerous new alien species, though the most effective antagonists are the Borg, old enemies from *TNG*. The Delta Quadrant is the home territory of the Borgs, so they are especially prominent there, showing up in numerous episodes to threaten *Voyager* as she makes her way homeward. Indeed, one of the crucial crew members (at least from the fourth season onward) is a former Borg drone, designated as Seven of Nine (Jeri Ryan). Originally a human girl by the name of Annika Hansen, Seven of Nine was assimilated by the Borg as a young child, apparently along with her scientist parents, who were attempting to explore the Delta Quadrant. The Hansens thus probably became the first humans ever assimilated by the Borg collective. Years later, in the episode "Scorpion, Part II" (September 3, 1997), which kicked off *Voyager*'s fourth season, Seven of Nine is rescued by Janeway—after an interesting turn that sees the *Voyager* crew momentarily in alliance with the Borg in a battle against Species 8472, a new alien race (created for the series entirely by computer animation). Seven of Nine is disconnected from the Borg collective and most of her Borg implants are removed, but her human identity has been almost entirely lost during her years of assimilation. Thus, with the help of the rest of the crew, she has to undergo a long and arduous (but sometimes extremely humorous) journey of rediscovery as she struggles to reestablish her humanity, providing through her ongoing development an important new plot strand for the series. Still another plot strand was provided by the occasional attempts of the Borg to recover their former drone, as in the rousing Season Five two-parter "Dark Frontier" (both parts originally broadcast February 17, 1999).

Officially, Seven of Nine was added to the crew of *Voyager* because the producers felt that the series lacked a character in the vein of Spock, Data, and Odo. Unofficially, many observers felt that the striking and shapely Ryan, clad after her rescue from the Borg mostly in skin-tight bodysuits, was hired to add sex appeal to the series. The latter was certainly a major effect of the change, but the seemingly incongruous combination of Seven of Nine's unerring logic and scientific brilliance with her provocative physical appearance made her far more interesting and complex than mere eye candy. Meanwhile, like all Spock characters, she provided an important outsider's view of the rest of the crew.

In any case, *Voyager* was hardly lacking in vaguely Spockian characters even before the arrival of Seven of Nine. In fact, one of the most striking things about the series was its proliferation of Spock characters. Whereas the three earlier *Star Trek* series had tended to have one such character on each crew (Spock, Data, Odo), *Voyager* had not one but four characters who seemed designed to tap into the tried-and-true formula for success. Seven of Nine is the most successfully Spockian of these characters, but the Vulcan lieutenant (eventually lieutenant commander) Tuvok (Tim Russ), *Voyager*'s security and tactical officer, is clearly meant to build on some of Spock's popularity, even if he lacks Spock's half-human hybridity. As a black Vulcan, Tuvok participates in *Star Trek*'s famed ethnic diversity, while his penchant for logic and deadpan delivery clearly recall those of Spock, even if he is a man of action who lacks Spock's knowledge of science. For example, as the first episode begins, Tuvok has infiltrated the crew of Chakotay's ship as an undercover agent for the Federation. It is, in fact, during an attempt to recover Tuvok from the Maquis ship that *Voyager* is propelled into the Delta Quadrant to begin with.

The most surprising Spock character aboard *Voyager* is B'Elanna Torres (Roxann Dawson), the ship's half-human, half-Klingon chief engineer. Though she occasionally shows the passion and temper typical of Klingons in the *Star Trek* universe, B'Elanna (partly because she has largely repudiated the Klingon side of her heritage since childhood) strives to approach all problems she encounters through very un-Klingon-like logic and calculation, in a mode very reminiscent of Spock. This approach is appropriate to her engineering specialty, which had helped to make her a brilliant student at Starfleet Academy. Her inability to come to terms with her own dual heritage (something that often plagues Spock in *TOS*) contributes to personal difficulties that eventually drive her out of Starfleet and into the Maquis rebellion and Chakotay's crew, whence she joins the crew of *Voyager*.

In the course of *Voyager*, B'Elanna develops via the typical *Star Trek* strategy of gradual humanization, following in the footsteps of the Spock characters from all of the earlier *Star Trek* series. Eventually, she is married to Paris, *Voyager*'s brash young pilot and the scion of a long line of Starfleet officers—though a man with a decidedly checkered past. Indeed, B'Elanna helps Tom overcome some of his own personal demons, just as he helps her to come to terms with her heritage and with herself. Ultimately, the two of them become the joyful parents of a daughter in the culmination of one of the many warm-and-fuzzy moments that became the trademark of *Voyager*.

A Spock character somewhat in the vein of Data is *Voyager*'s chief medical officer, in this case simply known as the Doctor (Robert

Picardo), nameless because he is actually a computerized projection, an "Emergency Medical Hologram." As such, he is, like Data, literally a product of computer technology. Though intended originally merely as a supplement for more conventional medical personnel in case of emergencies, the Doctor finds himself the only trained doctor aboard *Voyager* when the rest of the medical staff is killed during the initial passage into the Delta Quadrant. This new responsibility helps the Doctor to develop his personality, aided by the acquisition of an "autonomous holo-emitter" that allows him to function outside of sick bay—and even to go on away missions outside the ship. Meanwhile, even more than Data, he is gradually humanized through the series, growing in personality until he substantially outstrips his original programming, eventually becoming what is clearly an independent sentient being with his own feelings and dreams. Nevertheless, like Data, he often has difficulty convincing others that he should be regarded as a living being, despite his growing depth of character and appreciation for the arts, especially music.

Ultimately, the Doctor even develops a fondness for daydreaming, as when he fantasizes about taking command of the ship as an "Emergency Command Hologram" in "Tinker, Tenor, Doctor, Spy" (October 13, 1999). He even develops his once-meager personal skills to the point that he plays a key role in training Seven of Nine to develop such skills of her own. Meanwhile, his fantasy life comes to include the former Borg drone as well, so that, in addition to giving her singing and dancing lessons, he also falls in love with her. This relationship is never consummated, though the Doctor does at one point—in the episode "Body and Soul" (November 15, 2000)—occupy Seven of Nine's body when his program is downloaded into her remaining cybernetic implants.

In the complex two-hour finale, "Endgame" (May 23, 2001), *Voyager* and her crew manage to get safely back home via a Borg transwarp hub, but not until after a complex sequence of events that involves Janeway traveling back from an alternate future to assist the crew (and her former self) in outwitting the Borg. The series was thus brought to a neat conclusion and a happy ending, restoring at least some of the *Star Trek* optimism that *DS9* had seemed to question. On the other hand, *Voyager* and her crew accomplished relatively little—except to get back where they started.

If the overlap in broadcast times led to inevitable comparisons between *DS9* and *Voyager*, the series to which *DS9* was most often compared was that *other* space-station series, *Babylon 5*. *Babylon 5* began its run with the syndicated broadcast of its pilot episode, "The Gathering," in February 1993, just one month after the broadcast of the first episode of *DS9*. The regular weekly broadcasts of the series did not begin until January 1994, but throughout *Babylon 5*'s five-year run, the similar space-station settings would make comparisons between it and *DS9* inevitable. Also, despite the fact that it lacked the advantage of the *Star Trek* brand name and its low-budget computer-generated special effects looked a bit like a video game, *Babylon 5* held its own in these comparisons, attracting a loyal core audience that followed it through its entire run. This run was unique in that series creator J. Michael Straczinski had conceived, from the beginning, an epic five-year plot arc. Practical considerations, such as budgets and cast changes, necessitated certain modifications in the plot as the series went along, but, by and large, Straczinski and the producers of the series were able to stick to the original plan, producing a series that still stands as the epitome of continuous-plot SFTV.[5] Given this scope, *Babylon 5* was also able to produce well-defined characters, complex and interesting relationships, and a number of compelling ideas about the future.

The title of *Babylon 5* is taken from the name of the giant (far larger than DS9) space station aboard which the series is primarily set. Designed as a sort of interstellar United Nations, the station was built to provide a place where various space-going species could meet and mingle, exchanging ideas and goods—and hopefully gain the sort of mutual understanding that would prevent the outbreak of warfare among different species and planets. The principal builder and sponsor of the station is Earth, and the series repeatedly hints that, as a species, humans have a special place and destiny in the universe. As in the *Star Trek* universe, Earth seems to have a single world government, which in this case also holds sway over a number of colonies in outer space, including the Babylon 5 station. However, this future Earth is fraught with social, political, and economic problems, which sets it apart even more than *DS9* from Gene Roddenberry's vision of a utopian future in which such problems have been solved by technological progress.

Humanity in *Babylon 5* is considerably less advanced (especially technologically) than many of the other species aboard the station. Indeed, a primary motivation for the Babylon project is the Earth-Minbari War of ten years earlier, which started essentially as a misunderstanding after an Earth ship, in the midst of the first contact with the Minbari, fired upon and destroyed a Minbari ship, killing a key leader. In the subsequent conflict, Earth itself is nearly destroyed by the vastly superior forces of the Minbari Federation, though the Minbari suddenly and unaccountably (though we learn the reason in the course of the series) halt their advance just as they are about to attack Earth itself, instead surrendering and ending the war. Some jingoists on Earth therefore declare the war a victory, but most Earth leaders realize that the forces of Earth are no match for many of the alien civilizations in the galaxy, so the Babylon project is conceived as an attempt to avoid conflicts with those species.

The Babylon project has a strong utopian dimension in its vision of interspecies cooperation and understanding. Indeed, it is repeatedly described in the voice-overs that begin the early season episodes as "our last, best hope for peace," echoing the words used by John Kennedy to describe the United Nations in his 1961 inaugural address. It is, in fact, strongly supported (and partly sponsored) by several species other than humans, especially the Minbari. At any given time, the station has a population of approximately 250,000 people from more than twenty different species, all treated, at least theoretically, as equals. (All sentient species are referred to as "people" in the series, though nonhumans are frequently referred to as "aliens" as well.) Of this population, 42 percent are aliens, so that humans are in only a slight majority. On the other hand, the Babylon project is haunted by darkness from the very beginning. For one thing, some on Earth view it simply as a stalling tactic designed not to prevent war but merely to delay it until Earth can build its military forces to a sufficient level to be able to take on alien species such as the Minbari with a reasonable chance of victory. For another, the Babylon 5 station has that numerical designation because it is the fifth in a series of such stations, the first three having been mysteriously destroyed while still under construction and the fourth having disappeared just after completion. Thus, the Babylon 5 station is surrounded, from the very beginning, by an aura of danger and by the suggestion that there are dark and mysterious forces in the universe that oppose its mission.

The station itself is a work of advanced engineering that makes it a science fiction setting in the grand tradition, suggesting as it does that technology, by the year 2258 when the series begins, will have advanced far beyond anything available at the end of the twentieth century. Five miles long and weighing 2,500,000 tons, Babylon 5 is essentially a city spinning in space, complete with artificial gravity, a variety of atmospheres (to accommodate species who do not breathe oxygen), and an impressive array of high-tech computer and communications gadgets that help the station to run smoothly. The series features extremely advanced space-travel technology as well—as it would have to do in order for the various species that frequent the station to be able to get back and forth between the station and their home worlds. In this case, interstellar travel is accomplished by the use of "jump gates" that open gateways into the shortcut of "hyperspace," allowing ultrafast travel between points in normal space.

One is tempted, in fact, to say that the Babylon 5 station is a miracle of technology, except that, unlike many science fiction programs, *Babylon 5* makes it clear that the station was built with extensive human (and some alien) labor and that it was very expensive to build. In fact, due to cost overruns and budget shortfalls, some areas of the station have been left unfinished. Meanwhile, such practical problems also often plague the day-to-day operations of the station, which again require a significant contribution from human labor. For example, the various ships that come to the station to engage in trade must be loaded and unloaded by actual dockworkers, though advanced machinery does aid in the effort. Indeed, a key moment in the first season occurs in the episode "By Any Means Necessary" (May 11, 1994), when these dockworkers threaten to go on strike due to low wages and difficult working conditions, a situation caused by the fact that political maneuvering back on Earth has resulted in a cut in the station's promised manpower budget.

The budget gets even tighter after worsening political conditions on Earth cause the station to declare its independence from Earth authority during the third season. This declaration eventually leads to all-out interstellar war between the official government of Earth and an alliance led by Babylon 5, leading to even greater shortages on the station. We are constantly reminded during *Babylon 5* that all of the technology we see costs money. And the limited nature of the resources available to the station causes social problems and inequities on the station itself. In particular, while the major characters (who are in positions of authority aboard the station) generally live in relatively comfortable conditions, the station's workers have far less luxurious accommodations. The station even includes an extensive underclass of unemployed "lurkers" who occupy an unfinished area of the station known as "down-below." Here they live in hardship and squalor, scratching out a meager existence in a dingy world of poverty and crime. Despite this darkly pessimistic reminder that the poor may be with us always, the economics of scarcity that reign on Babylon 5 can have comic results as well, as in the episode "Hunter, Prey" (March 2, 1995), in which the station is ordered to develop a plan for marketing Babylon 5 merchandise galaxy-wide as a way of generating some additional cash.

This satirical swipe at 1990s capitalism shows the tendency of the series to mix considerable humor with its often taut drama. It also reminds us that capitalism remains a force in the twenty-third century and indicates one of the ways in which the future world of *Babylon 5* differs dramatically from the world of its *Star Trek* predecessors, in which capitalism has given way to an egalitarian system of universal affluence, at least on Earth. The action of *Babylon 5* (which spans the years 2258–2262) is roughly contemporaneous with that of the original series of *Star Trek* (which takes place roughly in the years 2266–2269), and the technology of the series is almost as advanced as that of *Star Trek*, with the exception of signature *Star Trek* devices such as transporters and replicators.

In terms of social and political development, however, the twenty-third-century Earth of *Babylon 5* seems, if anything, to have deteriorated relative to the late twentieth century in which the show was produced. One of the major elements of the five-year plot arc is the decline of Earth into a dystopian state, marked especially by the assassination of Earth president Santiago in a plot involving Vice President Clark, who becomes the new president and turns out to be working in league with a mysterious and sinister alien race known as the Shadows. If the future Earth of *Babylon 5* thus has substantial social and political problems, the same can be said for most of the alien races in the series, even though they are often much more technologically advanced than Earth. The series thus consistently suggests that advanced technology does not necessarily lead to social and political enlightenment.

Babylon 5 deals extensively with such social and political problems, while its individual characters tend to have far more personal problems than the characters of *Star Trek* and most other SFTV series. Further darkness is added to the series by the presence of the Psi Corps, a sort of secret police organization charged with regulating the activities of the numerous telepaths who began appearing on Earth a hundred years earlier—thanks, we eventually learn, to the manipulations of an advanced alien race known as the Vorlons. The Psi Corps seems to be accountable to almost no one, and some of its members seem bent on using the power of the corps to carve out their own personal empires, usually in direct opposition to Babylon 5 and its command staff.

In the first season of *Babylon 5*, the station is commanded by Commander Jeffrey Sinclair (Michael O'Hare), who gets the post after several more senior officers are passed over at the insistence of the Minbari. Indeed, throughout the first season there are hints that Sinclair has a special relationship with the Minbari, though the exact nature of this relationship is unknown to us (or to him) until the Season Three two-part episode "War without End" (May 16 and 23, 1996). In this complex and event-filled episode, the mystery of the disappearance of Babylon 4 is also solved when we learn that Sinclair took that station back one thousand years in time, where it became a key resource for the Minbari in their first war against the Shadows. In the process, Sinclair himself is transformed into a Minbari, becoming Valen, the greatest of all Minbari leaders. It also becomes clear (especially with supplemental information from the 1998 made-for-TV movie *In the Beginning*) that the Minbari's discovery that Sinclair would become Valen was what caused them to halt their assault on Earth. At the same time, Sinclair remains part human, and his descendants have invested the Minbari (many of whom seem excessively concerned with their racial purity) with a substantial mix of human DNA.

At the beginning of the second season, Sinclair goes off to Minbar to serve as a special ambassador (and secretly to head up the Rangers, an elite clandestine force training to do battle with the Shadows). He is replaced as the head of Babylon 5 by Captain John Sheridan (Bruce Boxleitner), the only human commander to have scored a victory against the Minbari in the Earth-Minbari War. The Minbari (especially the warrior caste) understandably have their doubts about the choice of Sheridan in the beginning, but he turns out to be a paragon of courage, leadership, and statesmanship. He soon wins over the crew of Babylon 5 and most of the Minbari, especially Delenn (Mira Furlan), the Minbari ambassador. On the other hand, Sheridan's independence and refusal to compromise his integrity sometimes put him at odds with the government back on Earth, culminating in his declaration of Babylon 5's secession from Earth's authority in "Severed Dreams" (April 4, 1996), one of the key episodes in the developing plot arc of the station's problematic relationship with Earth.

By the fifth season, Sheridan hands over command of Babylon 5 to newcomer Captain Elizabeth Lochley (Tracey Scoggins), while he himself ascends to the presidency of the Interstellar Alliance, a new political entity that grows out of the alliances formed during the Shadow War and the war with Earth. The second in command of Babylon 5 through its first four seasons is Lieutenant Commander (later Commander) Susan Ivanova (Claudia Christian), who starts out as a rather no-nonsense, by-the-books military officer, though she gradually evolves into a more human character who turns out, among other things, to have a rather wacky sense of humor. Ivanova has had a troubled past, which sometimes still haunts her, but she remains consistently on the side of the good, a fine military officer whose courage under fire is never in question, though she does sometimes seem very much out of her element when performing the diplomatic duties that her position on the station sometimes requires.

Doctor Stephen Franklin (Richard Biggs) is a brilliant surgeon and an unmatched expert in the physiology of the wide range of alien species that he is required to treat as the chief medical officer on the station. A figure of unquestioned virtue, he is also a courageous man of action, and his operations in the series go far beyond those he performs in the station's medical center. A driven workaholic, he also has his personal demons, as when his desire to get more work done leads to excessive consumption of pharmaceutical stimulants and eventually to drug addiction.

The final key member of the station's command staff is Security Chief Michael Garibaldi (Jerry Doyle). A particularly close confidant of Sinclair, who has selected him to head the station's security force despite a checkered background colored by alcoholism, the cynical Garibaldi is at first a bit wary of Sheridan, but he soon evolves into one of Sheridan's most trusted supporters. On the other hand, at the end of the third season, he is abducted by mysterious forces, which we later learn to be the Psi Corps. Due to mind-altering treatments during his captivity, Garibaldi engages in a plot that nearly leads to Sheridan's death, though he ultimately recovers and helps to save not only Sheridan but Earth as well.

Of the aliens on *Babylon 5*, the Minbari are probably the most important. They are an ancient and highly sophisticated people whose technological capabilities go well beyond those of Earth. In addition,

they are one of the few races on the show that seem to have a relatively well-functioning social and political system, at least through
the first three seasons. Minbari society is strictly divided into three
castes—religious, warrior, and worker—each of which has radically
different values and worldviews. All three castes have ostensibly equal
status and power, though we see little of the worker caste in the series, and Minbari society seems to be dominated by the other two
castes. The society is held together by a finely wrought system of
checks and balances, although by the fourth season this system
breaks down, and the religious and warrior castes find themselves
at civil war with one another. The warrior caste, not surprisingly, wins
this war, though they are prevented from gaining total domination of
Minbari society through the efforts of Delenn.

In addition to serving as the Minbari ambassador to Babylon 5,
Delenn is unique in that, at the end of the first season, she decides
to undergo a transfiguration that makes her half human so that she
can further the relationship between the Minbari and humans, whom
she sees as constituting the other half of the Minbari soul. The only
sign of her transformation is that she now has hair, and she still seems
thoroughly Minbari in her attitudes and behavior, though many
among the Minbari now regard her as suspect. Meanwhile, Delenn's
half-human status furthers a developing romantic relationship with
Sheridan, leading ultimately to marriage and to an important political
partnership as well. Delenn herself proves to be a strong and effective military leader as the series progresses (succeeding Sinclair as
the leader of the Rangers), though she also maintains a number of
traditional traits of the nurturing female.

In addition to Delenn and the other Minbari on the station (including Delenn's aide, Lennier, played by SFTV veteran Bill Mumy), the
principal alien representatives on the station come from the Centauri
Republic, the Narn Regime, and the Vorlon Empire, all of which have
official ambassadors on the station. These ambassadors themselves
constitute an important part of the cast of characters. One of the distinctive features that sets *Babylon 5* apart from most science fiction
television is the extent to which aliens are portrayed in the series as
complex individuals rather than simply as stock representatives of
distinctive alien races, while the alien races themselves tend to be
more complex and varied than in many series. For example, G'Kar
(Andreas Katsulas), the Narn ambassador in the first two seasons,
initially seems to be the truculent representative of a warlike race,

vaguely reminiscent of *Star Trek*'s Klingons, but made even more stereotypical by their reptilian appearance. As the series progresses, however, G'Kar becomes a much more positive, even spiritual character, especially after it becomes clear that Narn aggressiveness is mostly a response to their earlier conquest and enslavement by the Centauri. Indeed, when war breaks out between the Centauri and the Narn in Season Two, it quickly becomes apparent that the Centauri are the aggressors. A quick Centauri victory (thanks largely to the aid of the Shadows) then makes G'Kar a genuinely tragic character. Stripped of his ambassadorial title due to the fall of his government, he remains aboard Babylon 5 attempting to lead his people in an ongoing resistance to Centauri oppression.

The Centauri (transparently modeled after the Roman Empire) are an ancient and highly advanced race, though their once vast empire is, at the time of the series, in a state of serious decline. Moreover, Centauri politics seem to consist of little more than an unending series of self-serving intrigues. The Centauri have a long history of relations with Earth, having been the first alien species encountered by earthlings, one hundred years before the setting of *Babylon 5*. After this initial encounter, the Centauri supplied Earth with a number of technological advances, including jumpgates.

The Centauri ambassador on Babylon 5, Londo Mollari (Peter Jurasik), initially seems to be little more than an affable buffoon, more interested in partying than in politics—an impression furthered by the fact that the Centauri are among the silliest-looking aliens on science fiction television. They outwardly appear to be entirely human, except that the women always shave their heads, while the men wear their hair in a fanlike array extending across the top of the skull. Appearances, however, can be deceiving, and the Centauri have a number of nonhuman characteristics, such as two hearts and six sets of genitals, which can be used in combination to reach increasing heights of sexual pleasure. In *Babylon 5*, appearances can be deceiving in other ways as well. As the series proceeds, the ambitious and conniving Mollari (who will one day become emperor of the Centauri Republic, thanks partly to his own Machiavellian machinations) becomes a more and more sinister figure. For example, it is he who plays a central role in aligning the Centauri with the Shadows in the war against the Narn, though he also attempts to repudiate the Shadows soon after that war is won, realizing (almost as if he is waking from hypnosis) that the price for their support is far too high. By the beginning of the fourth season, Mollari swings back in the direction of virtue, spearheading the assassination of the crazed Centauri emperor, Cartagia (Wortham Krimmer), and granting independence to the newly conquered Narn home world.

The death of Cartagia leaves Mollari in a position eventually to succeed to the throne, fulfilling his lifelong ambition, but in a way that brings little joy, leaving him with dangerous enemies and awesome responsibilities. G'Kar and Mollari are well-rounded characters, with good sides and bad sides, personal triumphs and personal tragedies. On the other hand, one could argue that this depth of characterization, which goes so far beyond that of most aliens in SFTV, is achieved at the expense of making them seem less like aliens than eccentric humans. The same, however, cannot be said for Vorlon ambassador Kosh (voiced by Ardwright Chamberlain), the most enigmatic (and the most alien) of the alien ambassadors aboard the station. Virtually nothing is known about Kosh, or the Vorlons as a whole. The reclusive Vorlons have little truck with the other races that inhabit the galaxy, and, as *Babylon 5* begins, no outside visitor has ever returned from Vorlon space. Kosh is made even more mysterious in that he speaks in riddles and that no one has ever actually seen him: he appears outside his own quarters on the station only inside an "encounter suit," presumably designed to provide an atmosphere in which he can live.

In the course of the series, we learn that the Vorlons are a particularly ancient race, one of the First Ones, who inhabited the galaxy long before most of the current civilizations had reached outer space. As the series proceeds, Kosh develops from a minor character on the margins of the action to an important ally of the station in its developing war against the Shadows. His support for Babylon 5 and its allies leads, in the episode "Interludes and Examinations" (May 9, 1996), to his death at the hand of the Shadows. However, he is soon replaced by another ambassador, also called Kosh, who simply explains, in typically enigmatic Vorlon fashion, that "we are all Kosh." However, the second Kosh finds humans and their problems irrelevant, indicating a shift in the attitude of the Vorlons toward humans in relation to the Shadow War.

A major part of *Babylon 5*'s continuous plot arc involves these Shadows, who had been defeated in a massive galaxy-wide conflict one thousand years earlier, henceforth disappearing from the galaxy. As the series proceeds, we learn that they are gradually gathering their forces in an attempt to regain their former power. In so doing, they make a secret alliance first with the Centauri Republic and then with Earth, though it is clear that the Shadows have no compunctions about turning on their former allies. In the course of the third season, the conflict that had been slowly building throughout the first two seasons finally erupts into full-scale war, with the Shadows and their allies opposed by an alliance consisting of Babylon 5 and other former Earth colonies, the Minbari, and a number of other loosely aligned races, including (for a time), the enigmatic, almost godlike Vorlons. It turns out that the Vorlons are merely using the alliance as pawns in their long-running battle against the Shadows, but the war ultimately ends when the Vorlons and Shadows are both convinced to move on beyond the galactic rim, leaving the galaxy to the younger, less advanced races.

In addition to its continuous plot and complex characters, the most striking and memorable aspect of *Babylon 5* is the encyclopedic range of its references to literature, religion, myth, and other aspects of the Western cultural tradition. Science fiction (including SFTV) itself is one of the most important sources for the series.[6] The most prominent of such references is the frequent appearance of Walter Koening (*Star Trek*'s Chekhov) as Alfred Bester, an evil (mostly) operative of the Psi Corps. The casting of Koenig obviously acknowledges the importance of *Star Trek* as a predecessor to *Babylon 5*, but the naming of Koenig's character makes the allusions even richer, because it makes him the namesake of the author of such classic science fiction texts as *The Demolished Man* (1953), which envisions a future world in which telepaths play a number of key roles, including that of policemen.

Babylon 5 came to a relatively graceful end, with a final episode set twenty years beyond the main action—and originally filmed, incidentally, at the end of the fourth season, when it looked as if that would be the last. In the episode, Sheridan lives on, even as the series ends: rather than simply die, he exits the galaxy, following the Vorlons and Shadows to the mysterious realm beyond the rim, thus anticipating the movement of *DS9*'s Sisko to live among the "prophets." The universe of *Babylon 5* lived on as well, with the advent of Straczynski's follow-up series, *Crusade*. Several cast members of *Babylon 5* made guest appearances on *Crusade*, and the station itself sometimes figures there as well. *Crusade* is something of a throwback to the original *Star Trek* model: its principal setting is aboard a starship, which, like the original *Enterprise*, is engaged in a five-year mission of exploring the galaxy. But *Crusade*'s *Excalibur*, commanded by Captain Matthew Gideon (Gary Cole), is on a far darker mission with much higher stakes: as the series begins, the entire Earth has been infected by a plague initiated by the sinister Drakhs, former minions of the Shadows. This plague, we learn, takes about five years to run its course, by which time all life on Earth will be wiped out. Gideon and his *Excalibur* crew thus have that amount of time to find a cure and save the planet.[7]

Unfortunately, *Crusade* itself had even less time. After a number of squabbles with the TNT cable network, on which the show was broadcast, the series was unceremoniously canceled thirteen episodes into the first season. Some of these episodes showed promise, though the series never really got going, despite having *Babylon 5* as background—though it should also be remembered that *Babylon 5* itself only really hit its stride in the third season. As it was, the most notable episode of *Crusade* was probably "Visitors from Down the Street" (August 25, 1999), a hilarious takeoff on *The X-Files*, in which the *Excalibur* encounters an alien man and woman who have been doggedly investigating the possibility that their planet has long been explored (and interfered with) by visitors from Earth.

By poking fun at *The X-Files*, "Visitors from Down the Street" was actually very much in the spirit of *The X-Files* itself, which often relieved its generally dark tone with self-parody. In fact, episodes such as "Jose Chung's *From Outer Space*" (April 12, 1996), which parodies many of the basic elements of the series, were among the most popular and successful in the long history of the series, which ran from September 10, 1993 to May 19, 2002. All in all, though, *The X-Files* was dark indeed, in terms of both its distinctive (and highly influential) noir look and its content, which featured a variety of monsters, gruesome crimes, and sinister conspiracies. In that sense, and in the sense of its influence and popularity, *The X-Files* is perhaps the primary example of the dark turn taken by SFTV in the 1990s.

The central concern of *The X-Files* is a secret plot by alien invaders to take over the earth. As such, *The X-Files* was an alien-invasion series somewhat in the tradition of *The Invaders*. Indeed, the series acknowledged this important predecessor by featuring several guest appearances by Roy Thinnes, who had starred as David Vincent, the lone voice crying out against the alien intruders of *The Invaders* (forty-three hour-long color episodes in 1967–69).[8] However, *The X-Files*

went far beyond other alien invasion series in the cynicism and paranoia with which it treated this motif. David Vincent could never convince the authorities that an invasion was under way; in *The X-Files*,
the authorities not only know about the invasion plot, they are part
of it. The invasion involves not a simple onslaught but a vast, intri-
cate, long-term plot, with the help of certain elements within the U.S.
government. *The X-Files* takes popular suspicions that the government
is involved in a campaign to cover up evidence of UFOs to a whole
new level, suggesting that the government not only hides such evidence but may even be involved in the alien invasion. Indeed, the
series is unremittingly cynical about the government, which appears
capable of any and all nefarious and dastardly activities. As a result,
the protagonists never know whom to trust ("trust no one" is an
underlying theme of the series) and are even unaware of certain dark
secrets about themselves and their own pasts.

The X-Files is driven by the determination of FBI Special Agent Fox
Mulder (David Duchovny) to investigate the "X-Files," a collection of
unsolved cases involving paranormal phenomena, especially UFO
sightings and alien abductions. Though gifted with boyish charm and
a wisecracking sense of humor, Mulder is something of a fanatic,
dedicated to unraveling the mysteries of the X-Files at any cost. He
is also a brilliant Oxford-educated psychologist, though his abiding
interest in paranormal phenomena (which seems to have been triggered largely by childhood trauma caused by the disappearance of
his sister, Samantha, apparently by alien abduction) has caused him
to be regarded as something of a kook, earning him the nickname
"Spooky." Meanwhile, Mulder's fierce dedication to his offbeat investigations leads the FBI to assign fledgling agent Dana Scully (Gillian
Anderson) to work with him and to keep an eye on him. A trained
medical doctor with a reputation for dispassionate scientific objec-
tivity, Scully is seen as a counter to Mulder's potential for excess—
but also as a way of keeping tabs on him to prevent him from probing
into areas that are better left alone. Indeed, one of the crucial premises of the series is that many of the cases in the X-Files involve a
vast international conspiracy carried out by the Syndicate, a mysterious group that includes the participation of officials highly placed
in the U.S. government. However, other mysterious figures in the
government (and even within the Syndicate) sometimes lend aid and
support to Mulder and Scully, further complicating the picture. As the
series proceeds, Scully remains the voice of conventional reason, but

she also begins to grant that Mulder's theories might have more validity than she first believed, while Mulder himself experiences occasional bouts of skepticism. In the meantime, Mulder and Scully become genuine friends as well as professional allies, their bonding and mutual respect providing one of the key elements of the series. Indeed, the relationship (complete with growing sexual tensions) between the two protagonists was a key to the success of the series, as was the basic attractiveness of the protagonists themselves.

In its ongoing exploration of the alien invasion/government conspiracy motif, *The X-Files* joins series such as *Babylon 5* in the trend toward continuous plot arcs in SFTV of the 1990s. However, the majority of episodes of *The X-Files* involve stand-alone investigations into various paranormal phenomena that are not really part of the main plot arc. In these so-called monster-of-the-week episodes, Mulder and Scully battle werewolves, vampires, mutants, and other relatively traditional supernatural creatures. Sometimes these creatures are not even truly supernatural but are merely particularly bizarre criminals, especially serial killers, adding still more flexibility to the series.

These episodes, at their best, could be quite riveting, though they could be a bit far-fetched. However, it was the arc of sequentially connected alien-invasion episodes that was the real heart of *The X-Files*. This central arc itself went through so many twists and turns over the years that it was not really as continuous as the plot arcs of, say, *Babylon 5*. On the other hand, it was especially effective due to the detective-story theme of the ongoing investigation, which invited viewers to join Mulder and Scully in trying to piece together the various clues that accumulated over time.[9] However, *The X-Files*, in keeping with the postmodernist mode of epistemological skepticism for which it became renowned, does not neatly answer all of its important questions, leaving a number of loose ends, even after the final two-part episode "The Truth" (May 19, 2002), which leaves Mulder and Scully together and openly in love at last, but booted out of the FBI and on the run from powerful forces within the government.

Despite the many unanswered questions, a roughly coherent outline of the overall story behind the plot arc can be pieced together, though only with considerable analysis and guesswork. It seems, to begin with, that some sort of alien "life force," known as the Black Oil because of the way it appears in its free state, appeared on Earth millions of years ago (perhaps arriving from outer space, perhaps evolving on Earth). This virus subsequently becomes the central force in the later invasion of Earth, which is thus complicated by the fact that the "alien" invaders were on Earth long before human beings. That they are, in fact, merely trying to reclaim their earlier home from human interlopers dramatically complicates the terms of the invasion, which is thus not nearly as simple as the usual "good humans versus bad aliens" scenario.

The virus, which appears to be sentient, can enter living beings and take over their bodies, something it seems to have done to a group of alien visitors (the so-called gray aliens of UFO lore), who arrived on Earth thousands of years ago. Some of these aliens subsequently left, while others remained on Earth in hibernation. In an effort to regain control of the planet, the Black Oil has periodically abducted and taken over humans throughout the years and, at the time of the series, seems to be stepping up its efforts toward eventual reclamation of the planet, efforts that are expected to culminate in the return of the main alien force in an all-out invasion from space in the year 2012. Meanwhile, agents of the Black Oil/aliens have been working with the Syndicate (which began its operations after the discovery of the aliens at Roswell, New Mexico, in 1947) to prepare the way for the invasion, in return for which the members of the Syndicate and their families will be allowed to live on as human-alien hybrids that would be immune to the Black Oil virus. However, some members of the Syndicate, including the seemingly sinister "Cigarette-Smoking Man," a.k.a. C.G.B. Spender (William B. Davis), are apparently secretly working to undermine the invasion by developing a vaccine against the virus.

The invasion plans become even more horrifying when it begins to appear that the Black Oil intends not merely to take over the human race but to eradicate it, replacing humans with gray aliens by gestating the latter within human hosts (who are, unfortunately, killed by the process). These gray aliens will then occupy the earth, presumably serving as better hosts for the Black Oil. It is this plot that Mulder and Scully work to subvert, though various factors complicate the scenario, including the appearance of a rival group of aliens opposed to the Black Oil, and the development (apparently via the same genetic research being used to develop the human-alien hybrids) of a race of "supersoldiers" who may eventually serve as hosts that the Black Oil virus would prefer even to the gray aliens (but who may also eventually serve as a powerful counter to the Black Oil).

In the course of their investigations, Mulder and Scully both become infected by the virus, meanwhile discovering that all human beings apparently carry traces of the alien DNA, extending the hybridity theme that underlies the series and further effacing the already blurry boundary between "us" and "them" that is one of its hallmarks. The two agents, having become lovers, also have an infant, William, who may hold an unspecified key to foiling the invasion, perhaps due to genetic characteristics acquired from the fact that his parents have been infected with the virus. Mulder himself also seems, for reasons that are never made entirely clear, to be a particular threat to the invasion. He is thus targeted for death by conspiratorial forces still working within the U.S. government at the end of the ninth and last season of the series, even though virtually all of the members of the Syndicate are wiped out in the Season Six episode "One Son" (February 14, 1999) by the aliens who are opposed to the virus (and, who, in one of the series' most unlikely turns, have made themselves immune to it by sewing shut all of their bodily orifices, thus allowing the virus no point of access).

If all of this seems a bit complex and confusing, it was even more so as it emerged piecemeal over the nine years of the series. A distinguishing feature of *The X-Files* was its refusal to wrap things up in neat packages or even to make clear distinctions between good guys and bad guys. As such, the series resonated with the feelings of many viewers that they themselves were living in a world populated by sinister forces beyond their control or understanding. Among other things, the open ending of the series left room for possible subsequent feature film follow-ups, one successful theatrical film (1998's *The X-Files: Fight the Future*) having already been produced during the run of the series. But the loose threads left dangling at the end of the series were entirely appropriate given the consistent refusal of the series to provide neat and unequivocal answers to the various questions it posed.

This lack of closure, combined with the dark look and the basic detective-story texture of the series, made *The X-Files* genuinely different from most other SFTV series, despite the fact that it openly acknowledged a variety of television predecessors, ranging from *The Twilight Zone* to *Night Stalker* to *Twin Peaks*, in addition to *The Invaders*. Indeed, *The X-Files* was consistently self-conscious about its status as a television program, often alluding to other programs and to its own placement on the Fox Network. Mulder, whose quips often allude to various works of American popular culture, seems to be a particular fan of *The Simpsons*, while in "Nisei" (November 24, 1995) Mulder acquires a bootleg tape of an alien autopsy that Scully describes as "even hokier than the one they aired on the Fox Network." Meanwhile, one entire episode of *The X-Files*—"X-Cops" (February 20, 2000)—is shot as if it is an episode of the Fox "reality" show *Cops*.

Non-Fox shows are also part of the allusive framework of *The X-Files*, as when "The Post-Modern Prometheus" (November 30, 1997) sets itself against the background of *The Jerry Springer Show*, suggesting in a mode of self-parody that *The X-Files* (often criticized for its violence and abject subject matter) might be pandering to some of the same lowbrow tastes as does the Springer show. Of course, *The X-Files* also often engages in dialog with the supposedly wholesome television programming of the past. The episode "Home" (October 11, 1996), for example, is set in the seemingly idyllic small town of Home, Pennsylvania, which is both campily similar to and horrifyingly different from the Mayberry, North Carolina, made famous by *The Andy Griffith Show*.

Early in "Home" a group of kids playing baseball discovers the body of a horribly deformed infant buried under home plate. Mulder and Scully are then called in to investigate. When they arrive, Scully begins a scientific examination of the burial scene, while Mulder plays with a baseball left by the kids in the earlier scene and dreams of returning to the simple days of childhood and living in such a peaceful small-town community, with "no modems, no faxes, no cell phones." Scully then reminds Mulder that he would go nuts without a cell phone. She also sardonically compares Mulder's vision to the legendary TV town of Mayberry, at which point the local sheriff arrives and introduces himself, to Mulder's astonishment, as Andy Taylor (Tucker Smallwood).

"Home," in fact, features a number of such self-consciously ironic elements (Taylor's deputy is even named "Barney"), many of which refer specifically to the television tradition of idyllic small towns, of which Mayberry is the paradigm. But the town of Home is no Mayberry, as evidenced not only by the initial burial of the deformed baby but by the fact that Taylor is black and both Taylor and Barney are brutally killed by the baby's family, the Peacocks, a veritable walking catalog of inbred white-trash stereotypes. Television, "Home" reminds us, is not what it used to be, but then perhaps it never was.

In some cases, *The X-Files* is even more openly critical of television and its cultural power. "Wetwired" (May 10, 1996) clearly recalls films such as *The Manchurian Candidate* (1962) and *Videodrome*

(1983) in its suggestion of the use of television for psychological manipulation. Indeed, the darkness with which classic science fiction motifs are treated in *The X-Files* is typically more reminiscent of science fiction film (or even film noir) than SFTV, just as the look of the series often seemed more typical of film than television. For example, the sinister and conspiratorial nature of the alien-invasion motif recalls classic films such as *Invasion of the Body Snatchers*, while the virus motif recalls any number of films, of which *The Andromeda Strain* (1971) is probably the classic case. Many commentators found Scully's activities in the series reminiscent of those of FBI Agent Clarice Starling (Jodie Foster) in *The Silence of the Lambs* (1991), while the motif of gestating aliens within doomed human hosts recalls the horrifying images of the *Alien* series of films, which featured another strong female protagonist in Sigourney Weaver's Ripley.

Some episodes referenced film predecessors quite overtly and extensively. In "Monday" (February 28, 1999), the same day is relived over and over, à la the film *Groundhog Day* (1993), while "Triangle" (November 22, 1998) openly models itself on *The Wizard of Oz* (1939). Similarly, "The Post-Modern Prometheus," shot in black and white, campily mimics *Frankenstein* (1931) in a mode of postmodern pastiche. Other film allusions were more subtle or fleeting, as when the conflict of testimonies in the comic vampire episode "Bad Blood" (February 22, 1998) clearly echoes Akira Kurosawa's classic *Rashomon* (1950); when a scene in "Dreamland" (November 29, 1998) mimics the hilarious mirror scene from the Marx Brothers' *Duck Soup* (1933); or when we learn that José Chung is the author of *The Caligarian Candidate*, a thriller that deals with mind control and whose title links it to *The Manchurian Candidate*, with a dash of *The Cabinet of Dr. Caligari* (1920) thrown in for good measure.

Such allusive episodes often gave *The X-Files* a campy, postmodern air, but the ultimate darkness of its vision was never in doubt. Within the context of the affluence of American society in the 1990s, the paranoid tone of the series might seem surprising. However, the obsessive focus of *The X-Files* on the threat posed to mainstream American society by a variety of outside "Others"—whether they be aliens, foreigners, vampires, lunatics, or just poor Southern whites (often treated in the series as sinister rednecks)—may be entirely understandable. On the one hand, the boom of the 1990s helped many wealthy and even middle-class Americans to accumulate assets that gave them more to lose than ever before. On the other hand, this increase in the wealth of well-off Americans led to an increasing gap between their affluence and the poverty of the poor masses both at home and abroad. As a result, wealthier Americans had every reason to feel uncomfortable with their new prosperity, both because much of that prosperity was gained at the expense of poor workers worldwide and because it made sense to expect those workers to resent this situation. Thus, the richer Americans became, the more threatened and embattled they felt, and the paranoia of *The X-Files* responded perfectly to this mind-set.

In addition, that *The X-Files* was merely representative of a larger trend toward darker visions in the science fiction television of the 1990s helps to verify that this darkness participated in something much broader than the particular creative visions of Chris Carter and the rest of the *X-Files* production team. By the later years of the decade, millennial tensions (including the Y2K scare) led to even more darkness, culminating in Carter's own *Millennium* (also on Fox, 1996-99), perhaps the darkest television series of the entire 1990s, though it dealt more with a motif from the gothic and horror traditions than science fiction. By the beginning of the new century, the stock market bubble had burst; the shocking events of September 11, 2001, then seemed to ratify the fears of the previous decade. But such events also made the world seem a more complex and unpredictable place than it had ever been before: the simple oppositions of the cold war seemed almost refreshing by comparison. It was perhaps this new sense of unpredictability that contributed to a turn, in the SFTV series of the early years of the new millennium, away from representations of the future altogether.

Books, books, everywhere . . . Book-lover Henry Bemis, the last man on earth, sinks into despair surrounded by the stacks of books he can no longer read because he has broken his glasses in "Time Enough at Last" (*The Twilight Zone*).

The humans on the planet Luminos invite a diseased Ralph Cashman into their midst, knowing he will infect them with the Luminoid disease that will render them useless as slaves in "A Feasibility Study" (*The Outer Limits*).

The starship *Enterprise, the* iconic science fiction image of the 1960s (*Star Trek: The Original Series*).

Spock in love. Mr. Spock, having been infected by mysterious spores on the planet Omicron Ceti III, relaxes with his new love, Leila Kalomi, in "This Side of Paradise" (*Star Trek: The Original Series*).

Spock in heat. McCoy, Kirk, and Spock beam down to the planet
Vulcan, where Spock has been driven by the mating lust of *pon farr*
in "Amok Time" (*Star Trek: The Original Series*).

Riker, Picard, and Troi on the bridge of the new *Enterprise* in *Star
Trek: The Next Generation*.

Klingons old and new. Captain Koloth (above) in "The Trouble with Tribbles" (*Star Trek: The Original Series*) and Mr. Worf (below) of *Star Trek: The Next Generation* and *Star Trek: Deep Space 9*.

Data confronts his evil twin, Lore, in "Datalore" (*Star Trek: The Next Generation*).

Captain Picard as Locutus of Borg in "The Best of Both Worlds" (*Star Trek: The Next Generation*).

Sisko, Bashir, and O'Brien don vintage Starfleet uniforms after traveling back in time in "Trials and Tribble-ations" (*Star Trek: Deep Space Nine*).

Gul Dukat, the chief Cardassian villain of *Star Trek: Deep Space Nine*.

A typical late 1940s earthling male. The professor in "Little Green Men" lights butts for himself and his best gal (*Star Trek: Deep Space Nine*).

Kira and Odo commiserate in "The Begotten" (*Star Trek: Deep Space Nine*).

Number Six hooked up to a brain control device in "A, B & C" (*The Prisoner*).

Paul Foster consults with a purple-wigged technician on the moon base of *UFO*.

Two formidable science fiction beauties. Mrs. Emma Peel (above) of *The Avengers* was a genuine icon of the 1960s. Max Guevara (below) of *Dark Angel* was younger and less sophisticated than Mrs. Peel but gifted with super strength and super sex appeal.

The Eagle has landed. One of the eagles of *Space: 1999* sits on its launch pad.

The Doctor and Romana react to conditions on Ribos in "The Ribos Operation" (*Doctor Who*).

Franklin, Ivanova, Sheridan, and Garibaldi prepare to spring into action in *Babylon 5*.

Scully and Mulder get a briefing from Deputy Barney in "Home" (*The X-Files*).

Aliens approach in "One Son," cloaked in typical *X-Files* obscurity.

Makeup in space. Pa'u Zotoh Zhaan and Ka D'Argo of *Farscape*.

Puppets in space. Rygel (above) and Pilot (below) are two key members of the cast of *Farscape*.

Colonel O'Neill tests the open wormhole with a finger in *Stargate SG-1*.

Teal'c takes aim in *Stargate SG-1*.

CHAPTER 5

Back to the Future: Science Fiction Television in the New Millennium

Programs such as *The X-Files*, *Babylon 5*, and *Deep Space Nine* made the 1990s the richest period thus far in the history of American science fiction television. The situation continued to look bright as SFTV moved into the new millennium. True, *Babylon 5* and *Deep Space Nine* were no longer being broadcast, and *The X-Files*, beginning its eighth season in fall 2000, was in decline after the departure of David Duchovny at the end of the previous season. Nevertheless, an interesting collection of science fiction programs was still on the air in the year 2000. For one thing, *Voyager* was still on, representing the *Star Trek* franchise. Even though *Voyager* was canceled in 2001, it was replaced that same year by *Enterprise*, still another entry in the *Star Trek* sequence. In addition, several promising new programs that had begun broadcasting in the late 1990s were still on the air in 2000, including the alien-invasion series *Earth: Final Conflict* (which began airing in syndication in 1997, based on an idea by *Star Trek* creator Gene Roddenberry from the 1970s). *Stargate SG-1* (which had started in July 1997 on the Showtime cable network and later moved to the Sci Fi Channel) was also on, as were *Lexx* (a joint German-Canadian production that began as a series of TV movies in December 1997 and survived as a series until 2001 on Sci Fi) and *Farscape* (an impressive production of the Jim Henson Company that began airing on Sci Fi in March 1999 and continued into spring 2003). Meanwhile, the year 2000 saw the birth of *Andromeda* in syndication and James Cameron's *Dark Angel* on Fox, in what had become a rare case of a science fiction series on a major network. On the other hand, by summer 2003, of these series only *Stargate*, *Andromeda*, and *Enterprise* were still producing new episodes, though all of the others were still appearing as reruns or on DVD.

While the series appearing early in the new millennium represent a variety of innovations in SFTV, they tend collectively to turn away from imaginative visions of the future. Often they simply focus on the present; when they do project a future, it is seldom a golden future of technology-driven marvels. For example, *Farscape* and *Stargate* are set in the present time of the production of the series, while *Lexx* begins thousands of years in the past and ends up in the present. *Andromeda* and *Enterprise* are set in the future, but *Enterprise* is a prequel to the earlier *Star Trek* series, while *Andromeda* is set in a far future, by which time galactic civilization is in a state of collapse, though technology is still quite advanced relative to the present time of the series' production. Similarly, in *Dark Angel*, set in Earth's near future, American civilization is in a serious state of decline.

Together, the vision embodied in these series has much in common with recent developments in literary science fiction, such as cyberpunk, which has sometimes been criticized for its loss of the ability, so central to much earlier science fiction (and to SFTV series such as the first *Star Trek*s), to imagine a golden future driven by technological progress. In the case of science fiction television, there is also a strong element of nostalgia in this seeming turn away from the future. With half a century of SFTV behind them, series of the early twenty-first century often allude to their predecessors, inviting their audiences into an "in" group of viewers who will recognize these allusions. In addition, many earlier series have been resurrected for rebroadcast on cable, especially on the Sci Fi Channel, while, in addition to the new series that were in production at the beginning of the new millennium, there were also new versions of old classics such as *The Twilight Zone* and *The Outer Limits*.

The new version of *The Outer Limits*, which began airing on the Showtime cable network in March 1995, stayed in production for seven years (eventually shifting to the Sci Fi Channel in its seventh season), with a total of 154 episodes being produced. This series was very much in the spirit of the original, down to the use of an almost identical "control voice" narration to open each episode. However, there were changes, including a much more open and frank treatment of sexual themes, facilitated by the appearance of the series on a pay cable channel with far less censorship than the broadcast networks. This new openness created significant new possibilities for the series, though this was not always good news. One of the best-known episodes of the new series was the truly lame first-season "Caught in the Act," in which audiences were apparently supposed to feel compensated for a preposterous premise and incredibly hokey resolution by the sight of a topless Alyssa Milano in the central role of a good-girl coed made rapacious when her body is taken over by an alien entity desperate for love. Other episodes were a bit better, exploring (generally from a very masculine point of view) the implications of technology that previous chaste science fiction series had left untouched, as when lonely men have sex with beautiful android women ("Valerie 23") or simulate sex with lusty hologram women ("Bits of Love").

The new *Outer Limits* also employed substantially better special effects than the original, although, again, this advance sometimes led to the replacement of thoughtfulness with spectacle. However, the series did still occasionally try for depth, while episodes often ended with ironic twists reminiscent of *The Twilight Zone*. Meanwhile, *The Twilight Zone* itself went back into production with its second reincarnation, reemerging on UPN in fall 2002. Episodes of the new series were clearly modeled on those of the old (including direct remakes and sequels), and the format of an opening narration was continued, this time with actor Forest Whitaker in the narrator's role so memorably played by Rod Serling in the original series. The new series attempted to overcome the original series' indecision between half-hour and hour-long formats by airing two half-hour episodes in a one-hour block every week. There was also a conscious effort to update the series for new young audiences (such as the development of episodes that focus on rap music and other forms of contemporary culture), but the jury remained out as the series, going into its second season in fall 2003, had not quite found its niche, despite its attempts at hipness.

Hip, in fact, has been a key byword for science fiction series going into the twenty-first century. But hip, of course, is always a thing of the present, not the future, and this turn to hipness can be taken as part of SFTV's turn away from the future. With *Earth: Final Conflict*, set only in the very near future and featuring attractive young protagonists, even Gene Roddenberry–inspired science fiction turned toward hipness and away from the future. This series, in fact, is generally more reminiscent of *The X-Files* than of *Star Trek*, though that might partly be because Roddenberry died in 1991, well before the series actually became a reality.

In *Earth: Final Conflict*, an advanced alien race, the Taelons, arrives on Earth, calling themselves the "Companions" of Earth's people and promising to use their advanced technologies to help bring about a new era of peace and prosperity on the planet. The aliens are generally welcomed with open arms, though some humans remain suspicious that the Companions may have dark ulterior motives. These humans form an underground resistance that works to undermine the growing power of the Taelons. William Boone (Kevin Kilner), appointed director of interspecies relations for the U.S. government, joins this underground, providing the series with a strong, if complex (because he at first still believes the Taelons may yet be a great benefactor to humanity), initial protagonist.

As the first season proceeds, Boone, joined by ex-marine Lili Marquette (Lisa Howard) and others, begins to discover more and more evidence of alien treachery, including the fact that the Taelons are building a secret colony on the moon and that they are conducting secret experiments on human subjects on Earth. Meanwhile, Boone's own wife is killed on the orders of Ronald Sandoval (Von Flores), an FBI agent working as an attaché to Da'an (Leni Parker), the Taelon ambassador to the United States. When magnate Jonathan Doors (David Hemblen), head of the Doors International conglomerate and leader of the Resistance, goes public with concerns that the Companions may in fact be enemies of humanity, he gains some support but fails to prevent the aliens from gaining additional power. Their human allies (who are given cyberviral implants that increase their mental capacities but also supposedly ensure their loyalty to the Taelons) become more and more numerous, while some on Earth even worship the Companions as gods. Taelon power on Earth is further enforced by the Volunteers, a group of their allies who act as storm troopers to stamp out all opposition, increasingly converting the earth into an alien-dominated police state.

Boone is (apparently) killed at the end of the first season, but the series manages to go on. At the beginning of the second season, a new protagonist emerges in the person of Liam Kincaid (Robert Leeshock), the offspring of an alien renegade (inhabiting the body of Sandoval) and a human mother. Immediately after his birth, Kincaid develops into a fully grown human-looking adult, though his DNA carries traces of his alien ancestry. Later, Kincaid, now a major in the U.S. Army, goes on to become the personal protector of Da'an and is even allowed to forgo the usual implant because Da'an suspects his Taelon ties. Kincaid is thus placed in an ideal position to work for the Resistance, though the situation is complicated by a power struggle within the Taelon hierarchy, which leaves Da'an's rival (and, as it turns out, offspring), Zo'or (Anita La Selva), as the leader of the Taelons, with Sandoval as his security chief—and head of the Volunteers.

In Season Three, Kincaid (with his alien side now seemingly deemphasized) is joined by the beautiful Renée Palmer (Jayne Heitmeyer) in a partnership against the aliens. However, Palmer, who heads the division of Doors International devoted to developing Taelon technology for marketing on Earth, is a powerful and independent woman with an agenda of her own, and her sometimes antagonistic relationship with Kincaid is a far cry from Scully's partnership with Mulder in *The X-Files*, though sparks of sexual chemistry do sometimes occur between Palmer and Kincaid. But *Earth: Final Conflict* in other ways grows more and more reminiscent of *The X-Files* as it proceeds: plots and counterplots proliferate, and things often are not what they seem.

Eventually, Kincaid and Palmer discover that the Taelons have a history of genetically altering other species to make them tools of their own power and that they are now involved in a variety of genetic experiments on humans. These experiments are partly aimed at the production of Taelon-human hybrids due to the fact (something of a science fiction cliché) that the Taelons themselves are a dying race and need an injection of human energy to revitalize themselves. *Earth: Final Conflict* employs a number of such science fiction commonplaces, as when the communitarianism of the Taelons (they are all linked into a giant Commonality, a sort of hive mind) is opposed to the individualism of humans. All in all, though, the series is unusually complex, eschewing the easy "us versus them" oppositions that often inform alien-invasion series. Despite the existence of the Commonality, individual Taelons do have their own motivations, and they are far from being totally united in their attitude toward humans. In addition, individual Taelons are multidimensional. Da'an is presented in a particularly sympathetic light, but even Zo'or, the chief Taelon villain, has a sympathetic side. Similarly, there are both good and bad humans, and individual humans tend to have complex motivations.

Thus, even Sandoval, the chief human villain, can sometimes be the object of sympathy, though he can also often be far more villainous than the Taelons. In addition, again echoing *The X-Files*, many of the most sinister machinations in the series are performed not by aliens but by secret "black ops" organizations within the U.S. government.

The situation is complicated still further by the appearance of other alien races, such as the individualistic Jaridians, archenemies of the Taelons. By the middle of the fourth season, in the episode "The Summit" (January 22, 2001), it becomes clear that both the Taelons and the Jaridians are offshoots of a single ancestor species, the Atavus, which split into the two new rival species eight million years earlier. Both of those species are now dying and both hope to use human DNA in one way or another to repair their genetic faults, while Da'an (unsuccessfully) attempts in this episode to effect a rejoining with the Jaridians in order to resurrect the more hardy Atavus form.

By the end of the fourth season, this attempt has led to the resurrection of the Atavus and to the virtual destruction of the Taelons and Jaridians. Kincaid is apparently killed as well, leaving Palmer alone to lead the fight against the seemingly vicious, vampirelike Atavus, who are now bent on a conquest of the earth. In the fifth season, a tougher and more muscular Palmer (now clad in denim, leather, and muscle shirts) carries on the battle, in a mode perhaps modeled after Linda Hamilton's Sarah Connor in the film *Terminator 2* (1991), including the fact that many regard her as insane when she attempts to convince them that the Atavus even exist. Palmer is, however, still aided by J Street, and even occasionally by William Boone, who turns out not to have been killed years earlier but merely to have been kept in stasis by Sandoval. Boone is, however, killed in the ensuing action, after a brief romantic fling with Palmer. Most of the fifth season is extremely dark, with the Atavus appearing to be a purely evil foe. However, the season and the series end on a decidedly Roddenberry-like note of conciliation. Kincaid reemerges, now sharing the universal consciousness of all alien species; he then helps Palmer to gain control of the Taelon mother ship, which they use to return the surviving Atavus (who aren't all bad, after all) to their home planet. Then Kincaid and Palmer set out with the lone surviving Taelon on a new mission to explore the galaxy in the name of humanity.

The Canadian-produced *Earth: Final Conflict* thus ultimately returns to the *Star Trek* model, despite its earlier forays into darkness. Not so for *Lexx*, another Canadian series. Though chock full of traditional science fiction formulas and techniques, *Lexx* is more a parody than science fiction proper. It depends for most of its effects on the ways its treatment of standard science fiction themes deviates from (and sometimes openly mocks) conventional expectations and on the fact that it focuses so heavily on themes (especially sexual ones) that have typically been avoided (or at least treated with kid gloves) on SFTV, even though they have been prominent in science fiction literature since the 1960s.

Still, both this parody and exploration of unusual themes work only for audiences who understand the traditions of the genre. Thus, even the unprecedented *Lexx* depends, in its own way, on a certain element of nostalgia, or at least of recollection. *Lexx*, like most of the best science fiction series, develops an elaborate mythology that explains conditions in its fictional world and provides a basic backdrop against which the action of the series occurs. In the case of *Lexx*, however, the mythology may be a bit too elaborate, almost to the point of ridiculousness. Like all of the best satire, *Lexx* depends for its impact precisely on going a bit too far, on creating exaggerated situations that help audiences to see its subject matter in a new light. In the mythology of *Lexx*, there are two parallel universes: a universe of light (in which the initial action is set), and a universe of darkness, ignorance, and evil (which turns out, in a not-so-subtle ironic reversal, to be the universe in which our own Earth exists). The light universe, however, is a pretty dark place in its own right, dominated by the dystopian regime of "His Divine Shadow," the mystical (and brutal) head of the Divine Order and ruler of the League of 20,000 Planets, centered on the capital planet of the Cluster.

In the first season—a series of four two-hour made-for-television movies—a revolt against His Divine Shadow triggers a chain of events that leaves the main characters in flight from the Cluster aboard the stolen *Lexx*, a gigantic insect that has been genetically engineered by His Divine Shadow to serve not only as high-speed interstellar spacecraft but also as the most powerful destructive weapon in the universe, able to destroy entire planets with a single blast. Unfortunately, the *Lexx* can only be controlled by the holder of the "key," a sort of magical energy force that can only be carried by one person at a time. In this case, by sheer accident, the key ends up in the person of everyman Stanley Tweedle (Brian Downey), a low-level security guard who had previously been sentenced to death for a minor infraction. As captain of the *Lexx*, the selfish, cowardly, and lecherous Stan has power that contrasts sharply with his decidedly unheroic nature, creating numerous incongruities and opportunities for comedy and satire.

Also aboard the *Lexx* are an escaped love slave, Zev Bellringer (Eva Habermann), and a former "divine assassin," Kai (Michael McManus), the last of the heroic Brunnen-G, a race of romantic warriors destroyed by the forces of His Divine Shadow. As outlined in the initial season, Zev was raised in a small cubicle on the planet B3K expressly to serve as a wife, but turns out to be unsuited for her intended role in life: physically unattractive, she also resents her husband-to-be and insults him upon their first meeting. As a punishment, she is sent to the Cluster to undergo conditioning to be a love slave, which involves a physical conversion that makes her look like the fetching Habermann and a psychological conditioning that revs up her libido and also supposedly prepares her so that she will fall hopelessly in love with the next man she sees, who will presumably be her new master. However, the process goes awry during this final stage. In the ensuing chaos, Zev's DNA is mixed with that of a deadly Cluster Lizard, endowing her with courage, aggressiveness, and superhuman strength and speed. Meanwhile, the final conditioning is done not on her but on the decapitated head of 790 (voiced by Jeffrey Hirschfield), the robot in charge of her conditioning process. As a result, the ridiculous-looking robot head (which contrasts sharply with the generally sophisticated special effects of the series and is reminiscent of the intelligent toaster of the early *Red Dwarf*) falls madly in love with Zev, whom he subsequently attempts doggedly to seduce, even though he has no body. His advances to Zev (which include the composition of a variety of obscene love songs and poems) provide some of the series' campiest comic moments. Later in the series, 790's role becomes even more hilarious after an accident causes him to believe that he is female and to shift his desires to Kai. Afterward, the unscrupulous 790 is so desperate to have Kai to him/herself that he/she continually tries to get rid of the rest of the crew, making the head a liability somewhat in the mode of Dr. Smith of *Lost in Space*.

At the beginning of Season Two, *Lexx* switched to a more conventional series format, which caused Habermann to leave the show due to other commitments. However, borrowing a motif from *Doctor Who*, the show was able to continue her character by regenerating her, this time as Xev Bellringer (now played by the voluptuous, swollen-lipped Xenia Seeberg), whose exaggerated sexual attributes well match her accelerated libido, which leaves her anxious to have sex with virtually any man in the universe—except, of course, poor Stan, who is desperate to have sex with her. If all of this sounds preposterous, then the interpersonal dynamics of the crew of the *Lexx* become even more bizarre with the inclusion of Kai, the man in the universe that Xev desires most of all. Kai is handsome, deadly, and indestructible. Unfortunately, his powers and his lack of fear come mostly from the fact he was killed two thousand years earlier by His Divine Shadow, then reanimated for use as an assassin, powered by a substance called proto-blood. Subsequently, Kai fulfills his prophesied role as the killer of His Divine Shadow, after which he continues to operate on a continually diminishing supply of proto-blood, the shortage of which requires him to be kept mostly in cryostasis, thawed out for use only in crises, during which he frequently saves the other crew members from disaster. Meanwhile, being dead, he has no feelings or emotions and thus cannot return Xev's affections. McManus's deadpan delivery (which largely involves statements of the various things that "the dead" do not do—such as think, feel, or care much about anything) is another central running joke in the series.

Each of the three full-length seasons of *Lexx* focuses on a single continuous plot and theme. In the second season, the *Lexx* and its crew run afoul of the evil mad scientist Mantrid (Dieter Laser, in a genuinely hilarious over-the-top performance), who creates a race of self-replicating drones (robot arms, actually) that eventually devour and destroy the entire light universe by using its material to create more drones. Not to worry, though; at the end of this season, the *Lexx* and its crew manage to escape into the dark universe to continue their adventures there. Before leaving the light universe, however, they experience a number of preposterous adventures that allow the series to satirize numerous aspects of life on Earth, despite the fact that they occur in a completely different universe. For example, in the episode "791" (February 5, 1999), 790 finally acquires a male cyborg body, which will presumably allow him to have sex with Xev at last. Unfortunately, the cyborg is gay, so the newly embodied 790 ends up trying to have sex (anal rape, actually) with a horrified Stan instead, though Kai removes the head from the cyborg body in the nick of time. In a somewhat similar gender-bending motif, Stan and Xev finally have sex in the episode "Love Grows" (January 22, 1999). Unfortunately, for Stan, toxic wastes have caused their genders to be reversed, so that, during the act, he is a woman, while Xev is a man, leading him to conclude afterward that the whole experience didn't really count.

In "Lyekka" (December 25, 1998), the *Lexx* encounters the down-home, good-old-boy crew of a primitive space capsule from the planet Potato Hoe, the hokey culture of which is suspiciously earthlike. Indeed, their cornball emphasis on "virtues" and "values" is reminiscent not only of a great deal of terrestrial political rhetoric, but also of the wholesome themes of more conventional science fiction series such as *Star Trek*. This episode also introduces Lyekka (Louise Wischermann), a man-eating plant that takes on the appearance of a beautiful young woman once desired by Stan. Lyekka, who becomes a recurring character in the series, basically means well, but her nature makes her highly dangerous and (by the fourth season) nearly leads her and her kind to devour the entire population of Earth. In this episode, meanwhile, she merely eats the astronauts from Potato Hoe, using their proteins to construct the regenerated Xev.

Lexx's satire on good-old-boy culture (which is so extreme that it can ultimately be read as a satirical commentary on such satires) is even more outrageous in the episode "White Trash" (January 29, 1999), in which the crew discovers that a family of escaped convicts (who also turn out to be hillbilly cannibals) have stowed away on the *Lexx*, which is so large that any number of weird creatures can be hidden on board at any given time. The hillbillies hijack the *Lexx* and take it to their planet, then lure Xev down to the surface for a redneck gang-rape party. Luckily, Kai (as usual) saves the day, and the *Lexx* blows up the planet, though Pa, the leader of the hillbilly family, manages to get back on board the *Lexx*, where Lyekka promptly eats him.

Season Two also includes such episodes as "Lafftrack" (January 8, 1999), in which the *Lexx* visits "TV World," a resort planet designed to allow visitors to act out roles in their favorite television series, accompanied by casts of androids. The planet has long been abandoned (the two planets that sponsor it destroyed each other in a ratings war), but its technology still operates, so the crew of the *Lexx* is able to participate in various ridiculous programs—much to their own peril, as it turns out. Stan's performances, in particular, are so bad that he is consigned to be decapitated as part of "The Specialty Show," which parodies the tendency toward violent spectacle in earthly television. Indeed, the programs on TV World serve as parodies of a variety of television genres, such as soap operas and game shows. This episode thus illustrates the tendency of *Lexx* to use its science fiction motifs to construct exaggerated situations that allow for commentaries on the inflated and formulaic nature of a variety of cultural forms, including all conventional television programming, science fiction or otherwise.

"Lafftrack" is indicative of the tendency of individual episodes of *Lexx* to focus on specific genres or individual works as objects of parody. For example, "Twilight" (March 5, 1999) is basically an extended parody of zombie films such as *Night of the Living Dead*, while "Woz" (March 19, 1999) is an extended takeoff on *The Wizard of Oz*. "Wake the Dead" (February 12, 1999) plays out very much like a typical slasher film (complete with the requisite girl-in-the-shower scene, accompanied by music similar to that played during the famous shower scene from *Psycho*), as a gang of teenage delinquents from outer space boards the *Lexx* with murderous results. This episode incorporates other allusions as well, as when 790, tossed aside by a Kai momentarily intent on murdering the entire crew, remarks, "Oh, the horror," recalling the dying remarks of Kurtz in Joseph Conrad's *Heart of Darkness* (or Francis Ford Coppola's *Apocalypse Now*). The episode then ends with a shot of a spinning door passing the *Lexx* in space, very much in the mode of the opening graphics of *The Twilight Zone*.

In the third (and possibly weakest) season of *Lexx*, the crew members awake in the dark universe after four thousand years in stasis to find themselves trapped in the vicinity of an opposed pair of warring planets, unable to move on because the starving *Lexx* is too weak from hunger to fly. These planets, one covered mostly by ocean (the water planet) and one by searing deserts (the fire planet), turn out to be thinly veiled allegorical stand-ins for heaven and hell. In the meantime, these extreme settings provide a variety of opportunities for the kinds of exaggerated situations that are the stock-in-trade of *Lexx*. For example, in the season's fourth episode, "Boomtown" (February 27, 2000), Stan discovers a water-planet island utopia on which the inhabitants are devoted to around-the-clock sexual pleasure. Surrounded by a bevy of willing young beauties, Stan seems to have realized his fantasies at last—until his partners' insatiability leads him to realize that it is indeed possible to have too much of a good thing.

By the end of the third season, both planets are destroyed by the *Lexx*, with the destruction of the fire planet sending all the evil souls condemned to reside there to another distant planet where they might feel at home—which turns out to be Earth, of course. In the fourth season, the *Lexx* travels to Earth as well, bringing the series to a hilarious climax in which its satire and parody reach a new peak thanks to the ability to address the foibles of Earth culture all the more directly. Of course, the culture of Earth, seen from the perspective of such outsiders as the crew of the *Lexx*, appears particularly bizarre, and one of the strengths of the fourth season is its depiction of Earth as one of the strangest places ever visited by the *Lexx*, even as the planet itself is presented as nothing particularly special, except that the earth is described as being at the center of the darkest part of the dark universe. Otherwise, however, it is treated as entirely un- remarkable, as a completely typical example of a "type 13 planet" in its last stages of development, approaching the point where these particularly uninteresting planets almost invariably end up destroy- ing themselves.

The fourth season of *Lexx* parodies a wide range of terrestrial cul- tural products, from women-in-prison movies to adult films, from Dracula stories to Japanese monster movies, from *Apocalypse Now* to Shakespeare's *A Midsummer Night's Dream*. Thus, the episode "P4X" (July 27, 2001) finds Xev as a woman-in-chains in the Texas Prison for Women, where she becomes an online star after her tribulations are Webcast on the Internet. In "Fluff Daddy" (September 14, 2001), Stan fulfills (sort of) his dream of joining the porn industry. In "Walpurgis Night" (August 24, 2001) and "Vlad" (September 7, 2001), the gang travels to Transylvania to visit Dracula's castle, which Kai suspects is harboring another survivor from the Divine Order. "A Midsummer's Nightmare" (January 15, 2002) is largely a takeoff on Shakespeare, while "Apocalexx Now" (March 29, 2002) features an outrageous trip to Vietnam, in which Kai, Xev, and Lyekka travel upriver in a small boat, echoing the journey that provides the cen- tral plot strand of *Apocalypse Now*, though this time the journey ends with the nuclear destruction of Vietnam by order of the president of the United States. "Viva Lexx Vegas" (April 5, 2002) parodies the whole Las Vegas scene, meanwhile coming off as a sort of combina- tion of a mummy movie and a gangster flick. Finally, in "Lyekka vs. Japan" (April 19, 2002), a gigantic Lyekka threatens to crush Tokyo beneath her colossal feet, recalling any number of early Japanese monster movies.

As usual, television comes in for considerable mockery as well, especially in "Xevivor" (August 10, 2001), which lampoons *Survivor* and other reality television series, while also commenting on the lengths to which television executives in general are willing to go to get higher ratings. In this episode, a preposterously exploitative re-ality program (set on remote Zig Zig Island), features Xev (already something of a celebrity due to her earlier Internet exposure) as the prize, while a group of heavily muscled, he-man hunks compete for the right to have a night of sex with her. Stan, meanwhile, manages to become a contestant as well, though he seems to have little chance of winning. Then the hunks start to disappear one by one, killed off, as it turns out, by another army of alien replicant drones that has invaded the earth. In a motif that could occur only on *Lexx*, these replicants (essentially carrots with mechanical legs) take their victims by shooting up their anuses, then possessing their bodies and turn-ing them into killer zombies.[1] Of course, Kai eventually rescues Xev and Stan from the island, while later in the series the *Lexx* (newly invigorated by eating Holland) destroys the asteroid base of the carrot drones, rendering them inoperative. (Unfortunately, a second, larger asteroid ship appears, leading to the destruction of the earth, the *Lexx*, and Kai, though a new baby *Lexx* is reborn, carrying Xev and Stan off toward a new home planet.)

The fourth season of *Lexx* includes the series' most explicit politi-cal satire as well. In a sort of ongoing gag, various personages from previous seasons are reincarnated on Earth, generally as powerful political figures. Thus, Prince (Nigel Bennett), the satanic ruler of the fire planet from Season Three, now resurfaces as the evil head of the Bureau of Alcohol, Tobacco, and Firearms (ATF)—and possibly the most powerful figure on the planet. Meanwhile, his minion from the fire planet, Priest (Rolf Kanies), is now the president of the United States, though he continues to take his orders from Prince, to whom he remains a fawning bootlicker despite his new title. And the can-nibalistic wicked witch Giggerota from earlier seasons (Ellen Dubin) now reappears as Miami real estate agent G. G. Rota, eventually also becoming the first female pope (and ultimately a snack for Lyekka).

Such figures allow the series to skewer the U.S. government, the Catholic Church, and other images of authority on Earth. Other po-litically motivated groups, from right-wing militias to idealistic young environmentalists, come in for considerable satirical commentary as well. Ultimately, however, while *Lexx* is almost certainly the funniest and most outrageous science fiction television series ever produced, it is very limited in its appeal, largely because none of the characters are really likable. Like everything else in the series, the characters are exaggerated, more caricature than character proper. As a result, it is impossible for viewers to identify with the characters—and the series—in the way they typically have for most popular science fiction series.

The first two *Star Trek* series serve as the prototypes for these kinds of character-driven science fiction television. However, one turn-of-the-century series may go beyond even *Star Trek* in its ability to produce compelling characters—and even more compelling relationships among characters. In fact, the Australian-produced *Farscape* combines genuinely interesting characters (and relationships) with tense drama, quirky humor, and some of the most spectacular visuals in the history of science fiction television to produce what has widely been described as the first truly adult series in the genre. The program attracted many loyal fans over the years—and a storm of protest when the series was canceled by the Sci Fi Channel in fall 2002, its last episodes to be broadcast in the first part of 2003.

Created by Rockne S. O'Bannon (who had earlier written the 1988 film *Alien Nation*, which inspired a TV series on Fox that ran for a single season in 1989–90), *Farscape* was made by the Jim Henson Company partly as a showcase for their capabilities in combining computer-generated images and advanced puppetry to produce highly sophisticated special effects. As a result, *Farscape* is a very technically impressive series with some of the best effects—and most interesting-looking aliens—ever to appear on science fiction television. Indeed, the entire look of the series, including backgrounds and general color schemes, is absolutely gorgeous. Much of the content is quite interesting as well, as *Farscape* takes to a whole new level the *Star Trek* premise of a multiethnic crew aboard a huge starship that almost has a personality of its own. Indeed, *Moya*, the *Farscape* starship, is an intelligent life-form in her own right, dedicated to serving her crew but sometimes also with an agenda of her own. She can communicate with the crew only through the intermediary of Pilot, a highly specialized being (played by an extremely sophisticated puppet) who has a special rapport with the ship but can also communicate with the other species aboard. The upper part of Pilot's multi-armed body operates various controls and communicates with the crew; the rest of his body consists of a network of neural tentacles that extend throughout *Moya*, furthering his connection with her. Pilot takes great pleasure in serving the crew, but his first loyalty is to *Moya* whenever there is a conflict.

Of course, *Lexx* had already done the living ship idea (and the Vorlons of *Babylon 5* use living ships), but the motif comes off somewhat more effectively in *Farscape*, partly because of the interesting symbiotic relationship between *Moya* and Pilot and partly because *Moya* simply has more personality than *Lexx* or the Vorlon ships, though she also becomes one of the few genuinely alien aliens in science fiction television. Despite her otherness, *Moya* is a highly positive character with which audiences can easily sympathize, though she is at times almost a stereotypical nurturing female. *Moya* feels a great responsibility to take care of her crew, while much of the first season centers around the fact that *Moya* becomes pregnant, behaving erratically and eventually producing an offspring for which she feels genuine affection. *Moya* is perhaps also more interesting than *Lexx* because she is totally peaceful (and unarmed), whereas *Lexx* is an unmatched destructive force. On the other hand, *Moya*'s baby, *Talyn*, is born bristling with armaments, the product of genetic experiments to try to produce just such an armed living vessel. Meanwhile, as the series evolves, the formidable *Talyn* becomes an important character in his own right.

Only one member of *Moya*'s crew, handsome young American astronaut/scientist John Crichton (Ben Browder), is from Earth, or even human, for that matter. As the series begins, Crichton goes on an experimental spaceflight in which he and his craft are sucked into a wormhole. He emerges from the wormhole in a distant portion of the galaxy in the midst of a space battle, his sudden appearance causing the crash of one of several attack craft that are swarming about a huge vessel, on which he takes refuge. On that vessel, which turns out to be *Moya*, he meets a strange, alien crew of escaped convicts, who eventually become his comrades. *Farscape* is very much an ensemble show, and in many ways the various crew members are roughly equal in importance. However, Crichton remains a sort of anchor point for audiences, given that he is a contemporary earthling from the same culture as the viewers. Indeed, this sort of identification provides one reason for the popularity of present-time science fiction series, while Crichton's emergence in a distant part of the galaxy still involves him with the kind of advanced technologies that are the stock-in-trade of science fiction.

Contemporary popular culture (mostly American) provides a crucial part of Crichton's dialogue, which is peppered with various allusions to this culture, a motif that creates a sort of dramatic irony in that audiences will generally understand his references, while no one else on *Moya* ever has any idea what he is talking about. Crichton's almost constant flow of references spans everything from *Animal House* to a variety of classic television programs, from *The Wizard of Oz* to Kentucky Fried Chicken. *Star Trek* (of course) is a particular favorite, though his references to that near-sacred text of TV science fiction are sometimes less than reverent. Thus, in the two-part episode "Self-Inflicted Wounds," Crichton responds to one character's complaints about conditions aboard a sabotaged and seemingly dying *Moya* by sarcastically exclaiming, "Welcome to the Federation starship SS *Butt-crack*!" Most of the episode "Revenging Angel" (August 10, 2001) occurs inside Crichton's mind as he lies in a coma, giving us a good look at his thoughts. These thoughts turn out to consist primarily of a patchwork of quotations from contemporary American popular culture, including references to Marilyn Monroe, *Forrest Gump*, *Who Framed Roger Rabbit?*, the Oscars, and a variety of children's cartoons. Indeed, much of the episode is in animation, playing out as a *Road-runner* cartoon, with Crichton as the Roadrunner. In this episode, Crichton identifies *Star Trek*'s Kirk as his boyhood hero but is quickly reminded, "That was a television show—and he did Priceline commercials!"

This constant flow of pop cultural allusions might eventually become annoying rather than amusing, except that Crichton's style of speech and thought actually has an understandable motivation. Lost in a distant part of the galaxy and immersed in a totally alien environment, his constant references can be taken as an attempt to hold on to his own cultural identity, the tenuousness of which partly accounts for his growing instability in Season Three. Earth culture also impacts the plots of individual episodes as when, in the two-part "Self-Inflicted Wounds" (March 30 and April 6, 2001), an alien ship picks up a transmission of *The Three Stooges*, making Crichton feel that Earth must be somewhere nearby. Individual episode titles ("Back and Back and Back to the Future," "Won't Get Fooled Again," "Suns and Lovers") are often allusive to modern and contemporary Earth culture. That these titles are often humorous reinforces Crichton's quips as a source of the hip humor that underlies the drama of the series. The dialogue and content of some episodes, especially in specific scenes, can also be quite humorous, involving such motifs as a variety of comic interspecies misunderstandings and Crichton's tendency to go a bit bonkers under extreme pressure.

Despite Crichton's centrality, the dynamic interrelationships among the crew are the key to the success of *Farscape*. Because each member of the crew is from a different species, they have widely varying personalities, making for especially sharp character differentiation. For example, the large and powerful Ka D'Argo (Anthony Simcoe), marked by his distinctive facial tattoos and tentacles, is a Luxan warrior, a creature of violence. Bold and impulsive, he is set (at least initially) against the somewhat more human-looking (but entirely blue) Pa'u Zotoh Zhaan (Virginia Hey), an 812-year-old tenth-level Delvian priest. Zhaan, however, is in many ways even more alien (in human terms) than D'Argo, given that she is a plant, while he is at least an animal. Devoted to the pursuit of spirituality and inner tranquility, Zhaan seems the opposite of D'Argo in numerous ways, some of which come a bit close to gender stereotyping, with her feminine soulfulness opposed to his macho muscularity. On the other hand, the gendered opposition between D'Argo and Zhaan is not nearly as simple as it might first appear. D'Argo is a warrior with a sensitive heart of gold; his experiences of camaraderie with the others aboard ship (and especially the influence of Zhaan) help him to get in touch with his softer side. Zhaan, meanwhile, has a violent side left over from her pre-priest days as a creature driven by hatred and emotion. Indeed, while both D'Argo and Zhaan had been imprisoned for the murder of their mates, it turns out that D'Argo was framed for the murder of his wife, Lo'Lann, while Zhaan really did kill her lover, whom she felt had become a danger to the entire Delvian community with his lust for power.

Lo'Lann was a member of the completely human-looking Sebacean species and had actually been killed by her own brother in an action motivated by racial hatred over the thought of her marriage to a Luxan. A third member of *Moya*'s crew, Officer Aeryn Sun (Claudia Black), is also a Sebacean. In particular, she is a former member of the highly trained military group known as the Peacekeepers, mercenaries who hire themselves out to the highest bidder for use as soldiers, police, and even prison guards. Indeed, *Moya* had formerly been captured by the Peacekeepers for use as a prison ship, and her original crew are all former prisoners who had taken over the ship in a mutiny just before Crichton's arrival. In the subsequent action, Aeryn is declared contaminated because she has too much contact with the rebels, forcing her to join her former enemies.

If D'Argo and Zhaan are sometimes set off as an opposed pair, then the same can also be said of Crichton and Aeryn, though in this case the usual gender roles are less conventional. Aeryn, trained for a life of discipline and destruction, is still working to overcome her military background, while Crichton is much more sensitive (and has much more of a sense of humor). However, as with D'Argo and Zhaan, the two tend to influence one another, blurring the sharpness of the boundary between them. As the series progresses, in fact, the two develop a distinct sexual tension. In the late first-season episode "A Human Reaction," the two even make love, though the experience is somewhat clouded by the fact that both are involved in a sort of virtual reality experiment being conducted by alien scientists (from an advanced race known as the "Ancients," to test whether their race would be welcome if they migrated to Earth—their planet, in a time-honored science fiction cliché, having now been rendered uninhabitable). The Ancients conclude, incidentally, that Earth isn't for them: reconstructing a virtual Earth from Crichton's memories, they find earthlings savage and xenophobic.

By the third season, the Crichton-Aeryn relationship reaches a fever pitch and becomes a major plot line. Meanwhile, if the relationship between Aeryn and Crichton suggests that she is not all that inhuman, the fact is that all of the aliens aboard *Moya* have suspiciously human characteristics, perhaps with the exception of Pilot and *Moya* herself, though even the very alien-looking Pilot begins to display more human reactions and emotions as the series proceeds. Even the fifth crew member, the very alien-looking Rygel XVI (again played by a sophisticated puppet, though the haughty Rygel hilariously declares in one episode that he is "nobody's puppet"), displays many very recognizable human characteristics. He is a lovable scoundrel who constantly gets the other crew members in trouble with his selfish and unprincipled behavior, but he comes through for them in a pinch when they need him the most. Rygel is the former Dominar of the Hynerian Empire, once the ruler of over 600 billion subjects but now deposed by his own brother, who sent him into imprisonment by the Peacekeepers. Rygel's constant eating fuels his tendency to burp and fart frequently, and his helium farts (which cause those around him to talk in chipmunk voices, sometimes at the most inopportune moments) are a stock source of humor in the series. He is also hopelessly venal, constantly scavenging and maneuvering in an effort to find ways to profit from the various difficult situations in which the crew members constantly seem to find themselves. Yet he is also a skilled negotiator and diplomat, qualities that are frequently of great value as the crew encounters one alien culture after another.

Much of the initial plot of the series is driven by the fact that the Peacekeepers are determined to recapture *Moya* and her crew. And they are even more dedicated to this mission after Crichton arrives, because it turns out that the craft that crashed upon Crichton's appearance from the wormhole had been piloted by the brother of Peacekeeper Captain Bailar Crais (Lani John Tupu, who also supplies the voice of Pilot), who then swears vengeance for his brother's death. To escape the Peacekeepers, *Moya* flies off into the Uncharted Territories, leaving her and her crew free for the moment but also totally lost. Much of the subsequent action is then motivated by the attempts of the crew to find their way back to their various homes, encountering one strange alien civilization after another—all with the Peacekeepers still hot on their trail.

Along the way, *Moya* periodically picks up new crew members, with the cast gradually expanding in the course of the series. Near the end of the first season, the crew is joined by the enigmatic Stark (Paul Goddard), a Banik slave rescued from captivity at a Peacekeeper base. Half mad from his extended torture at the hands of the Peacekeepers, Stark at first makes only occasional appearances in the series, but he is fully installed as a crew member by the end of Season Two. In this season, he is seemingly killed, his atoms dispersed into space. However, we later discover that he is able to reconstitute himself because he is actually a creature of energy who uses his human-looking body only as a container. Meanwhile, we learn that he is a "Stykera," one who has a special affinity with the dying, whose suffering he can sense from long distances. Stark becomes something of a soul mate to Zhaan, but his fluctuating sanity and erratic behavior make him a rather problematic member of the crew, which he leaves in the third season, only to return near the end of the fourth.

Also problematic (and also added to the crew near the end of the first season) is the willowy Chiana (Gigi Edgley), a member of the highly advanced Nebari race. The very youthful Chiana is a combination street urchin, thief, con artist, and prostitute, and the fact that she is an escaped prisoner helps her to fit right in with the *Farscape* crew, even if she is a bit younger and more immature than the other crew members. Among other things, she adds balance to the show, providing a partner for Rygel in much the way that Crichton teams up with Aeryn and that D'Argo and Zhaan constitute a pair. Indeed, Chiana and Rygel quickly establish an odd sort of bond, though it certainly takes some time before Chiana, accustomed to getting by entirely on her own, can feel that she is genuinely a member of the group.

The extremely sexy Chiana also adds a touch of spice and opens up new, racier plot options. Quite young herself, she also seems intended to help the show appeal to a younger audience. The same things might be said for another young female character who gradually becomes a full-fledged crew member in the course of Season Three. Joolushko Tunay Fento Hovalis (Jool for short, played by Tammy MacIntosh) is a member of the Interion species, which, we are told, may be closely related to humans. She is also quite attractive, which might account for some of the initial friction between her and Chiana, though most of this friction seems class-based. As opposed to Chiana, educated on the streets, Jool has led a relatively privileged life and has attended all the best schools. As a result, she is spoiled, pretentious, and (especially at first) almost insufferably arrogant and self-centered. However, she is also extremely intelligent and knowledgeable, which comes in quite handy and helps her gradually to fit in. Jool's education is especially valuable because she is able to step in for Zhaan as the ship's doctor after Zhaan (due to the departure of Hey) is killed off in "Self-Inflicted Wounds."

After spending Season Three with the crew, Jool leaves to pursue her own work as an archaeologist at the beginning of Season Four, though she is quickly replaced by the somewhat similar-looking Sikozu Svala Shanti Sugaysi Shanu (Raelee Hill). Sikozu is a member of the Kalish species, who have long been oppressed by the evil Scarrans, whom they much despise. Sikozu brings a number of interesting mental and physical characteristics to the show, meanwhile illustrating the ability of the series to move forward smoothly even with a number of changes in the cast, though Crichton and Aeryn remain the anchor characters throughout. Ultimately, the courageous Sikozu is a far more interesting and effective crew member than Jool had been, especially after, late in the season, she turns out to be a genetically engineered member of the Kalish underground, able to emit radiation that kills Scarrans (who are otherwise virtually indestructible) almost immediately. The fourth season also sees the addition of Utu-Noranti Prolatong (Melissa Jaffer), a witchlike, three-eyed old woman from the planet Trask. Noranti adds considerable humor to the show with her horrid cooking, poor hygiene, and uncouth ways, while her spells also add an additional weapon to the crew's arsenal.

During the second season, Chiana and D'Argo strike up a torrid sexual relationship, even as the sexual sparks between Crichton and Aeryn increase as well. The D'Argo-Chiana relationship crumbles at the beginning of Season Three, when Chiana (partly out of fear of commitment in her relationship with D'Argo) also begins an affair with D'Argo's half-Sebacean son, Jothee (Matt Newton), illustrating the way in which *Farscape* is willing to boldly go where no science fiction television has gone before. In this and other ways, Chiana's questionable (and generally self-serving) morals provide a major source of complexity in a series whose characters are far from the paragons of the first two *Star Trek* series. *Farscape* also gained energy late in the first season with the addition of a new, more evil and repulsive villain and pursuer, Scorpius (Wayne Pygram), though Crais continued to make periodic appearances as well. The handsome Crais was a complex villain made somewhat sympathetic by the torments he suffered due to the death of his brother and by troubled memories of his own past, as when he and his brother were turned over by their father to the Peacekeepers for training in early childhood. However, the new villain, Scorpius, is hideously ugly and unremittingly evil. Scorpius is part Scarran (an evil and repulsive alien race) and part Sebacean, which proves to be a very problematic combination, given that these two species seem to have completely incompatible needs. For example, Scarrans love heat and Sebaceans hate it, so Scorpius has to wear a thermal regulator suit to help achieve a balance, while a weird cylindrical implant in his head contains cooling rods to help with temperature regulation.

As a villain, Scorpius draws upon a number of motifs from science fiction tradition. For example, he is the inventor of the Aurora Chair, an interrogation device that (often very painfully) extracts memories from those who are placed in it. This chair thus recalls classic texts such as *1984* and *A Clockwork Orange*, among many others. Scorpius initially seems both totally evil and single-minded, driven almost exclusively by a desire to master the technology of creating and maintaining traversable wormholes for use in interstellar space travel. He thus has a special interest in Crichton, partly because of Crichton's prior experience in traveling through a wormhole, but mostly because he is convinced that the Ancients have planted knowledge of wormhole technology deep in Crichton's brain, even if Crichton himself is not conscious of this. Much of the action of the second season is motivated by the fact that Scorpius, while interrogating Crichton in the Aurora Chair in Season One, planted a chip in his head that is designed to extract the wormhole knowledge but that also causes Crichton to see tormenting visions of Scorpius (whom he addresses as "Harvey" in another of his pop cultural references), who is, in this sense, literally inside his head. As the series proceeds, Crichton's internal conversations with Harvey are typically set in imaginary settings such as scenes from old movies, such as World War II and classic horror films.

By the end of the second season, Crais (who has now become *Talyn*'s pilot and only crew member) has become a much more positive character, partly because of his relationship with *Talyn*. Thus, in the rousing three-part sequence late in the second season, "Liars, Guns, and Money" (January 5–19, 2001), Crais and *Talyn* come to the rescue of *Moya* and her crew, who have gotten themselves into a seemingly hopeless situation in an attempt to storm a heavily fortified Shadow Depository (initially in order to acquire funds to pay a ransom to free Jothee, but ultimately to rescue Crichton from Scorpius, who now holds him captive). Eventually, Crais becomes a full-fledged member of *Moya*'s crew, but he and *Talyn* are both killed at the end of Season Three, sacrificing themselves to save all the others—and to throw a huge monkey wrench into Scorpius's efforts to develop wormhole technology.

The epic "Liars, Guns, and Money" is indicative of the tendency of *Farscape* to grow grander and more cinematic as the series proceeds. Indeed, this trilogy, which includes numerous spectacular, large-scale battle scenes, is really part of a five-part sequence that also includes the subsequent cliff-hanger at the end of the second season, "Die Me, Dichotomy" (January 26, 2001), and its resolution at the beginning of Season Three, "Season of Death" (March 16, 2001). Though season-ending cliff-hangers had become a cliché in science fiction television by this time, "Die Me, Dichotomy" is particularly effective. Filled with frenetic action that brings together numerous strands from earlier in the season, this episode leaves the various characters in particularly dire straits. Aeryn, for example, appears to have been killed, while the bulk of *Moya*'s crew prepares to go their separate ways, dispersing across the galaxy. Scorpius appears triumphant and on the verge of acquiring his long-sought wormhole technology. And, in the concluding shot of the season, Crichton lies screaming, strapped into a surgical chair; Scorpius's chip has been removed at the expense of destroying Crichton's power of coherent speech, while the only surgeon capable of restoring his speech appears to have been killed by Scorpius.

In "Season of Death," Zhaan manages to revive Aeryn (though this drains her own energies and contributes to her decline toward death), and Crichton recovers his speech, though a residual Harvey remains inside his mind even without the chip. Nevertheless, before Season Three is over, Crichton himself is killed, this time once and for all. Luckily, however, this is *Farscape*, and there is already an extra copy of Crichton on the scene due to the fact that he has been "twinned" (another old *Star Trek* motif), so that, for an extended period of the season there are now two of him, apparently identical, and both speaking in quotations from popular culture. Indeed, much of Season Three proceeds with two Crichtons (distinguished by different-colored T-shirts) after he is twinned by the evil Kaarvok (Shane Briant) in "Eat Me" (April 29, 2001), one of many *Farscape* episodes to draw strongly upon horror film motifs. These two twins operate relatively independently, with the black-shirted Crichton joining Aeryn, Crais, Rygel, and Stark aboard *Talyn*, while D'Argo stays aboard *Moya* with Chiana, Jool, and the green-shirted Crichton.

It is the black-shirted Crichton who pursues a torrid sexual relationship with Aeryn during this period, his subsequent death allowing the series to replay the growth of this relationship, now between Aeryn and the green-shirted Crichton, complicated by Aeryn's memories of her relationship with the black-shirted Crichton. Much of the action of Season Four revolves around Aeryn's gradually growing ability to accept the green-shirted Crichton as the same man she had earlier loved so dearly, a situation complicated by the fact that she is now pregnant, apparently by the black-shirted Crichton, though she claims the paternity is uncertain. Meanwhile, the fourth season sees a partial rehabilitation even for Scorpius, who essentially becomes a member of *Moya*'s crew, demonstrating the extreme flexibility and unpredictability of character development in *Farscape*. Indeed, one of the highlights of the fourth season is the three-parter "We're So Screwed," which largely consists of the crew's attempts to rescue Scorpius from captivity at the hands of the evil Scarrans. Indeed, by this time we have discovered that much of Scorpius's seeming evil is actually motivated by an attempt to stop the Scarrans from moving forward with their plans to colonize the galaxy, while his hatred of the Scarrans turns out to derive largely from his mistreatment at their hands, especially during his childhood as a much-abused half-breed in their midst.

Unfortunately, events related to the rescue of Scorpius cause the Scarrans to set their sights on Earth itself. In the fourth and last season, Crichton leads the crew of *Moya* in a desperate (and ultimately successful) effort to save Earth from a Scarran invasion. Meanwhile, this season (almost) ends on a romantic note, as Aeryn accepts Crichton's marriage proposal and admits that the baby is unequivocally his (though this presumably means his black-shirted incarnation). At this moment, however, an unidentified alien craft swoops down and blasts them both to smithereens. Of course, given Stark's earlier resurrection, there is no reason why they couldn't return. Indeed, this episode was originally shot not as the conclusion of the series but merely as a season-ending cliff-hanger. It ends as D'Argo screams with despair (echoing Crichton's scream at the end of Season Two), while the screen displays the announcement: "TO BE CONTINUED." The cancellation of the series subsequent to the filming of this episode throws that announcement into doubt, though of course there is always the possibility of an eventual feature film (or television special) to give the series a proper wrap-up.

Unfortunately, fairly quick cancellations have recently been the norm for science fiction television series. Of course, most network attempts to break into the science fiction genre in recent years have been dismal failures in terms of ratings. For example, NBC's extremely interesting 1996 alien invasion/government conspiracy series *Dark Skies* (which drew considerable attention because of the connection of its creative team—and its premise—with *The X-Files*) lasted only a single season of nineteen episodes, even though it attracted a core audience of die-hard fans. Even *Dark Angel,* one of the most hyped science fiction series of recent years, made a big initial splash but failed to survive its second season. The series was cocreated by *Titanic* and *Terminator 2* director James Cameron, and the Fox Network clearly hoped to parlay Cameron's name recognition into big ratings. Fox's hopes for success seemed reasonable, and the series did indeed get a great deal of attention after its premiere in fall 2000, no doubt largely because of the Cameron connection.

Dark Angel is set in a 2019–20 postapocalyptic, depression-ridden America described as "just another broke ex–super power" and "just another Third World country." In this case, marking recent changes in the global political situation as the show went on the air, the apocalypse came not from a cold war–style nuclear holocaust but from a terrorist assault on computer systems via an "electromagnetic burst" from a satellite high above the earth, leading to an all-out collapse of the American economy. In the series, this collapse is still very much in effect, and the various characters have to scramble to survive in a world of poverty, shortage, and squalor. Meanwhile, these conditions have offered the opportunity for particularly corrupt and unscrupulous forces to gain control of both the government and the business world, leading to oppressive conditions reminiscent of such dystopian classics as George Orwell's *1984*.

On the other hand, the show also suggests that these oppressive conditions merely represent an intensification of tendencies that were already in place before the "burst" rather than a completely new departure. Central to the series is Project Manticore, a sinister attempt to create and train genetically engineered supersoldiers that was well under way before the collapse. The protagonist of the series, beautiful young Max Guevara (Jessica Alba), had been among a group of these genetically enhanced children who escaped from Manticore's high-security facility back in the year 2009, before the collapse of America. We eventually learn that a total of twelve children escaped, though Max has spent the years between 2009 and 2019 not knowing whether she was the only survivor. As a result of her background, Max has superhuman speed, reflexes, and senses—but she is also bitter, cynical, and emotionally inaccessible. In addition, just as Superman had his Kryptonite, Max has her weakness, making her seem a bit more human and thus making it easier for audiences to identity and sympathize with her. In this case, Max has a flaw in her genetic design that causes her to have severe seizures if she is not constantly medicated with Tryptophan, a food supplement very difficult to procure in the depression-plagued world in which she lives.

In the pilot episode, Max meets up with Logan Cale (Michael Weatherly), a man who is her opposite in virtually every way, especially after a shooting in this episode leaves him crippled and confined to a wheelchair. In addition, as the scion of an extremely wealthy family, Logan has led a protected life as opposed to having the hardships encountered by Max. He is also extremely idealistic, and now uses his wealth, which seems to have survived the general economic collapse, in the interest of a variety of projects to do good and battle the crime and corruption that reign supreme in the society around him. For example, he uses the sophisticated computer center with which he has surrounded himself periodically to interrupt the mind-numbing television broadcasts, which are designed to procure the obedience (or at least apathy) of the general population, with minute-long messages from "Streaming Freedom Video," revealing the truth about various criminal operations and corrupt political figures.

Logan, at least ten years older than Max, serves as a sort of mentor, helping her to overcome the cynicism to which she clings by enlisting her aid in his personal fight for justice. However, especially after his shooting, he is just as emotionally closed off and repressed as she is, and the two of them go through the two-year run of the series unable to make the move to overcome the emotional barriers between them, despite the numerous indications of a powerful mutual sexual attraction. The show thus seeks to create some of the same sort of unresolved sexual tension between Max and Logan that *The X-Files* had drawn upon for so many years between Mulder and Scully. In this case, however, the motif never quite clicks, and the Max-Logan relationship never quite resonated with audiences of *Dark Angel* the way the Mulder-Scully relationship had with viewers of *The X-Files*.

Dark Angel had relatively high production values from the very beginning, sporting a noir look that clearly owed a great deal to *The X-Files* (and perhaps *Blade Runner*), but that was also highly appropriate to the setting of the series in a 2020 dystopian America. It also didn't hurt that the almost ridiculously beautiful Alba (who somehow manages to be both smoldering and cherubic) immediately became something of a TV sex symbol as the series began airing. Add in a basic science fiction scenario that addressed a number of extremely contemporary concerns and issues, and *Dark Angel* seemed to have a real shot at success. However, even though *Dark Angel* was heavy on action and eye candy, it was light on truly imaginative science fiction concepts once it got beyond the reasonably intriguing basic premise. In fact, the series quickly became an almost conventional crime-fighting series, but with a superhero in the central crime-fighter role, somewhat in the mold of Batman, another dark loner. There was also, for good measure, a dash of *The Fugitive*, as Max spent much of her time evading the hapless attempts of Manticore head Donald Lydecker (John Savage) to recapture her and the other Manticore escapees. Finally, in the second season, the enemies battled by Max and Logan were themselves often superhuman (or at least nonhuman), bringing in another clear *X-Files* influence.

These various generic strands never quite came together, though, and *Dark Angel* ultimately depended largely on violent fight scenes and on the sex appeal of Alba to attract audiences, the latter situation encouraged by her tight (typically black leather) costumes and by titillating revelations, such as the fact that (due to feline DNA added to her genetic mix) Max goes into heat three times a year, making even the geekiest of males almost irresistible to her. Unfortunately, this attempt to tap into the sex and violence formula that has made so many American television series successful tended to dilute, rather than reinforce, the science fiction setting of *Dark Angel*, so the series ultimately appealed only to a relatively small (if sometimes extremely devoted) core audience.

This audience was understandably upset at the cancellation of the show, though Fox continued its unusually strong commitment to the science fiction genre by replacing *Dark Angel* in 2002 with *Firefly*, an outer space adventure set five hundred years in the future and featuring a renegade spaceship crew doing battle against the oppressive forces of official authority in a dystopian intergalactic future. The basic scenario of *Firefly* recalled such predecessors as *Blake's 7* and *Farscape* (while sometimes also strongly echoing the Western genre), but again the series never drew a large audience, and it was canceled before making it through even a single full season, continuing the bad luck of science fiction series in the early twenty-first century.

On the other hand, Fox did score a moderate success with the animated series *Futurama*, a sort of science fiction sitcom that in some ways looks back to predecessors such as *Red Dwarf*. Of course, the most important predecessor of *Futurama* was Fox's highly successful animated sitcom *The Simpsons*, created by Matt Groening, who also created *Futurama*. It is thus no surprise that *Futurama* features many of the same kinds of in-jokes and hip pop cultural references that helped to make *The Simpsons* so successful. In addition, just as *The Simpsons* derived much of its humor from its irreverent treatment of the sitcom tradition, *Futurama* relied heavily from the very beginning on parodic references to the entire tradition of science fiction television, which has sometimes suffered from a certain self-seriousness. *Star Trek*, as usual, is crucial to the allusive texture of *Futurama*, as when, in the first episode, we find that the head of Leonard Nimoy has been preserved in a jar in a "head museum" as one of the crucial figures in the history of the series' future world.

Set in the year 3000, *Futurama* focuses on Fry, a lowly pizza delivery boy from the late twentieth century who is accidentally frozen in a suspended animation machine (*Futurama* doesn't worry much about technological verisimilitude) only to awake one thousand years into the future. Once he arrives in this astounding new world, he finds that he is able to get a new job as, well, a delivery boy. Indeed, despite the high-tech nature of the future society of *Futurama*, in most ways very little has changed since Fry left his own world in 1999. Thus, the satire of the series is clearly aimed at our own contemporary world, and *Futurama*, like most of its contemporaries in SFTV, has no real interest in imagining a different future. On the other hand, the best science fiction typically uses its settings in distant times or on distant planets simply to provide a fresh perspective on the here and now, and in this sense *Futurama* is typical of much science fiction, despite its comic and parodic elements.

Fry is joined in *Futurama* by a variety of offbeat characters, including his would-be love interest, Leela, an alien woman with a talent for martial arts who is also quite beautiful—if you can only get past the fact that she has only one large eye in the middle of her forehead. Perhaps the central comic figure in the series is the foul-mouthed, ill-tempered robot, Bender, who guzzles alcohol, chomps cigars, and generally makes a nuisance of himself, all the while somehow remaining lovable. Together, the three intrepid voyagers travel about the galaxy making deliveries for the Planet Express Delivery Service, meanwhile encountering a wide range of strange aliens, harrowing (but hilarious) adventures, and close calls, all in the interest of a good-natured send-up of the entire science fiction genre. Indeed, the references to science fiction in the series go well beyond the obvious nods toward *Star Trek* and other well-known predecessors to include a variety of more complex and sometimes esoteric allusions, as in the episode "Fear of a Bot Planet" when the three heroes travel to the planet "Chapek 9," which is inhabited entirely by androphobic robots. Only real science fiction fans would realize that the name of this planet derives from that of Karel Čapek, the Czech science fiction writer who is credited with coining the term "robot" in his 1920 play *R.U.R.* Perhaps more fans, however, would recognize that the title of the episode refers to the classic 1990 hip-hop album *Fear of a Black Planet*, by the group Public Enemy, a connection that reinforces the status of this episode as a satire (albeit a lighthearted one) on racism.

Futurama began airing in 1999, the year Fry was originally frozen, and continued through five seasons into summer 2003, making it one of the longest-running science fiction series of recent years. Indeed, of the true SFTV series being broadcast at the beginning of 2000, only *Stargate SG-1* was still on the air with new episodes at the end of 2003. The latter series, based on the 1994 Roland Emmerich film *Stargate*, must surely take the prize for the most promising and innovative basic concept among SFTV programs on the air at the beginning of the new millennium. In the original film, archaeologists working in Egypt discover a strange circular object that turns out to be an alien transportation device. When properly operated, the device, or "stargate," establishes a stable wormhole between itself and a similar device on a distant planet. Travelers then merely have to step through one stargate and they will emerge from the other, having traveled vast distances essentially instantaneously. After American archaeologist Daniel Jackson (James Spader) manages to translate the hieroglyphic code that explains the operation of the stargate, an American military team, led by Colonel Jack O'Neill (Kurt Russell), goes through the gate with Jackson and discovers itself on the distant planet of Abydos, where the people live in a culture that closely resembles that of ancient Egypt on Earth. They are, however, enslaved by their cruel gods, led by the evil Ra (Jaye Davidson). A little investigation reveals that these gods are actually Goa'ulds, snakelike alien parasites who take over the bodies of humans and use them as hosts. The people on Abydos, meanwhile, actually are descended from ancient Egyptians, who were taken there through the stargate by the Goa'uld. The Americans (of course) manage to defeat the aliens, liberate the human population, and return safely to Earth, though Jackson stays behind to study the civilization of Abydos—and to be with the beautiful young Abydonian woman Sha'uri (Mili Avital), whom he weds.

The television series *Stargate SG-1* picks up pretty much where the *Stargate* film leaves off, though with important changes in casting. O'Neill is now played by TV veteran Richard Dean Anderson (best known for the hit 1990s series *MacGyver*), while the part of Jackson is played by relative newcomer Michael Shanks. Meanwhile, the stargate program becomes much more organized (and better funded), especially after it is discovered that there are numerous stargates all over the galaxy and that the Goa'ulds, still smarting from their defeat on Abydos, are bearing a serious grudge against Earth. To meet this threat, the Stargate Command (SGC), under the leadership of air force general George Hammond (Don S. Davis), is established in a secret underground facility in Colorado, while numerous teams of specialists are organized to go through the stargates in search of new life and new civilizations. However, unlike the explorers of *Star Trek*, the SGC is a military organization with a very clear military mission: to battle the Goa'uld wherever they find them and, in particular, to seek out advanced alien weapons technologies that will help Earth defend itself against the far more advanced technology of the Goa'uld.

Stargate SG-1, then, is fundamentally both a space-exploration and an alien-invasion series. On the other hand, the central importance of the war against the Goa'uld, while certainly providing fertile plot material, may ultimately be a limitation to the series as science fiction. All too often, *Stargate SG-1* becomes a fiction not of ideas but of action, descending to the level of a relatively conventional shoot-'em-up that relies for its audience appeal more on action and battle scenes than on thoughtful and intriguing science fiction concepts.

Nevertheless, such concepts do abound in *Stargate SG-1*. For example, the presentation of advanced technologies encountered in the exploration of various planets and in the battle against the Goa'uld is, predictably, a crucial component of the science fiction in the series. In this sense, of course, the real star of *Stargate SG-1* is the stargate itself, which obviously offers tremendous opportunities for the exploration of other worlds, however unlikely its scientific basis might be. For one thing, as with the wormhole of *Farscape*, the discovery of the stargate allows contemporary humans (rather than humans of some distant future) to interact with advanced technologies, making it easier for audiences to identify with the protagonists of the series. In addition, the fact that the characters come from the same cultural background as the audience facilitates the allusiveness of the series, which constantly refers to other works of twentieth-century popular culture. O'Neill (a sort of older and more cynical version of *Farscape*'s Crichton) is particularly given to such references, with *The Wizard of Oz* (in many ways an important predecessor of SFTV) and *Star Trek* (the prototype of all TV science fiction) being among his favorite sources.

In the course of the series, the ability to travel instantaneously to other worlds is supplemented by the discovery that, under certain circumstances, the stargate can be used for time travel and for travel into alternate universes, opening up still more possibilities for the exploration of standard science fiction themes. The series is thus highly flexible, if sometimes unfocused. There are virtual reality episodes, episodes featuring androids indistinguishable from humans, and even a look at a dystopian future (the fourth season's "2010"), in which the stargate program leads to contact with an alien species, the Aschen, who transform human society—but nearly exterminate the human race. Meanwhile, the fact that the stargate program is top secret (for fear that news of its findings—especially the impending Goa'uld threat—will lead to mass hysteria) enables episodes of intrigue that are highly reminiscent of *The X-Files*. In one ongoing motif, for example, a shadowy clandestine government intelligence organization, the N.I.D., dogs the SGC, hoping to put its findings to sinister uses. *Stargate SG-1* sometimes echoes the more comic aspects of *The X-Files* as well, as in the hilarious Season Four episode "Point of No Return," in which conspiracy buff Martin Lloyd (played by Willie Garson, who had guest-starred in two episodes of *The X-Files*) gets wind of the stargate program, forcing the SGC to pay attention to his various theories of alien invasion, government cover-ups, and so on—many of which might have come directly out of *The X-Files*. Lloyd (who himself turns out to be an alien) would then return the next season in the even spoofier "Wormhole X-Treme," a satire of TV science fiction (including *Stargate SG-1)* that again recalls the comic episodes of *The X-Files*, but is also at some points almost reminiscent of *Lexx*.

As the series proceeds, the stargate itself is supplemented by additional advanced technologies, including more and more emphasis on the type of interstellar spacecraft that had previously been the principal vehicles for space exploration in science fiction series. The Goa'uld, for example, have advanced spacecraft with hyperdrive technology that allows faster-than-light travel, echoing the warp drive made famous by *Star Trek*. They can thus travel even to places that do not have stargates and carry cargoes too large to fit through the gates. By the fifth season, the SGC, spurred by alien technologies, has developed its own faster-than-light interstellar ship, the *Prometheus* (though O'Neill wants to name it the *Enterprise* and wonders why it doesn't have phasers).

Other *Star Trek*–style technologies abound in *Stargate SG-1* as well, including the fact that the Goa'uld have matter transporter devices that resemble the transporters of *Star Trek*, though with a bit more hardware. Meanwhile, we learn that there are other races in the galaxy (and, in some cases, in other galaxies) that are even more technologically advanced than the Goa'uld. Indeed, befitting their nature as parasites, the Goa'uld seem to have developed very little technology of their own but have simply cannibalized it from other species, much as the Borg of *Star Trek* assimilate other technologies as they travel through the galaxy. The stargate system itself, initially thought to have been designed and built by the Goa-uld, turns out to be the product of "the Ancients." Apparently not related to the

Ancients of *Farscape* (such Ancients are a fairly common science fiction conceit), these Ancients were an incredibly advanced race from a much earlier time that seems to have been wiped out by some sort of plague, though some of the Ancients, we eventually learn near the end of the sixth season, seem not to have died in the usual sense but to have ascended to a higher plane of reality. The stargate travelers encounter a number of other advanced species as well, the most important of which is the Asgard, who turn out to be none other than the "gray" aliens of Roswell lore, providing still more links to science fiction traditions of the past. The Asgard are so technologically, intellectually, and spiritually advanced that they initially regard humans as primitive savages, though they eventually become allies of the humans against the Goa'uld, especially after their supreme commander, Thor, takes a special liking to O'Neill. Indeed, unlikely as it might seem, we learn early in the seventh season that O'Neill is a genetically advanced human, an evolutionary leap whose DNA might potentially help the Asgard (who have reproduced by cloning for thousands of years) solve their own increasing genetic problems.

In the course of the series, other advanced races join the Asgard, including the Tollan and the Nox, as *Stargate* gradually builds an extensive intergalactic mythology. One particularly important plot strand that occurs in numerous episodes involves the Tok'ra, a rebel group of benevolent Goa'uld who inhabit their hosts only if the hosts are willing, and who allow their hosts to continue as partners in the sharing of the host body—something like the Trills of *Star Trek*. The Tok'ra and the humans from Earth (generally referred to by aliens in *Stargate* as the Tauri) become important allies against the Goa'uld in the course of the series, even though certain tensions remain between the two groups. In "The Fifth Race" (January 22, 1999), we learn that the Asgard, the Tollan, the Furlings, and the Ancients once formed a mighty alliance (now long defunct) designed to oppose such evil as the Goa'uld throughout the known universe. We also learn in this episode that the Asgard find humans a quite promising species and believe that they may someday become the fifth great interstellar civilization.

Humans are, in fact, very much the dominant species in *Stargate*. For various practical purposes, SFTV has long been dominated by humans, and series such as *Star Trek* even attempted to explain the tendency of interstellar explorations to encounter humans virtually everywhere they go with a theory that the galaxy had earlier been seeded with humans (or at least human DNA) by some sort of superior beings. Indeed, the original *Star Trek* series episode, "The Paradise Syndrome" (October 4, 1968), can be taken as a sort of prototype for the various interstellar encounters with other humans in *Stargate*. In the *Star Trek* episode, a settlement of Native Americans has been transplanted to a distant planet by a race known as the "Preservers," where they continue to live and practice their original culture. Similarly, in *Stargate* the explorers encounter numerous humans who have been transplanted to various planets by the Goa'uld, beginning with their first encounter with humans in ancient Egypt, where they enslaved the Egyptians and installed themselves as the pantheon of Egyptian gods. This motif allows for some very interesting anthropological encounters—though it does not explain why most of the humans encountered in outer space seem to speak English. Most of these transplanted groups still maintain much of their original culture, and few of them have advanced as far (at least technologically) as has civilization back on Earth itself.

However, *Stargate* stops far short of equating civilization with technology. The advanced civilizations of the series tend to have extremely advanced technology, though the Nox live a simple, pastoral existence in which this technology remains virtually invisible. The Tollan, meanwhile, recognize the dangers of their own advanced technology. They are particularly opposed to sharing technology with less-advanced races, such as humans, which leads to considerable frustration for the SGC, given that Tollan weapons could be of huge benefit in opposing the Goa'uld.

This frustration grows even stronger in the episode "Pretense" (January 21, 2000), in which the *Stargate* crew saves the Tollan home world from a Goa'uld attack after excessive Tollan confidence in their own defense technologies makes them vulnerable. Yet the Tollan still refuse to share their precious technology, realizing how dangerous it might be in the wrong hands. Indeed, while *Stargate SG-1* generally endorses the value of technological advancement, warnings against overreliance on technology abound in the series. Thus, in "Nemesis" (March 10, 2000), even the generally wise Asgard are revealed to be in severe danger because overconfidence in their technology has left them vulnerable to attacks by an army of robot replicators. Indeed, these replicators are themselves the products of advanced technology, while their main goal (again echoing the Borg of *Star Trek*) is to assimilate advanced technologies wherever they can find them. This warning against the dangers of hypersophisticated technology is then driven home by the fact that the Asgard have to enlist the aid of the Tauri in fighting off the replicators, precisely because the replicators will not be able to anticipate the moves made by such a primitive foe.

The apparent invincibility of these replicators provides the cliffhanger ending to Season Three, though they are defeated (for the time being) in the Season Four opener, only to reappear in the first episode of Season Five. Meanwhile, the replicator motif shows the influence of the possibilities of nanotechnology on *Stargate SG-1*, one of the many ways in which the series (from its basic wormhole premise on up) seeks to tap into recent and contemporary trends in speculative science fiction. Of course, the replicator motif had already been done in *Lexx*, and a knowledge of the comic uses of the motif in that series makes it a bit harder to take the replicators of *Stargate* seriously.

In any case, despite its extensive intergalactic mythology, fancy science fiction hardware, and relatively advanced special effects, *Stargate SG-1* is ultimately character driven. The flagship team of the SGC is "SG-1" (thus the title of the series), led by O'Neill, who has to be coaxed out of retirement in the first episode to take the job. The team also includes air force captain (later major) Samantha Carter (Amanda Tapping), a brilliant young astrophysicist. Jackson is also added to the team, after Sha're (now played by Vaitiare Bandera, with the spelling of the character's name unaccountably changed in the credits) is captured in a retaliatory strike on Abydos by the Goa'uld "system lord" Apophis (Peter Williams). Sha're is then infested by a Goa'uld parasite and forced to become Apophis's queen, driving Jackson to join the SGC in an attempt to rescue her. The fourth member of the team is the inscrutable Teal'c (Christopher Judge), a Jaffa (elite Goa'uld guards who host larval forms of the Goa'uld parasite and thus retain some self-awareness and determination) who tires of participating in Goa'uld atrocities around the galaxy and decides to join the fight against them.

Stargate SG-1 depends heavily on the camaraderie among the members of SG-1 for its effects. The four members of the team (supplemented by the initially crusty Hammond, who eventually becomes a trusted ally) are constantly in severe danger, forging strong bonds of trust and genuine affection through their mutual experiences and reliance on one another for safety. As in *Star Trek: The Next Genera-*

tion, *Stargate SG-1* enhances and expands this motif of personal relationships by introducing us to the families of the major cast members. A major plot arc in the first years of the series involves Jackson's attempt to recover Sha're from the Goa'uld; later, after Sha're is killed, Jackson searches for the son of Sha're and Apophis, a boy who has inherited, via genetic memory, crucial secrets that could lead to the final defeat of the Goa'uld. O'Neill is something of a loner (who spends most of his leave time on solo fishing trips in remote locales), but he is largely that way because of a personal tragedy in his past that occurred when his young son accidentally shot and killed himself with a gun O'Neill kept in the house. Carter, meanwhile, is the daughter of an air force general, Jacob Carter (Carmen Argenziano), who is found to be dying of cancer but is then saved when he joins the Tok'ra. His new symbiote then cures his cancer, allowing him to live on and to join the fight against the Goa'uld.

Teal'c is similarly impervious to most diseases (as well as poisons, radiation, and so on) thanks to the presence of his symbiote. He is also a huge and powerful warrior, with superhuman strength. On the other hand, even Teal'c, though not fully human, is humanized by family relationships in the series. When he revolts against his Goa'uld masters, he is forced to leave his wife and child behind on his home planet of Chulak. In the episode "Bloodlines" (October 10, 1997), he returns to Chulak to try to prevent his son, Rya'c (Neil Denis), from taking a symbiote and becoming a slave to Apophis, finding meanwhile that he must battle against his own wife, Drey-Auc (Salli Richardson), who is furious with Teal'c for the hardships his rebellion has brought upon the family, who have now been declared outcasts. In this episode, we also meet Bra'tac (Tony Amendola), Teal'c's beloved 130-year-old Jaffa mentor. (Teal'c himself, we later learn, is 101 years old, the symbiotes also apparently bringing great longevity to their hosts.) The wise, virtuous, and courageous Bra'tac also now battles against the Goa'uld, becoming a recurring character in the series.

Teal'c, despite his background as a warrior, is also the Spock character of *Stargate SG-1*, making him, in a sense, a combination of Spock and *The Next Generation*'s Worf. Generally dispassionate, Teal'c reacts with a logic and stoicism to virtually every situation (sometimes with comic results), though he does, over time, learn to be more human thanks to his close interaction with the other members of the SG-1 team. In this sense, his evolution vaguely recalls that of Data in *The Next Generation* and Seven of Nine in *Voyager*.

Though series from *The X-Files* and *Babylon 5* to *Farscape* and *Stargate SG-1* have strongly challenged the dominant position once held by the *Star Trek* franchise in science fiction television programming, that franchise remained influential at the end of 2003. While *Enterprise*, the only *Star Trek* series currently in production at the time of this writing, has never quite found the loyal core audience of the earlier *Star Trek* series, it is still an important series, appearing weekly on a broadcast network, even if a minor one.[2] In addition, one of the most popular syndicated science fiction series at the end of 2003 was *Andromeda*, which, though not a *Star Trek* series in itself, is based on an original idea by Gene Roddenberry and is coexecutive produced by Majel Barrett Roddenberry. Indeed, that series is officially billed as "Gene Roddenberry's *Andromeda*," acknowledging its lineage while at the same time attempting to use the magic lure of the Roddenberry name to attract viewers.[3]

Enterprise, which began airing on UPN in September 2001, is a prequel to the original *Star Trek* series, set approximately ninety years after eccentric scientist Zefram Cochrane developed Earth's first warp drive, introducing a decaying, postapocalyptic Earth to interstellar travel in the year 2063, then quickly leading to contact between humans and the much more advanced Vulcans. This contact then contributes to a new age of enlightenment and technological progress on Earth and, ultimately, to Earth's central role in the development of Starfleet and the United Federation of Planets. The maiden voyage of the titular *Enterprise* (registry number NX-01) takes place in 2151, placing the action of the series in the early years of Starfleet and at a time when the Federation is still being organized. This setting places *Enterprise* a little more than a century before the setting of the original *Star Trek* series, allowing it to fill in a great deal of background for all of the earlier *Star Trek* series. As a result, while *Enterprise* does take place 150 years into our future, relative to the earlier *Star Trek*s, it involves a projection not into the future but into the past. Thus, rather than appearing futuristic, the technology of the series actually looks old-fashioned to viewers who are accustomed to the earlier series, a situation reinforced by the intentionally retro look of the title sequence that opens each episode.

The *Enterprise NX-01* is commanded by Captain Jonathan Archer (Scott Bakula), who, on his first assignment, must hastily assemble a crew to undertake a mission to return a wounded Klingon (who has crashed on Earth) to his home world. Something of a throwback to

James T. Kirk (though Bakula lacks William Shatner's campy charisma), Archer is a strong, virile figure of paternal authority toward his crew and the ship, which his own father helped to design and build. Of the crew, Commander Charles "Trip" Tucker III (Connor Trineer), the ship's Floridian chief engineer, serves as a sort of right-hand man to Archer, whom he has known for years. Adventurous and bold, Tucker is a highly competent engineer, though he is a bit impulsive and lacks the diplomatic skills that are sometimes needed as the *Enterprise* voyages outward to encounter new life and new civilizations. The ship's weapons and tactical officer is Lieutenant Malcolm Reed (Dominic Keating). Descended from a long line of British naval officers, Reed is initially a bit reclusive, though one plot arc of the series involves his gradual willingness to open up to the rest of the crew and to accept them as a kind of family. The pilot of *Enterprise* is young Ensign Travis Mayweather (Anthony Montgomery), who was born in space and grew up on spaceships. The final crucial human member of the crew is the communications officer, Ensign Hoshi Sato (Linda Park). Gifted with great linguistic skills, Ensign Sato plays a far more crucial role on the *Enterprise* than did her predecessor, Uhura, in the original series.

Though the *Enterprise* is Earth's first deep-space craft (capable of reaching warp five), the crew already includes aliens. One of the most interesting members of the crew is the chief medical officer, Dr. Phlox (John Billingsley). Both highly competent and highly unconventional, Phlox (from the planet Denobula) continues the long line of important (and generally colorful) *Star Trek* medical officers. The final central member of the crew is the perfectly logical, highly intelligent, and extremely beautiful subcommander, T'Pol (Jolene Blalock), who is obviously linked to the original Spock, but whose skin-tight outfits and deadpan delivery of dialogue clearly identify her as the direct successor (or predecessor) of *Voyager*'s Seven of Nine. T'Pol is placed aboard the *Enterprise* as an advisor at the insistence of the Vulcans, who fear that the humans on board will need her wisdom and logic to stay out of trouble in the unfamiliar situations they will encounter in deep space. Indeed, the Vulcans refuse to supply the star charts that the *Enterprise* needs for navigation unless T'Pol is allowed to go along, despite Archer's strong objections, which are not personal but racial. Archer has a strong suspicion of all Vulcans and resentment of what he sees as their meddling and condescension where humans are concerned.

However, despite initial tensions, T'Pol is gradually able to win over Archer and the rest of the crew. Indeed, like Seven, she becomes humanized in the course of the series, as her loyalties gradually shift from the Vulcan High Command to Starfleet—and especially to Archer himself, for whom she develops a strong (if rather illogical) romantic attraction, one that becomes mutual (if not acted upon), thus making Archer and T'Pol the requisite unrequited couple that had by this time become almost obligatory in science fiction series. At one point, T'Pol opts out of a prearranged Vulcan marriage in order to stay aboard the *Enterprise*, thus enabling the sexual tension between her and Archer to continue to build. By the end of the second season, in the cliff-hanger episode "The Expanse" (May 21, 2003), T'Pol even resigns her commission with the Vulcan High Command in order to accompany Archer and his crew on a highly dangerous mission that the Vulcans have ordered her to forgo.

Vulcans, in general, play a crucial role in *Enterprise*, acting as mentors and guides for Earth, though this role also sometimes leads to considerable tension between the two cultures. However, Archer is certainly not alone among humans in his suspicions and antagonism toward them, which often turn out to be justified when a number of Vulcans in the series prove to be less than paragons of virtue. In addition, the Vulcans of the series often prove excessively confident in their own knowledge and understanding of the universe, which sometimes makes it difficult to adapt when they encounter new things that contradict their previous experience. Among the original pantheon of *Star Trek* alien species, Klingons also feature significantly in *Enterprise* as one of the first hostile species encountered by humanity in its movement outward into the galaxy. *Enterprise* also features some new enemies of humanity, the Suliban, a mysterious nomadic race made particularly formidable by technology imported from the future as part of the temporal cold war, an event in which the *Enterprise* becomes inadvertently involved. In addition, at the end of Season Two, Earth itself comes under attack from still another foe, the Xindi, who also get information from this future. This time, the information shows that Earth forces will eventually destroy the Xindi home world, so the Xindi plan to launch a preemptive strike to destroy Earth. Season Three then moves to a vaguely continuous plot arc (though not nearly as much as the ten-episode sequence with which *Deep Space Nine*—and its Dominion War—had ended) in which the *Enterprise* and her crew venture into the Expanse in an attempt to locate the Xindi and prevent them from destroying Earth.

In *Enterprise*, the galaxy is clearly a very dangerous place—far more so than in the earlier *Star Trek* series. Part of this danger occurs because the earthlings of the series know so little about the galaxy, though this situation also gives the series an even greater sense of discovery than its predecessors in the franchise, even though we largely know where those discoveries will lead. Much of what the crew of the *Enterprise NX-01* encounters is completely new, each encounter adding significantly to their knowledge of the galaxy. Meanwhile, the temporal cold war, first introduced in the early episode "Cold Front" (November 28, 2001), remains a mysterious motif in *Enterprise*, and this war provides the series' only real projection into the future. In this case, however, the future appears mysterious (as does the exact nature of the war), though it clearly involves extremely advanced technologies. At the same time, the time-travel motif suggests an effective simultaneity to all periods of history that tends to undermine the whole notion of history as we know it.

Andromeda also projects an advanced future that represents little real historical progress. The premise of the series, which began its fourth season in syndication in fall 2003, relies on the projection of a future intergalactic alliance known as the Systems Commonwealth, a political entity (described in the series as the greatest civilization in history) that clearly has much in common with *Star Trek*'s United Federation of Planets. Meanwhile, the existence of the Commonwealth is predicated on the development of much the same advanced technology (especially for faster-than-light intergalactic space travel) that is crucial to the Federation. Beyond this basic similarity, however, *Andromeda* projects a rather different future than that envisioned via the basic optimism of *Star Trek*. For one thing, the Commonwealth is not centered on Earth, which occupies a rather marginal position and which joined the Commonwealth thousands of years after its original evolution from the Vedran Empire, centered on the planet Tarn Vedra. More important, *Andromeda* is primarily set not during the glory days of the Commonwealth, but three hundred years after it has collapsed in the wake of the chaos created by a large-scale revolt on the part of the Nietzscheans, one of the key members of the organization. The Nietzscheans are genetically engineered superhumans who viewed themselves as superior to the other groups that constituted the Commonwealth, which they saw as increasingly weak and conciliatory, especially in the light of a treaty negotiated with the Magog, a particularly brutal race (given to the eating of human flesh) who had for some time been at war with the Commonwealth. In another example of looking to the past rather than the future, the Nietzscheans, inspired by the thought of nineteenth-century Earth philosopher Friedrich Nietzsche (with a dash of right-wing thinker Ayn Rand thrown in for good measure), believe that power is the principal motivation driving all life and that those who are strong enough to seize power are justified in doing so. Unfortunately, the Nietzschean rebellion (followed by considerable infighting among different clans or "prides" of Nietzscheans) leads not to strength but to anarchy, which opens up much of the Commonwealth (including Earth itself) to attacks by the Magog. Indeed, the envisioned fall of the Commonwealth is clearly modeled in many ways on the fall of the Roman Empire on Earth, with the period following that fall becoming a sort of galactic Dark Age in which intellectual and technological progress come to a standstill while violent forces continue to rock the galaxy.

The basic scenario of *Andromeda* is triggered when the starship *Andromeda Ascendant* (aka the XMC-10-284), the pride of the Commonwealth fleet, is ambushed by a huge armada of Nietzschean ships at the beginning of the rebellion. Captain Dylan Hunt (Kevin Sorbo) orders his crew to abandon ship in escape pods, while he himself stays aboard, among other things fighting off his own Nietzschean first officer's attempts to take over the ship. The *Andromeda Ascendant* subsequently escapes the Nietzscheans when it is drawn into the event horizon of a black hole. Meanwhile, Hunt and his ship are trapped in the event horizon, frozen in time due to the time dilation effect of the black hole's immense gravitational force, until they are pulled free three hundred years later by an enterprising salvage ship, the *Eureka Maru*, hoping to make a killing by selling off the high-tech ship.

Surprised to find Hunt on board and alive, the salvagers initially battle against him for control of the ship, but eventually join on as his crew, with the *Maru*'s captain, Beka Valentine (Lisa Ryder) becoming the new first officer (acting executive officer is her official title) of the *Andromeda*. A gifted space pilot, Valentine, the daughter of a space smuggler, was in fact born on a spaceship and has never lived on a planet. The imported crew also includes a Nietzschean, Tyr Anasazi (Keith Hamilton Cobb), and a Magog, Rev Bem (Brent Stait). Converted to the "Way" (a powerful religious force sweeping the galaxy in much the same way that Christianity swept across Europe in the wake of the fall of Rome), Rev Bem is now a holy man, having renounced the usual brutish violence of his race in favor of pacifism and mysticism. He is thus virtually the opposite of the typical Magog. On the other hand, the large and well-muscled (we know because he spends lots of time with his shirt off) Anasazi, who serves as security officer and is something of a darker version of *Star Trek: TNG*'s Worf, is in many ways a prototypical Nietzschean, though his Nietzschean individualism is driven to an extreme due to the fact that his own pride has been exterminated by Nietschean infighting. Partly for that reason, Anasazi has a huge chip on his shoulder, though he gradually and grudgingly learns to respect Hunt (a nonengineered human from Tarn-Vedra) after a great deal of early hostility between the two.[4]

The other crew members to come over from the *Maru* are human tech-whiz Seamus Harper (Gordon Michael Woolvett)—the only crew member who is from Earth—and the highly mysterious (and initially purple-skinned, though her skin color becomes more human as the series proceeds) young alien woman Trance Gemini (Laura Bertram), who is essentially Harper's opposite. Very good with plants and people (and possibly able to see into the future), Gemini is a complete klutz with computers and machines, while Harper seems to have an instinctive feel for virtually anything mechanical or electronic. In fact, he has a neural implant at the base of his brain that allows him to interface directly with computerized systems. Harper's skills, of course, turn out to be incredibly invaluable in getting the *Andromeda* back into operating condition while also helping to maintain the ship's highly automated systems, including the army of droids and bots that fills out a crew that had once numbered more than four thousand. These systems, meanwhile, are also managed by a central artificial intelligence, perhaps descended from Zen, the supercomputer that provides the brain of the *Liberator* in *Blake's 7*. In this case, however, the artificial intelligence is integrated into the ship, essentially making the *Andromeda Ascendant* a sentient being in its own right. Indeed, one of Harper's most important contributions is the creation of Andromeda, or "Drommie" (Lexa Doig), a lifelike android personification, or "avatar," of this artificial intelligence (though she, or it, also has numerous other holographic and robotic avatars). Efficient and businesslike, but equipped with great beauty (and often rather scantily clad), Drommie sometimes questions Harper's motivations in her physical design, though her sexual attractiveness should presumably be something of an asset to her as she clearly develops an infatuation for Hunt.

Romantic sparks occasionally fly between Hunt and Valentine as well, but in general *Andromeda* focuses on real action more than potential romance, as the idealistic Hunt tries to inspire his new crew to join him in his quest to rebuild the Commonwealth and thus restore civilization to the galaxy, battling Nietzscheans, Magog, and a whole panoply of other violent adversaries along the way. The special effects of *Andromeda* are top-notch, and many of the outer space battle scenes are among the most impressive to have appeared on series television, even if the heavy reliance on such scenes tends to detract from the thoughtfulness of the series and its exploration of an imaginary future. Meanwhile, much of the success of the series depends on the chemistry among the various crew members, which is in some ways made even more important than in *Star Trek* due to the fact that they are essentially alone in a hostile universe. On the other hand, except for Rommie, who is completely devoted to Hunt and his cause, the crew of the *Andromeda Ascendant* definitely has mixed motivations, and their interpersonal chemistry is often more reminiscent of *Blake's 7* than of *Star Trek*, with an idealistic leader holding together a band of renegades with mixed motives as they carry on a battle against huge odds.

Unfortunately, *Andromeda* never really achieves the interesting complexity of *Blake's 7* in this sense, despite the contrast between Hunt's idealism and the cynicism of most of his crew members. For one thing, Hunt is far too dominant in the series, and it is impossible to imagine *Andromeda* going on without him in the way that *Blake's 7* was able to continue without Blake, even though all of the major characters of *Andromeda* are given occasional episodes in which they are featured. For another, Hunt himself lacks Blake's personal complexity. He may be a bit obsessive, but he is also a figure of almost perfect virtue and heroism in his one-man war against barbarism. In short, Hunt is just a bit too perfect to be truly interesting as a character. He does have a few personal demons (mostly having to do with the fact that everything and everyone he ever knew—including his beloved fiancée, Sarah—are long dead), but in general he remains a quintessential idealist, traveling about the galaxy in his attempt to rebuild the Commonwealth, battling evil and anarchy.

Occasionally, *Andromeda* touches on topical issues, but these tend to be treated in rather banal and uncontroversial ways, with the crew of the *Andromeda* serving as intergalactic policemen in ways that are reminiscent of the global role of the United States in the early twenty-first century, despite the fact that they are outsiders who lack the power to enforce their vision on the galaxy. For example, in

"Slipfighter: The Dogs of War" (November 4, 2002), the *Andromeda* travels to the planet Marduk to destroy a Voltareum reactor so that it cannot be used in a project to develop weapons of mass destruction, thus almost eerily anticipating the U.S. invasion of Iraq in March 2003—except that the Mardukians really *are* developing weapons of mass destruction. In fact, the ideology of the Commonwealth (despite the fact that it does not originate on Earth) seems to be pure unquestioned Americanism, as when Hunt describes the Commonwealth as a "government of the people, by the people, and for the people" in the episode "A Rose in the Ashes" (November 27, 2000).

Andromeda, through the memories of Hunt, routinely looks backward, rather than forward, in time in search of images of a better world—or universe. It even looks back on other SFTV series, often featuring guest appearances by such actors as William B. Davis of *The X-Files*, John De Lancie of *Star Trek*, Michael Shanks of *Stargate SG-1*, and James Marsters of *Buffy the Vampire Slayer*. Indeed, science fiction television as a whole took on an increasingly retro feel as it moved into the twenty-first century, largely due to the prominence of the Sci Fi Channel, which has become more and more crucial as a sort of home base for the genre. Any number of former series have been resurrected on the network, and fans often turn to it for nostalgic re-viewings of the past rather than exhilarating looks into the future, indicating the same sort of nostalgia that has driven the production of new versions of series such as *The Twilight Zone* and *The Outer Limits*. Meanwhile, science fiction television series have been absolutely central to the explosion in DVD releases of classic television series in general, with SFTV series such as *The X-Files*, *Babylon 5*, *Farscape*, *Stargate*, and the various *Star Trek*s all having the kind of devoted core audience that makes such releases viable.

Of course, the Sci Fi Channel also continues to produce its own series, of which *Stargate SG-1* is clearly the most important. In recent years, however, the miniseries form has become more and more central to original programming on Sci Fi, including miniseries versions of Frank Herbert's classic science fiction novel *Dune* (2000) and its sequel *Children of Dune* (2003). The former is particularly epic in scope, attempting to capture the narrative grandeur of the original novel, though it fails to match the stunning visuals of the 1984 David Lynch feature film version (which itself failed adequately to reflect Herbert's narrative).

In December 2003, the network broadcast a miniseries update of *Battlestar Galactica*, while a major event on Sci Fi in December 2002 was *Taken*, the massive fifteen-hour alien-invasion/abduction series coproduced by Steven Spielberg. *Taken* is a kinder and gentler form of alien-invasion series, marked by the kind of sentimentalism of which Spielberg is the master. Nonetheless, the multigenerational scope of the series indicates the epic turn taken by Sci Fi miniseries. At the same time, the focus on previous science fiction classics such as *Battlestar Galactica* and *Dune* as sources of material for Sci Fi Channel miniseries indicates the way in which even these new productions contain a strong element of nostalgia. In *Battlestar Galactica*, for example, a key ingredient is the old-fashioned nature of the *Galactica* itself, while the sentimentalism of *Taken* is very much in tune with this turn to nostalgia.

This turn to sentimentalism and nostalgia can be related to the growing maturity (or perhaps exhaustion) of the genre of science fiction television. At the same time, it responds to larger trends as well. After all, by the beginning of the twenty-first century, what had once been the science fiction future was now the present day of the real world, a present that had not, in general, lived up to the expectations of the science fiction novels, films, and television series of earlier decades. While technological advances, especially in computers and communications, continued at a rapid rate, space travel (the heart of earlier science fiction visions of the future) had not lived up to previous expectations, and the space program had in fact slowed to a virtual standstill. In addition, many cultural commentators were proclaiming an end to the historical stage that, from the eighteenth to the twentieth centuries, had defined the historical process as progress. Some were even declaring the end of history itself, and collectively analysts of the global historical situation were finding it difficult to project a future in which progress would continue unimpeded. In this situation, it comes as no surprise that SFTV would also find such projections difficult. On the other hand, this more general loss of historical imagination probably makes science fiction as a whole more important than ever as a potential source of vision. And, given the cultural power of television as a medium, science fiction television may be our last best hope to recover the sense of confidence and wonder that propelled Western civilization from the Renaissance to outer space and cyberspace.

Notes

CHAPTER 1

1. For more information on science fiction radio in the 1950s, see James F. Widner and Meade Frierson, III, *Science Fiction on Radio: A Revised Look at 1950–1975* (Birmingham, AL: AFAB, 1996); and Patrick Lucanio and Gary Coville, *Smokin' Rockets: The Romance of Technology in American Film, Radio, and Television, 1945–1962* (Jefferson, NC: McFarland, 2002).

2. For more on science fiction television in the 1950s, see Lucanio and Coville, *Smokin' Rockets*; as well as Patrick Lucanio and Gary Coville, *American Science Fiction Television Series of the 1950s* (Jefferson, NC: McFarland, 1998).

3. On the science fiction novels and films of the 1950s, see M. Keith Booker, *Monsters, Mushroom Clouds, and the Cold War* (Westport, CT: Greenwood, 2001).

CHAPTER 2

1. Corey had appeared in thirty-six films from 1941 to 1951, before his blacklisting, then no more films until 1963. He did appear in an episode of television's *The Untouchables* in 1960, however.

2. David Buxton, *From the Avengers to Miami Vice: Form and Ideology in Television Series* (Manchester: Manchester University Press, 1990).

3. Alain Carrazé and Hélène Oswald. The Prisoner: *A Television Masterpiece*. Trans. Christine Donougher (London: Virgin Publishing, 1995).

4. That these original Klingons vaguely resemble Russians, or at least cold war stereotypes of Russians, gives the episode even more of a cold war flavor.

5. This ending is treated comically, but the same motif is treated much more seriously in an episode of the later *Enterprise* series, entitled, in fact, "The Communicator" (November 13, 2002).

6. The secular vision of *Star Trek* has sometimes been attributed to the vision of Roddenberry. On Roddenberry's hostility to organized religion, see David Alexander, "Gene Roddenberry: Writer, Producer, Philosopher, Humanist." *The Humanist* (March/April 1991): 37, 157.

7. "Amok Time" was written by Theodore Sturgeon, one of the leading science fiction novelists of the 1950s and 1960s. Sturgeon also wrote the episode "Shore Leave" (December 29, 1966). Other well-known science fiction writers who scripted episodes of *TOS* included Harlan Ellison, "The City on the Edge of Forever" (April 6, 1967); Norman Spinrad, "The Doomsday Machine" (October 20, 1967); and Richard Matheson, who had written numerous episodes of *The Twilight Zone* as well as *Star Trek*'s "The Enemy Within" (October 6, 1966). Indeed, the high quality of the writing of many of the individual episodes has no doubt been a key to the ongoing success of the series, though most agree that it was the overarching vision of Roddenberry that really held it all together.

8. Other than the *Enterprise* itself, the transporters are probably the most distinctive single piece of technology in *Star Trek*. Note, however, that an almost identical technology was in use on twenty-fifth-century Earth in the 1939 serial *Buck Rogers*.

CHAPTER 3

1. In the later series *Enterprise*, set a century *before* the original series, the featured ship is also the *Enterprise*, but now with the registry number NX-01. Thus, the ship of *TNG* retroactively becomes the sixth starship *Enterprise*, but the fifth to bear the registry number NCC-1701.

2. Crusher was replaced for the second season of the series by Dr. Kate Pulaski (Diana Muldaur), whose crusty demeanor was much more akin to McCoy's. However, Pulaski never quite meshed with the rest of the crew, and Crusher was brought back for Season Three and all subsequent seasons.

3. The Klingons of the series *Enterprise*, set in the century prior to the original series, also have prominent brow ridges, interestingly enough.

4. In *Nemesis*, Picard has another "son" of sorts, in that the villain of that film, one Shinzon (Tom Hardy), is a clone of Picard, driven to villainy due to his childhood mistreatment in a Romulan prison colony.

5. The most important "environmental" episode of *TNG* is "Force of Nature" (November 15, 1993), in which it is revealed that the overuse of warp drives is causing distortions in the fabric of space-time, leading the Federation to agree to limit that use until the problem can be solved.

CHAPTER 4

1. Quark's brother, the seemingly dim-witted Rom (Max Grodénchik), is even more of a departure. Quark shows little respect for his brother, a Ferengi with no head for business whatsoever. Yet Rom turns out to be a mechanical genius. Inheriting some of his father's talents and proclivities, Rom's son, Nog (Aron Eisenberg), becomes the first Ferengi to study at Starfleet Academy.

2. A similar point is made in the amusing episode "Little Green Men" (November 6, 1995), serving among other things as an homage to the science fiction films of the 1950s, in which Quark, brother Rom, and nephew Nog accidentally enter a time warp and crash their ship on Earth in 1947 (at Roswell, New Mexico, of course). Taken captive by the U.S. military, the Ferengi find the humans around them to be primitive, savage, and violent.

3. Jadzia is killed at the end of the sixth season, though the Dax symbiont lives on and is joined with a new host to become Ezri Dax (Nicole deBoer), who joins the *Deep Space Nine* crew as a new young officer at the beginning of Season Seven.

4. Other lines are unclear as well. In "For the Cause" (May 6, 1996), Sisko's own future wife, Kasidy Yates (Penny Johnson), is sent to a Federation prison for running supplies to the Maquis, while Michael Eddington (Kenneth Marshall), the seemingly by-the-books Starfleet security officer sent to help keep order on Deep Space Nine, turns out to be a Maquis leader working undercover.

5. The series seemed on the verge of cancellation through most of the fourth season, leading Straczynski and the show's producers to wrap up most of the initial plot lines prematurely in that year. The fifth season thus stands as a somewhat anticlimactic postscript to the rest of the series.

6. Famed science fiction writer Harlan Ellison served as conceptual consultant throughout the run of *Babylon 5*, actively working to help ensure that the ideas developed in the series were of a kind explored in the best of the genre.

7. This theme of global plague was revisited by Straczinski in his later *Jeremiah*, which began broadcasting on the Showtime cable network in March 2002. Adapted from an award-winning European graphic novel series, *Jeremiah* details the efforts of its title character (played by Luke Perry) to help restore a postapocalyptic world devastated by plague.

8. Spurred by the early popularity of *The X-Files*, *The Invaders* returned (on Fox, of course) as a four-hour miniseries in 1995. Thinnes, as Vincent, played a minor role in the miniseries, which focused on the tribulations of Nolan Wood (Scott Bakula), whose former infant autism seems to render him uncontrollable by the implants with which the aliens are gradually taking over the Earth's population.

9. This motif of viewer involvement explains not only some of the popularity of the series but also the fact that the series spawned an array of secondary texts, such as books and Web sites, rivaled only by the *Star Trek* franchise. These texts include a series of glossy season-by-season "official guides" published by HarperCollins; an array of "clue texts," such as James Hatfield and George Burt, *The Unauthorized X-Cyclopedia* (New York: MJF Books, 1997); Phil Farrand, *The Nitpicker's Guide for X-Philes* (New York: Dell, 1997); Jane Goldman, *The X-Files Book of the Unexplained* (New York: HarperPrism, 1996); even academic studies such as Jan Delasara, *PopLit, PopCult, and The X-Files* (Jefferson, NC: McFarland, 2000); and the volume of scholarly essays, David Lavery, Angela Hague, and Marla Cartwright, eds., *Deny All Knowledge: Reading The X-Files* (Syracuse, NY: Syracuse University Press, 1996).

CHAPTER 5

1. Actually, there is one late episode of *The X-Files*, "Badlaa" (January 21, 2001), in which a bizarre killer also takes his victims by crawling up their anuses and killing them from the inside. In this case, the killer is a legless Indian beggar with mystical powers, thus enacting a "terror from the Third World" motif.

2. Perhaps in an attempt to better tap into the *Star Trek* audience, the official title of the series was changed at the beginning of the third season (fall 2003) from simply *Enterprise* to *Star Trek: Enterprise*.

3. Barrett Roddenberry was also an executive producer of *Earth: Final Conflict*, which was similarly marketed as "Gene Roddenberry's *Earth: Final Conflict*."

4. Nevertheless, at the end of the third season, Anasazi abandons *Andromeda* and strikes out on his own, in a move Hunt regards as a betrayal.

Index

About the Author

M. KEITH BOOKER is Professor of English at the University of Arkansas. He is the author of many articles and books on modern literature and culture, including *Monsters, Mushroom Clouds, and the Cold War* (Greenwood, 2001) and *Strange TV: Innovative Television Series from The Twilight Zone to The X-Files* (Greenwood, 2002).